THE PHILOSOPHY OF IMMANUEL KANT

STUDIES IN PHILOSOPHY AND THE HISTORY OF PHILOSOPHY

General editor: Jude P. Dougherty

Studies in Philosophy and the History of Philosophy Volume 12

The Philosophy of Immanuel Kant

edited by Richard Kennington

THE CATHOLIC UNIVERSITY OF AMERICA PRESS
Washington, D.C.

Printed in the United States of America

Library of Congress Cataloging in Publication Data

Main entry under title:
The Philosophy of Immanuel Kant.
(Studies in philosophy and the history of philosophy; v. 12)
Includes index.
1. Kant, Immanuel, 1724–1804—Addresses, essays, lectures. I. Kennington, Richard, 1921–.
II. Series.
B21.S78 vol. 12 [B2798] 193 84-23887
ISBN 0-8132-0607-3

Contents

Foreword

The majority of the contributions in this volume were delivered in their original form as lectures in the Colloquium in fall 1981, School of Philosophy, the Catholic University of America.

While the Colloquium commemorated the bicentennial of the publication of the *Critique of Pure Reason*, it was devoted to the entire philosophy of Kant.

In order to gain a wider representation of Kantian themes, Professors Benardete and Dahlstrom were invited to contribute essays on the first *Critique*, and Professors Pippin and Shell were asked for contributions on Kant's moral and political philosophy.

RICHARD KENNINGTON

1 "A new epoch in the history of the world begins here and now"

HANS-GEORG GADAMER

Few books celebrate their birthday. Their first appearance is seldom an event of the magnitude of the death of Socrates, the birth of Jesus, the Hegira, or the beginning of the French Revolution. Could one see a quite well-known turn in philosophical thought as being of the same magnitude? More specifically, is Kant's *Critique of Pure Reason* commensurable with the occurrence of the French Revolution, even if only from a distance? In any case, these events are not unrelated. Kant said of the French Revolution that "such an event is never forgotten" and imperturbably perdures. As early as the publication of his third *Critique* (1790), he had appended an explanatory remark to the text expressive of his sympathy for the Revolution and his hope for freedom. In the same way, he understood his *Critique of Pure Reason* as a revolution in thought, comparable to the Copernican Revolution. In fact, those coming after him—Schiller and Goethe, Hegel and Marx, even the historical school—saw in his *Critique* the beginning of an epoch. Its significance was on the same level as the emancipation of the Third Estate. And thus it is no arbitrary characterization to describe the date of the appearance of the *Critique of Pure Reason* with a phrase that Goethe coined on the occasion of the bombardment of Valmy, which showed the invincibility of the French revolutionary armies: "A new epoch in the history of the world begins here and now."

An epoch is a span of time from which one reckons forward and backward. Even Goethe's phrase sounds like a late formulation of the astonishment experienced by Goethe the war reporter at Valmy. Similarly, the *Critique of Pure Reason* was a shock for which the intellectual

Translated by Professor John Donovan, Department of Philosophy, Georgetown University.

environment was in no way prepared. And yet, a decade after the outbreak of the French Revolution, Europe shuddered under the martial tread of the Napoleonic armies; and ten years after the appearance of the *Critique of Pure Reason,* the entirety of philosophical discussion centered essentially around the question of the true articulation and completion of the transcendental philosophy grounded in Kant.

What fundamentally constitutes an epoch? It was all too clear that no one expected an epoch-making work from the witty, elegant, and esteemed philosopher of Königsberg, the author of the *Dreams of a Spirit-Seer.* He seemed to the highly respected Göttingen philosophers, as we know from reliable evidence, to be a dilettante, and factually, the *Critique of Pure Reason* was for the most part incorrectly received. The critical review from Göttingen, authored primarily by Garve—a review to which Kant replied sharply in the *Prolegomena*—saw the book as an essentially flawed undertaking. Certainly, Kant deceived himself to the extent that he saw this critique of his major work as being based on a spiteful and superficial skimming of its contents. The fashion in which Garve—even with unjustifiable disclaimers—acknowledged himself to be the review's author would serve to show how much the *Critique of Pure Reason* had overtaxed its contemporaries.

To be sure, the transcendental dialectic, with its presentation of the antinomies, struck at the very heart of the prevailing Wolffian scholasticism, so that Mendelssohn labeled Kant the "all-destroyer." But in fact Kant began with Hume's skepticism, and was the first to pose the question of the possibility of metaphysics as a science in a positive and critical sense. There was a general lack of appreciation of the fact that he did not pose the question of metaphysics in a skeptical way. Kant himself saw that his train of thought demanded too much and wrote the *Prolegomena* as the kind of an interpretation and introduction which was meant not so much for a beginner as for a philosophy teacher. That is, he sought to introduce the new science of transcendental philosophy in such a way that it became intelligible from the perspective of Hume's skepticism, but at the same time appeared to justify in a new way the fulfillment of man's natural tendency towards metaphysics. It is apparent that the *Prolegomena*—just as many of the additions which Kant added to the second edition of the *Critique of Pure Reason*—attempted to afford the reader a better orientation. The reader was to understand that the new transcendental philosophy would be developed expressly in relationship to the English Enlightenment—to Locke and Hume on the one hand—but also in response to the Wolffian metaphysics that dominated the university system. Even the very effective comparison of his revolution in thought with the Copernican reversal—an analogy developed in the new preface to the second edition of the *Critique of Pure Reason*—served this purpose.

Certainly, the essential ground of the triumphant breakthrough in thought which the *Critique* was, and the foundation of its perduring influence, lay in the fact that Kant discovered the a priori presuppositions of the experiential sciences themselves—presuppositions not discoverable within the boundaries of experience, but rather grounding the possibility of all experience. The secondary task posed for philosophy by the edifice of science, because of the development of the mathematical science of nature, found a solution here which did justice to both of its aspects: the experiential sciences with their research orientation which must examine all dogmatic presuppositions through their own methodology, and the metaphysical tradition which had been part of the cultural history of the West since the Greeks, with its claim of eternal truths. Thus, the first decade following the appearance of the *Critique* fulfilled the expectations of contemporary thinkers on all sides of the intellectual spectrum. To be sure, there was the critique of dogmatic metaphysics. But in the very act of establishing the boundaries of knowledge, not only did the mathematical science of nature—this undeniable fact—find self-evident recognition, but also the rational fact of freedom, whose proclamation was a prelude to the ideals of the French Revolution.

Thus, perhaps, when we take a new look back, the Kantian *Critique* appears as the historical source for all of us, and one understands why Kant is highly esteemed by the various traditions on both sides of the ocean, which today appears more or less like a "canal." But the truly astonishing thing is that the appearance of the *Critique of Pure Reason* began an epoch which continues on right up to the present. In spite of Hegel, Nietzsche, Heidegger, and Wittgenstein, no one has known how to introduce a subsequent and deeper epoch-building work. In a certain sense, Kant appears to be correct when he announced in the Introduction to the *Prolegomena:*

> My intention is to convince all those who find it important to concern themselves with metaphysics that it is absolutely necessary to bracket their work, and to view all that has been done in this field up till now as if it were naught. . . .

Perhaps many may perceive the curtailment of the development of metaphysics as rooted in the work of Marx or Nietzsche without being considered foolish. And yet, in the end man's natural tendency toward metaphysics time and again seeks such foolishness and attempts it anew. Since Kant, the question "whether or not such a thing as metaphysics is at all possible"—which previously had not even been raised—is at least posed as a question. Since him, it is asked by all, even if there is a wide spectrum of expectations in regard to its answer. Thus, in fact, the task posited by Kant's *Critique of Pure Reason* remains, as does the epoch begun by it, right up to the present. But the question now is no longer the emancipation of a single class, but rather the issue of the status of mankind as such in a world civilization coalescing into a planetary unity.

And yet, anyone who began his university education as I did, at the time of the First World War, was confronted on all sides with an entirely different Kant who generally stood under the heading not of metaphysics, but rather—announced with no less passionate enthusiasm—of the theory of knowledge. Permit me to offer the testimony of one who was a young man at that time, in order to sketch out in the light of the historical influence of the *Critique of Pure Reason* the dimensions in which this great intellectual achievement moved. Historical influence can never be viewed as a closed totality. An endemic characteristic of the historical life of thinking spirit is that it deepens its own self-awareness, and by reflecting upon itself, recognizes itself in differing and new ways. What Kant means can never be decided in retrospect alone, but only with an eye to the future, in the development of thought in an open dialogue, a free exchange of question and answer. And this is a process in which each of us is not so much a questioner, but rather is interrogated by Kant.

How did the dominance of Neo-Kantianism, which was all-pervasive when I was a young man, come to be? It is not surprising that Kant's contemporaries and the thinkers of the next generation were rooted in his thought, and claimed to be its realization. The speculative development of Kant which followed soon after his writings—which we call German Idealism—is rooted with radical decisiveness in his Copernican Revolution. All of them, from Reinhold and Fichte on, intended to think Kant consistently through to the end, when they undertook to deduce, from the principle of self-consciousness, the whole of knowledge as the positings of reason. Now the role that self-consciousness, as the transcendental unity of apperception, played in Kant's *Critique of Pure Reason* was certainly of central significance for the centerpiece of his argument, the profound yet hard to interpret first transcendental deduction. It is through the synthetic unity of reason that the data given in the forms of intuition are united with objective validity to the constitutive categories of the understanding. Thus, without a doubt the principle of self-consciousness appears to be a decisive point in the argumentation constitutive of Kant's problematic. But it in no way discloses the principle from which the entire system of scientific knowledge can be developed. It is well known that Kant never once used the expression 'system' to characterize his own critical effort, even though the systematic unity of reason was ever so important to him. The spontaneous positing and normative self-regulation which Kant had recognized as practical reason was raised to the level of a first principle for the first time by Fichte—and Kant did not recognize his position in this move.

This clearly expresses that which, for his contemporaries, was authentically new in Kant. Kant's theory of the thing in itself, and the affection of sensibility through the thing in itself, appeared to almost all of them to be a dogmatic remnant from the metaphysics he had vanquished. The task which remained was to eliminate this remnant. Fichte went so far in his unbecoming impudence as to call Kant dense for not deriving his own construction of the *Wissenschaftslehre* entirely from the principle of self-consciousness.

This certainly does not imply that German Idealism wanted to breathe new life into the metaphysical idealism which Kant had opposed with good reason. Rather, it was a new attempt to ground metaphysics, and thus a new system of thought that necessitated speculative idealism as its consequence. It was not a question of doubting the reality of the external world, or an attempt to call the receptivity of our own perceptual faculties into question. Rather, at issue here was an understanding of the finitude and conditioned status of human nature, from the perspective of the spontaneity of reason. Reason, which recognized itself, recognized thereby that its limitations were its very own doing. In the same stroke it validated the rationality of empiricism by recognizing in the a posteriori of experience nothing but the impetus of thought. In this way German Idealism understood itself to be the authentic development of Kant, and to have brought transcendental philosophy to its true completion.

All this is well known. And everyone knows of the insoluble conflicts with empirical science which transcendental idealism of this kind engendered. Schelling's and Hegel's philosophy of nature, and also Hegel's construction of World History, and last but not least the transfiguring of the positivity of religion into the dialectical synthesis of thought offered a singularly great challenge to the experiential orientation of their contemporaries. The careful synthesis which Kant had advanced between the experiential standpoint of scientific knowledge and the requirement of reason was abandoned by German Idealism's "philosophy of identity."

In view of this conflict, a reconsideration of Kant was in the air, and in fact, the beginning of Neo-Kantianism stretches back to the epoch of Hegel himself. Above all, it was an all-encompassing demand for the dominating completion of thought, in a transcendental logic which Hegel initiated, that was in general bound to be judged in conflict with the progress of research. Added to this was the force of the Christian Church, which used all of its weapons against the speculative transfiguring of sacred history in Hegel's dialectical *Philosophy of Religion.* What is commonly called 'late Idealism' today, which originated in this theistic reaction to Hegel's gnosticism, may almost go unnoticed in view of the dominant position of German Idealism in the schools. We know today that the spokesmen of this critique of Hegel, among whom are Fichte's son and Immanuel Herman Weise, had laid the foundation for the real return to Kant, which would first occur a decade later. These thinkers followed Schelling's critique of Hegel's 'panlogicism', and his profoundly significant distinction between the categories 'ground' and 'existence' as they are predicated of God. (Cf. the origin of the term 'facticity', which in the Kierkegaard renaissance of the twentieth century gave new expression to the concept of existence—in the work of Heidegger and Sartre.)

It was in the 1860s that the phrase "back to Kant" became a popular slogan. A book by the young Otto Liebmann, which appeared in 1865, had more the character of a manifesto, and immediately found a greatly positive reception. In truth, there was already at an earlier date a recognition on the part of the empirical sciences of their own compatibility with Kant's theory of the a priori, which prepared the way. Obviously, it was the limiting of the a priori categories of the understanding to employment upon the appearances that the positive scientific orientation of this period discovered. The "thing in itself" was bound to appear as an unintelligible metaphysical residue, which was not consistent with the general thrust of the Kantian *Critique.* In fact it is true that the assertion of an attempt to explain the origin of appearances through the "thing in itself" which is supposed to "affect" the senses cannot count as 'knowledge' according to the authentic Kantian presuppositions. The category of causality can only find employment in the forms given in intuition. But that precisely signified that one could offer no further understanding of the logical postulate intrinsic to Kant's argumentation—that in every appearance something must be given that comes to appear there.

This was an age which Comte had not wrongly described as a "positivist" one. Fechner once gave this apt illustration: "A prominent Pole or Russian visited a large manufacturing plant in Berlin that was powered by a steam engine. He was taken on a tour of the entire plant, inspected all of its departments carefully, followed the relationship of the parts of the machinery, asked questions about all possibilities, conversed in a very sensible fashion with the foreman who was showing him around; in brief, he seemed to be completely oriented to the process whereby the plant ran. After he had gone through all of this, he asked, to the great consternation of the foreman: 'Won't you show me now also the place beneath all of this where the horses stand?' " Fechner finished the story with the sentence which sounded the death knell of the "thing in itself": "There are no horses below."

Thus, we've arrived at the point at which the magic phrase of the theory of knowledge up to 1919 was carved upon all the cathedrals, was for the first time formulated as a battle cry. In 1862 Eduard Zeller placed this frequently used phrase in the foreground in his inaugural lecture at Heidelberg. The lecture had the immediate purpose of returning to the idea of a transcendental logic, which in Hegel's school had been given a further development—to the careful Kantian attempt to mediate between empiricism and rationalism, the a posteriori and the a priori. In this way Zeller was able to invoke a renowned empirical researcher of Helmholtz's stature as an advocate for Kant. But it is an indication of how even the recognition of a priori elements in knowledge was formulated in a positivistic fashion when we hear Zeller say: "We are never forgetful that a priori elements are already contained in experience itself. When we separate them, we are able to identify for the first time that which is purely objectively given." Zeller is following Helmholtz entirely here, in as much as he distinguishes the concept of observation, which establishes the actual series of events, from the inferences which mediate—on the ground of experience—that which is "given" in observation. This corresponds entirely to Helmholtz's doctrine of unconscious inferences, through which only the scientific researcher can illustrate the Kantian a priori.

The birth of the "theory of knowledge" was thus a form of protest against the panlogicism of the Hegelians. Only as a consequence of this can we understand the return to Kant. Hence, the theory of knowledge believed that it was returning to Kant when it recognized "a given" as distinct from the categorical formulation of thought. Indeed, the given is treated as a first foundation, upon which thought must follow as a second step, primarily as a search for causes. When we remember Kant's central problematic, as for instance it is expressed in the letter to Marcus Herz in 1772, it is obvious that this has nothing to do with Kant: "To the extent that the image only contains the manner in which the subject is affected by the object, it is easy to see how it [the object] relates to this [subject] as an effect to its cause." That is, as a "determination of our minds." One may remind oneself of Kant's explicit exposition of his position—that it is a question of the justification of the use of the categories of the understanding alone, and this not so much for scientific knowledge, itself of great importance, as for the partly illegitimate, partly unavoidable extension of our thought beyond the boundaries of experience. In any case, it is a genetic-psychological reinterpretation of the transcendental problematic, and not its recovery, which paved the way for the theory of knowledge in this its first attack. It was able to place itself under Kant's mantle through the interpretation of Fries and his school. From here up to Nelson, the transcendental approach of Kant was understood anthropologically—that is, as geared to an empirical-genetic problematic.

The authentic rediscovery of the Kantian problematic was something radically other than such application of Kantian concepts to the "facts of consciousness." The fundamental thought of the new Kantianism lay in opposition to the orientation toward the given, and had its purest expression in the transcendental understanding's "construction" of the object through thought. The object is not "the given," but rather the "infinite task"—as Natorp's formulation puts it. One should not allow oneself to be deceived by the universal preeminence which Neo-Kantianism displayed at the beginning of our century. It is a matter of programmatic beginnings, which in looking back to the original text of Kant, discloses to us an entire history of Kant interpretation. In the *Critique of Pure Reason,* the problems of the theory of knowledge, especially the doctrine of the "thing in itself" and the doctrine of "affection," are placed in the foreground in this history of interpretation: this we see in Kuno Fischer in 1860, Otto Liebmann in 1865, F. A. Lange and Hermann Cohen in 1871, A. Riehl in 1875, Benno Erdmann, and so on. Before Neo-Kantianism really established itself and spread through the entire cultural world—to the Anglo-American as well as to the Latin and eastern Asiatic cultures—neither the southwest German nor the Marburg school was prominently known. The Polish philosopher W. Tatarkiewicz has quite aptly depicted how contingent it was to call Neo-Kantianism "the Marburg school," and how dogmatic it appeared for them to recognize themselves as the real descendants of Plato, Galileo, Descartes, and above all, Leibniz—all interpreted to be forerunners of the Kantian justification of mathematical natural science. Thus, the Polish thinker spoke from a time—at the beginning of our century—when Cohen had published his own system of pure knowledge, and Natorp his *Plato,* and the logical foundations of the natural sciences were becoming visible in the school of critical philosophy. The revival of transcendental thought, which sprang from the return to Kant, was in no way supported by the spirit of the times, which demanded psychology and not the critical theory of knowledge. Neither Fechner nor Wundt nor Dilthey nor Sigwart maintained the transcendental philosophy, and the same holds true for the philosophical historical research which was developing at that time. As described in the categories of Husserl or of Neo-Kantianism, all of this was psychologism or historicism.

It is from this constellation that one should understand that the authentic concern of Kant—the grounding of metaphysics in a new and uniquely viable foundation, namely, practical reason and the rational fact of freedom—was cast into the background by the rediscovery of Kant. That science has a priori presuppositions, and that the conditions of the possibility of experience are demonstrated in the givenness of science—these things certainly also express Kant's doctrine. But Kant had posed the *quaestio juris,* with what right may the a priori categories of the understanding be taken as objectively valid? from a metaphysical interest. And it is well known that Kant's answer to this question was neither developed in a psychological-genetic way, nor even limited to the justification of science.

Since Kant's followers had made the idea of a system, and its grounding in the supreme and foundational principle of self-consciousness, the central point, Kant's argumentation was essentially changed. When thought attempts to begin with itself, it can recognize nothing given in intuition outside itself. What was the return to Kant then supposed to mean? What other surety against the romantic employment of intellectual intuition could it offer? The answer lay in the adherence to the "purity" of mathematical natural science. Cohen's formula now was "the unity of consciousness." The "proof" of this "unanicity" through thought is the infinitesimal method. In the consideration of boundaries, in the concept of the infinite, all intuition and comprehension is subordinated and the true source of reality is obtained. It steps into the place of intuition and that which is given in it. This holds good not only for the purity of scientific knowledge, but just as much for the pure will and for pure feeling. Thus Cohen points to a science which serves as a model of the self-assertion of the pure will—the science of right.

However narrow or heavy-handed this might sound, in comparison to the dominant psychologism it succeeded in reinstating the transcendental concept of the a priori. To the extent that it finally returned psychology to a critically legitimizing sense, by that very fact it displayed the stamp of a retrieval of the Kantian problematic. Natorp's *General Psychology* had developed the idea of a transcendental psychology as research into consciousness as such, in which the various modes of our consciousness of objects find their unity. Husserl's research into regional correlations ought to be compared here.

The Object of Knowledge was the title of one of the most influential books leading to the ascendancy of Neo-Kantianism. Heinrich Rickert, a student of Windelband's, was its author. Such a title as this gives precise expression to the Marburg orientation toward the fact of science. Yet, it was not mathematical natural science alone that was considered. H. Lotze already had collected theoretical and practical philosophy under the concepts of validity and value, and, following Windelband, Rickert had sought the boundaries of the conceptual scaffolding of natural science. The widespread and central methodological debate concerning the foundation of the human sciences found its solution here from the viewpoint of Neo-Kantian methodology. The solution lay in the epistemological grounding of science. Moreover, it was right in character for the South German school to invert Dilthey's question concerning the architectonic of the historical world into the question of the object of the historical sciences. It is the value-content which makes an event into a historical fact.

The theory of value, which had no real expression in Kantian thought, was the most influential doctrine of Neo-Kantianism. It encompassed the distinction between the judgment which objectively ascertained facts and the subjectively grounded value judgment. Thus, Neo-Kantianism credited Max Weber also with determining the foundation of the social sciences. Indeed, Max Scheler and Nicolai Hartmann later on, in reaction to Neo-Kantianism, posited a phenomenology of value, which ascribed also to value an ideal inseity. And yet, the turn to a phenomenology of value was not unconnected with transcendental idealism. Husserl taught this directly, and the phenomenology of value had its place very early in his research program, and maintained its importance throughout his work. Of course, it was a thoroughly encompassing concept of transcendental justification which Husserl's phenomenology followed. It had nothing of the narrowness of the Neo-Kantian orientation toward the fact of science. Husserl saw Descartes' methodic doubt more as a prototype of his thought than Kant's transcendental turn, because he associated the latter with Neo-Kantianism as a mere epistemology of scientific understanding. His research sought the a priori of the entire life-world. Thus we must, in the end, apply to him that which is clearly the case for Windelband and Rickert: the result of the phenomenological research program is more likely to be a Hegel than a Kant.

A similar judgment can be made concerning the most brilliant representative of Marburg Neo-Kantianism. Ernst Cassirer with full consciousness extended the transcendental problematic beyond the perimeters of science to the entire field of the objectifications of culture. In his *Philosophy of Symbolic Forms* he elucidated, from the perspective of the activities of transcendental subjectivity, the vast field of that which Hegel had rendered accessible to logic and the logos under the rubric of "objective spirit."

And so it appears that, for these many decades spanning the age of the "back to Kant" movement which we call Neo-Kantianism, the noteworthy accomplishment that resulted was the following: the movement which advertised itself under Kant's name was more of a return to Fichte and Hegel. It is no less significant that the critique of Neo-Kantianism which arose during the First World War, armed with the weapons of the older critique of Hegelianism—especially Kierkegaard's existential dialectic—can be directly seen as the retrieval of the original Kantian position. It was mainly the metaphysical tradition of the eighteenth century which was the root of Kant's thought. One became able to see this for the first time with the self-destruction of Neo-Kantianism, which—in the case of Natorp and the late Fichte, the Heidelberg school, and, in the end, even Husserl despite himself—was oriented toward Hegel. Christian Wolff, the object of the shared disdain of the Neo-Kantians, again became of interest, for example to Picher, Nicolai Hartmann, Peter Wust, Heinz Heimsoeth, etc. This renewed interest led to a revaluation of rational metaphysics in the contemporary work of Kant scholarship. Thus it is significant that Nicolai Hartmann's renunciation of his idealist Marburg tradition did not result in a practical philosophy, but took the shape of a metaphysics of knowledge. Kant was no longer seen as an epistemologist, but again as a metaphysician, but, to be precise, as a metaphysician of knowledge, and not on the ground of practical philosophy, where he himself had grounded metaphysics anew.

It is surprising that the two original thinkers who are contemporaries for those of us who are older, and who successfully led the critique of idealism after World War I—Jaspers and Heidegger—both apprehended Kant under the heading of metaphysics. For both, the issue was the retrieval of metaphysics, and both turned to Kant for that purpose, of course in vastly different ways. Jaspers's philosophy of existence repeated in its way Kant's founding of metaphysics on practical reason. Heidegger saw, without taking practical philosophy into consideration, the true rediscovery of metaphysics in the *Critique of Pure Reason* itself. It was astonishingly close to the fundamental motivations of Kantian thought how Jaspers accomplished his rejection of the formal procedures of argumentation in Neo-Kantianism, and developed his "philosophy" in an entirely personal fashion. There is no direct reference to Kant, at least no more than to Plato, Plotinus, or Schelling, and perhaps Jaspers himself was unaware of how much his personal appropriation of the great tradition of philosophy stayed within the systematic framework of Kantian thought. Not only does the positing of boundaries correspond to the scientific world-orientation of the *Critique of Pure Reason,* and not only does the overstepping of such boundaries correspond to the boundary situations of human existence, to the primacy of practical reason. Even that which Jaspers calls metaphysics, the step over into transcendence and the reading of its ciphers, is a Kantian motif. Thus, Jaspers renews, in the vocabulary of his *Existenz*-philosophy, the postulates of practical reason which Kant had sketched out as the justification and fulfillment of man's natural tendency toward metaphysics. And it is a paradoxical fact that Jaspers's liquidation of Neo-Kantianism in fact led him nearer to the original Kant than the Neo-Kantian school itself stood. It seems to me that it is becoming clear that the thought of our cultural crisis is more and more, and with justification, directed towards this question: How is the natural tendency of mankind toward metaphysics to be mediated with the ethos and pathos of science, whose nameless power rules our civilization?

It is enough of a paradox that Heidegger, who from his early association with Husserl had fought Neo-Kantianism, reckoned Kant, as he himself expressed it later, as having provided him a "shelter" to help him find his way. Of course it also follows that, in as much as he opposed the ultimate grounding in the transcendental ego, he retrieved the Kantian doctrine of the two sources and validated the fundamental significance of receptivity. It is a paradox that he, attempting to get behind phenomenological idealism, and aiming at the temporality of Being, at "Being and Time," laid aside Kant's own grounding of metaphysics in practical reason. An immediate consequence was that for him the transcendental imagination (as was already the case in the work of Fichte) promised to serve as the hidden unity between the two sources of knowledge, and, despite this deeply hidden ground, in which he saw temporality, he was unable to seize upon it as an ultimate principle of all grounding. When Cassirer in Davos, in opposition to the fundamental Heideggerian reference to Kant as a metaphysician, maintained the foundational role of ethics in the grounding of metaphysics, Heidegger interpreted this reference to freedom immediately as the "self-liberating of freedom in man." This corresponds completely with Heidegger's later formulation that the essence of truth is freedom. For this statement fundamentally means that the essence of freedom is truth, which reveals but equally conceals. The primacy of the question of Being in relation to ethics, announced in the *Letter on Humanism,* is already applicable here. Likewise when Heidegger later, in his Kant portrait of 1929, saw an aggravation of his own path, Kant was for him perhaps not the metaphysician of practical reason but one of the few thinkers who had not lost sight of the question of Being, and fallen into the forgetfulness of Being characteristic of metaphysics.

In the meantime, a half century has gone by. It is part of the discipline of giving testimony not to go beyond what one has seen oneself. The account of an aging witness to the ambiguous return to Kant must be adjusted to a situation in which new problematics arise and new horizons emerge. The witness becomes a participant in the thoughtful confrontation with Kant which recognizes no discontinuity. This confrontation is proceeding in many directions. Among them I would like to point out two, in which Kant, again not as an epistemologist, but as a metaphysician, appears even for me as a partner in conversation. There is, in the first place, the central role which the problem of language, the theory of the symbol, and linguistics play in the present. Must not in the end even the fertile ambiguity which is rooted in Kant's concept of the "thing in itself" appear in a new light from this perspective? That a new problematic attains suggestive interfacing with an older viewpoint—this itself is directly taught in the *Critique of Pure Reason.* That which Herder had in mind in his murky critique of Kant's architectonic of the concept may be capable of a new determination by scholars with new analytical and logical insight. The inner relationship between word and concept, between the life of language and designation through the concept, points to a universality of reason, in which the oppositions of scientific daring and political and economic prudence can be mediated—the most pressing task of the contemporary world.

There is a second correlation which is not clearly expressed in the *Critique of Pure Reason.* I mean the significance which practical philosophy also has directly for the theoretical problems of knowledge for metaphysics. In the *Foundations of the Metaphysics of Morals,* Kant has shown with brilliant consistency the inner connection of practical reason with its justification in thought. Is there not adequate evidence for the natural tendency of man towards metaphysics in the fact that everyone attempts to complete it? Of course, a critique of this tendency is necessary, and indeed, precisely a critique uniting all counterpositions in the metaphysical spectrum. Kant saw in capacity to make judgments the unifying point of human rationality. Already the first generation of his followers was especially inspired by the *Critique of Judgment* with which Kant had completed his critical enterprise. This work appears to me today, in the entire multiplicity of its implications, a perduring heuristic guide for our thought. Two centuries of human experience, and a successor to older knowledge, a successor as diversified as there are various cultural and historical traditions, and which is attempting in the hermeneutic dialogue of the present to find unity—all of this found its origin in 1781 with Kant's *Critique of Pure Reason.*

"A new epoch in the history of the world begins here and now." And Goethe's text continues: "and you can say that you were there." Can we say that also of the birth of the *Critique*? That we were there? That we are there?

Heidelberg

2 The Originality of Kant's Distinction between Analytic and Synthetic Judgments

HENRY E. ALLISON

In most discussions of the topic, Kant's distinction between analytic and synthetic judgments is assumed to be fundamentally akin to distinctions drawn by some of his predecessors. Leibniz's distinction between truths of reason and truths of fact and Hume's between relations of ideas and matters of fact are the two most commonly cited. If it is acknowledged at all, Kant's originality is seen to lie in his extremely controversial contention that a subset of synthetic judgments can be known to be true a priori. It must be noted, however, that this textbook conception of the Kantian distinction ignores the fact that, in the second edition of the *Critique of Pure Reason,* Kant claims that not only the problem of the synthetic a priori, "but perhaps even the distinction between analytic and synthetic judgments, has never previously been considered" (B 19). Moreover, some three years later, in his response to Eberhard, who denied that Kant's thought is original in any significant respect, he again insists that prior to the *Critique* "this manner of considering judgment has never been properly conceived."[1] To be sure, Kant also expresses himself more cautiously, acknowledging that some of his predecessors, most notably Locke, Leibniz, and Crusius, came close to discovering the distinction.[2] Nevertheless, he consistently maintained the originality of the distinction as he articulated it.

[1] *On a Discovery, Kants gesammelte Schriften,* vol. VIII, p. 244. *The Kant-Eberhard Controversy,* ed. and trans. Henry E. Allison (Baltimore and London: Johns Hopkins University Press, 1973), p. 154.

[2] Cf. *Prolegomena,* §3, *Kants gesammelte Schriften,* vol. IV, p. 270, where Kant acknowledges finding, "einen Wink zu dieser Eintheilung in Locke"; *On a Discovery,* vol. VIII, pp. 245–46; *The Kant-Eberhard Controversy,* pp. 155–56, where he again mentions Locke as well as Crusius and the Wolffian logician Johann Peter Reusch; and the *Vorarbeiten zur Schrift gegen Eberhard,* vol. XX, p. 376, where he suggests that perhaps Leibniz understood nothing more with his distinction between the principles of contradiction and sufficient reason than his own analytic-synthetic distinction.

Not surprisingly, this claim has been challenged, first by Eberhard and then, in the twentieth century, by Arthur Lovejoy. Both insist, the latter with considerable erudition, that Kant's celebrated distinction is nothing more than a warmed-over restatement of a distinction that was already commonplace in the logical writings of the Leibniz-Wolff school.[3] The Eberhard-Lovejoy critique has, in turn, been dealt with in definitive fashion by Lewis White Beck, who champions Crusius as a genuine forerunner of Kant.[4] I believe that Beck is correct to the extent that Crusius exerted a significant (perhaps even decisive) influence on Kant, and that he probably came closer to anticipating the distinction than any of Kant's better-known predecessors; but I do not think that one can claim much more than that.[5] My concern, however, is not with historical questions regarding relative degrees of influence or approximation; it is rather with the philosophical reasons underlying Kant's insistence on the discontinuity of his analytic-synthetic distinction with the superficially similar distinctions of his predecessors. In brief, my thesis is that Kant's claim of originality reflects his understanding of the connection between the analytic-synthetic distinction

[3] Arthur O. Lovejoy, "Kant's Antithesis of Dogmatism and Criticism," in *Kant: Disputed Questions,* ed. Moltke S. Gram (Chicago: Quadrangle Books, 1967), pp. 105–30. I discuss Eberhard's views in *The Kant-Eberhard Controversy,* pp. 36–42.

[4] Lewis White Beck, "Lovejoy as a Critic of Kant" and "Analytic and Synthetic Judgments before Kant," in *Essays on Kant and Hume* (New Haven and London: Yale University Press, 1978), pp. 61–100; esp. 92–94 for the discussion of Crusius.

[5] As Lewis White Beck points out, J. S. Beck wrote to Kant in 1793 that Crusius's *Weg zur Gewissheit,* §260, provides a better indication of the analytic-synthetic distinction than the passages Kant had cited from Locke (*Kants gesammelte Schriften,* vol. XI, pp. 444–45). Crusius there argues against Wolffian dogmatism that the principle of contradiction is not the single principle of human cognition; in particular, he maintains that it is not sufficient to account for "the constitution [*Einrichtung*] of the concepts themselves." Here, as elsewhere, his main example is the causal principle. He contends that the proposition that something came into existence without a cause is absurd but not self-contradictory. As many scholars, including Beck, have noted, Crusius is thus a source of the essential lesson which Kant claimed to have learned from Hume and which supposedly awakened him from his "dogmatic slumber." At the very least, Crusius must be credited with a clear recognition of the need to provide an extra-logical principle for the explanation of some a priori truths. Presumably, this is what Kant himself had in mind when he remarked that Crusius "only refers to metaphysical propositions which cannot be demonstrated through the principle of contradiction" (*On a Discovery,* vol. VIII, p. 246; *The Kant-Eberhard Controversy,* p. 156). Kant's complaint is that Crusius did not proceed from this insight to the formulation of a universal distinction between kinds of judgments. His point could also be put by stating that Crusius hit upon the problem of the synthetic a priori without first having a clear conception of the nature of synthetic judgments in general. This is consistent with the fact that Kant's criticism of Crusius is essentially the same as his criticism of Hume; viz., he conflates subjective with objective necessity. For a comprehensive treatment of Kant's relationship to Crusius see Heinz Heimsoeth, *Metaphysik und Kritik bei Chr. A. Crusius,* Schriften der Königsberger Gelehrten Gesellschaft, Heft 3 (Berlin, 1926).

and his conception of judgment or, more generally, his account of discursive thought. The essential point is that in order to recognize the possibility of judgments that are synthetic in Kant's sense, it is first necessary to recognize the complementary roles of concepts and sensible intuitions in human knowledge. In other words, it is necessary to recognize that human thought is discursive in the sense indicated by Kant in the Transcendental Analytic. Since, as I shall try to show, Kant's predecessors did not regard human thought as discursive in this sense (as requiring a synthesis of concept and intuition), they were not able to arrive at the Kantian conception of a synthetic judgment (whether a priori or a posteriori).[6] Consequently, they can hardly be said to have arrived at Kant's analytic-synthetic distinction.

I

Discursive knowledge, which Kant sometimes characterizes simply as "thought" (*das Denken*), is knowledge by means of concepts.[7] In his *Lectures on Logic* Kant defines a concept, in contrast to an intuition, as "a general representation or a representation of what is common to several objects."[8] In light of this definition, he further points out that it is a mere tautology to speak of general or common concepts, as if concepts could be divided into general, particular, and singular. "Not the concepts themselves, but merely their use can be so divided."[9] In the parallel definition in the *Critique,* Kant remarks that a concept, again in contrast to an intuition, refers to its object "mediately by means of a feature [*eines Merkmals*] which several things may have in common" (A 320/B 377). In other words, due to its generality, a concept can only refer to an object by means of features which are also predicable of other objects falling under the same concept.

In the *Critique* Kant remarks that a concept "is always, as regards its form, something universal which serves as a rule" (A 106). As such, a concept functions as an organizing principle for consciousness, a means for holding a series of representations (themselves concepts) together in an "analytic unity." For example, to form the concept of body is to think together the features of extension, impenetrability,

[6]The general point that Kant's predecessors did not regard knowledge as discursive in Kant's sense is argued by M. Glouberman, "Conceptuality: An Essay in Retrieval," *Kant-Studien,* Heft 4 (1979), pp. 383–408. He does not, however, relate the issue to the analytic-synthetic distinction or to the question of Kant's originality.

[7]*Lectures on Logic,* §1, *Kants gesammelte Schriften,* vol. IX, p. 91.

[8]Ibid.

[9]Ibid.

figure, etc. (the components of the concept). To apply this concept is to conceive of some actual or possible object(s) under the general description provided by these features. This is equivalent to forming a judgment with respect to the object(s). Thus Kant claims that "the only use which the understanding can make of these concepts is to judge by means of them" (A 68/B 93), and he characterizes concepts as "predicates of possible judgments" (A 69/B 94).

Kant also distinguishes between pure (a priori) and empirical concepts and between the matter and the form of a concept; but only the latter distinction is directly relevant to our present concerns. By the content of an empirical concept, Kant means the sensible features that are thought in it as marks. These are derived from experience and correspond to the sensible properties of things. By the form of a concept, Kant means its universality or generality, which is the same for all concepts. The main point is that simply having a set of sensible impressions that are associated with one another is not the same as having a concept. The latter requires the thought of the applicability of this set of sensible impressions to a plurality of possible objects. With this thought these impressions become transformed into "marks," i.e., partial conceptions. This thought, however, is not itself derived from experience; rather, it is produced by a series of "logical acts" of the understanding that Kant terms "comparison," "reflection," and "abstraction."[10] These involve the combining together of the common sensible features shared by diverse particulars into the above-mentioned "analytic unity," while disregarding or abstracting from the differences.[11] Kant sometimes characterizes this whole process as "reflection" (*Reflexion, Überlegung*);[12] consequently, the concepts produced thereby are also called "reflected [*reflectirte*] representations."[13]

Although discursive knowledge is defined as knowledge by means of concepts, concepts alone are not sufficient to produce knowledge. Thought must have some content to conceptualize, and since it is essentially an organizing or unifying activity, it cannot produce this content from its own resources. The content must, therefore, in some way be given to the mind. Kant's generic term for the kind of representation that performs this essential epistemic task is 'intuition' (*Anschauung*). In the *Lectures on Logic* Kant defines an intuition, in

[10] Ibid., §6, pp. 94–95.

[11] Ibid., p. 95.

[12] Ibid., §5, p. 94. Cf. *Reflexionen* 2876 and 2878, *Kants gesammelte Schriften*, vol. XVI, pp. 555 and 557.

[13] *Lectures on Logic*, §1, p. 91.

contrast to a concept, as a "singular representation (*repraesentatio singularis*)."[14] He repeats this characterization in the parallel definition in the *Critique,* and, as befitting its presentational function, adds that an intuition "refers immediately to the object" (*bezieht sich unmittelbar auf den Gegenstand*) (A 320/B 377). An intuition can thus be characterized as a representation of an individual object, by means of which that object is present to the mind. Both the singularity and the presentational function of an intuition can be understood in terms of its immediacy.[15]

The above characterization is meant to apply to all kinds of intuition. Kant also insists, however, that all *our,* i.e., human, intuition, but not every conceivable kind, is sensible. Now 'sensibility' is the name Kant assigns to the receptive side of the mind, that is, its capacity to receive data (impressions) in so far as it is somehow "affected by objects." The linkage of intuition with sensibility thus means that all our intuition and, therefore, all our knowledge, depends upon the mind's capacity to receive data (impressions). By the same token, sensible intuition only provides the mind with the raw data for conceptualization, not with determinate knowledge of objects.[16] Actual

[14] Ibid.

[15] This is diametrically opposed to the interpretation advanced by Jaakko Hintikka, "On Kant's Notion of Intuition (*Anschauung*)," in *The First Critique, Reflections on Kant's Critique of Pure Reason,* ed. Terence Penelhum and J. J. MacIntosh (Belmont, California: Wadsworth Publishing Company, 1969), pp. 38–53, and related papers. Following Frege, Hintikka calls attention to the fact that in the *Lectures on Logic* Kant defines 'intuition' simply as a singular representation, and that he nowhere affirms a necessary connection between intuition and sensibility. An intuition is thus understood essentially as a singular representation corresponding to a singular term; immediacy is treated as a mere corollary of singularity. Now Hintikka is quite correct with regard to the question of the connection between intuition and sensibility, but it does not follow from this (as he seems to assume) that immediacy is not a defining characteristic of a Kantian intuition. The key point is that even non-sensible, i.e., intellectual, intuitions must be conceived of as presenting their object immediately to the mind. Thus, despite Kant's definition in the *Lectures on Logic,* singularity is not really a sufficient criterion for an intuition in the Kantian sense, even when the notion is divorced from any connection with sensibility. Hintikka's denigration of the immediacy criterion has also been criticized from a quite different perspective, and with no reference to the notion of an intellectual intuition, by Charles Parsons, "Kant's Philosophy of Arithmetic," in *Philosophy, Science and Method,* ed. Sidney Morgenbesser, Patrick Suppes, and Morton White (New York: St. Martin's Press, 1969), esp. pp. 570–71, and Kirk Dalles Wilson, "Kant on Intuition," *Philosophical Quarterly* 25 (1975), pp. 247–65.

[16] Interestingly enough, this whole issue is glossed over by Hintikka. He argues (op. cit., pp. 46ff.) that since the connection between intuition and sensibility is only established in the Transcendental Aesthetic, any reference to intuition in portions of the *Critique* that precede the Aesthetic either textually (the Introduction) or chronologically (the Transcendental Doctrine of Method) can be interpreted without any reference to sensibility. The motivation for such a reading is to find in the *Critique* a conception of syntheticity, and, more particularly, an account of the role of intuition in mathematics,

knowledge requires not only that the data be given in intuition, but also that they be taken under some general description or "recognized in a concept." Kant expresses this clearly in the famous formula:

> Intuitions and concepts constitute, therefore, the elements of all our knowledge, so that neither concepts without an intuition in some way corresponding to them, nor intuitions without concepts, can yield knowledge. (A 50/B 74)

It has been frequently noted, however, that there is a tension, if not a contradiction, between Kant's claim that sensible intuition requires thought in order to yield the representation of an object and the generic definition of 'intuition' as *repraesentatio singularis.*[17] The latter certainly suggests that an intuition is itself a representation of an individual object, quite apart from any conceptual determination. Perhaps the sharpest statement of the problem is by J. S. Beck, who comments in a letter to Kant:

> The *Critique* calls "intuition" a representation that relates immediately to an object. But in fact, a representation does not become objective until it is subsumed under the categories. Since intuition similarly acquires its objective character only by means of the application of categories to it, I am in favor of leaving out that definition of "intuition" that refers to it as a representation relating to objects. I find in intuition nothing more than a manifold accompanied by consciousness (or by the *unique "I think"*), a manifold determined by the latter, in which there is as such no relation to an object. I would also like to reject the definition of "concept" as a representation mediately related to an object. Rather, I distinguish concepts from intuitions by the fact that they are thoroughly determinate whereas intuitions are not thoroughly determinate. For both intuitions and concepts acquire objectivity only after the activity of judgment subsumes them under the pure concepts of the understanding.[18]

Kant's only extant response to this query is contained in a marginal note attached to Beck's letter. In it he remarks:

> To make [*Bestimmung*] a concept, by means of intuition, into a cognition of an object, is indeed the work of judgment; but the reference of intuition to an object in general is not. For the latter is merely the logical use of representation insofar as a representation is thought as being a cognition. When,

---

which is devoid of all of the "psychological" implications which, Hintikka assumes, arise as soon as intuition is understood in connection with sensibility. The point which Hintikka ignores, however, in this effort to modernize, i.e., de-psychologize, Kant, is the connection between sensibility and discursive knowledge.

[17] Most recently by Manley Thompson, "Singular Terms and Intuitions in Kant's Epistemology," *Review of Metaphysics* 26/2 (December 1972), pp. 314–43.

[18] Beck's letter to Kant, Nov. 11, 1791, *Kants gesammelte Schriften,* vol. XI, p. 310. English translation in Zweig, *Kant, Philosophical Correspondence, 1759–99,* pp. 180–81. Beck repeats essentially the same point in his letter to Kant of May 31, 1792.

on the other hand, a single representation is referred only to the subject, the use is aesthetic (feeling), in which case the representation cannot become a piece of knowledge.[19]

Although Kant does attempt to defend his definition of 'intuition', he really seems to concede Beck's main point; for he acknowledges that, apart from being conceptualized in an act of judgment, intuitions do not really refer to or "represent" objects at all. To be sure, Kant does suggest that, independently of judgment, an intuition refers to an "object in general," and this calls to mind the definition of 'appearance' in the *Critique* as the "undetermined object of an empirical intuition" (A 20/B 34). Nevertheless, it is clear in the present case that the assertion of a connection between intuition and an "object in general" is merely for the purpose of logical 'classification'. In other words, it is Kant's way of distinguishing between intuitions, which become objective, i.e., represent objects, by being brought under concepts in judgments, and purely subjective or aesthetic representations (feelings), which have no cognitive function.[20] It must not be forgotten, however, that Kantian intuitions can be brought under concepts, and that when they are they do represent particular objects. Thus, as I have argued elsewhere, it is necessary to distinguish between determinate or conceptualized and indeterminate or unconceptualized intuitions.[21] Only the former is in the full sense a *repraesentatio singularis.*

Unfortunately, this does not exhaust the complexity or, perhaps better, the ambiguity inherent in the Kantian conception of intuition. In fact, it only applies to one of three senses in which Kant uses the term: the sense in which it refers to a particular kind of representation or mental content. In addition to this more or less official sense of 'intuition', Kant also uses the term to refer both to the object represented, the *intuited,* and to the act of directly representing an individual, the *intuiting.* In short, it is necessary to distinguish a mental content, an object, and an act sense of 'intuition'.[22] Now, while it is generally clear from the context when the term is being used in the

[19] Zweig, *Correspondence,* p. 181.

[20] Cf. *Critique of Pure Reason,* B 66, *Critique of Judgment,* Introduction, VII, *Kants gesammelte Schriften,* vol. VI, p. 189.

[21] *The Kant-Eberhard Controversy,* pp. 80–82, and "Transcendental Schematism and the Problem of the Synthetic A Priori," *Dialectica* 35, no. 12 (1981), pp. 68–73. In these places, however, I have argued for the necessity of making the distinction in the case of pure intuition (the central text being B 160 note, where Kant distinguishes between a "form of intuition" and a "formal intuition"). The present claim is that a parallel distinction is required for empirical intuition as well.

[22] This threefold distinction was suggested to me by Lewis White Beck in his comments on an earlier version of this paper.

third sense, it is frequently difficult to determine whether it is being used in the first or second sense or, indeed, whether or not Kant himself conflates the two senses. Moreover, we shall see that a resolution of this question is crucial for the proper understanding of the Kantian conception of a synthetic judgment. First, however, we must consider Kant's general theory of judgment.

II

As already indicated, discursive knowledge is judgmental. It is in and through judgments that we apply concepts to given data, while concepts themselves are characterized as "predicates of possible judgments." Kant makes all of this quite explicit when he states that "we can reduce all acts of the understanding to judgments, and the *understanding* may therefore be represented as a *faculty of judgment* [*ein Vermögen zu urtheilen*]" (A 69/B 94). Accordingly, in order to understand more fully the significance of Kant's claim about the discursive nature of human cognition it is imperative to consider Kant's account of the nature of judgment.

Kant's general account of judgment in the *Critique* is contained in the section entitled "The Logical Employment of the Understanding," which serves as an introduction to the Metaphysical Deduction. His major concern here is to make explicit the connection between discursive or conceptual knowledge and judgment. This enables him to connect the pure concepts of the understanding with the forms or functions of unity in judgment. The initial claim is simply that every judgment involves an act of conceptualization and every such act involves a judgment.[23] Since this is the case, and since Kant's conception of concepts commits him to the doctrine that "no concept is ever related to an object immediately, but to some other representation of it, be that other representation an intuition or a concept," he proceeds to define judgment as "the mediate knowledge of an object, that is, the representation of a representation of it" (A 68/B 93). Apart from the mediated or indirect nature of the relation between concepts and objects in judgments, which is a consequence of the abstract, general nature of the concept, two points are to be noted about this definition. The first is that it implies that every judgment involves the cognition of an object, or at least the claim of such cognition. This, in turn,

[23] Cf. H. J. Paton, *Kant's Metaphysic of Experience* (London: George Allen and Unwin, 1936), vol. I, p. 251.

means that every judgment, simply qua judgment, is "objectively valid." Although Kant does not develop that point here, he does do so in the second edition Transcendental Deduction, where he distinguishes a judgment from a mere association of ideas, which only possesses "subjective validity."[24] The second is that it is perfectly general, and thus presumably applicable to analytic and synthetic judgments alike. It is followed immediately in the text by an explanation which contains a capsule account of his theory of judgment. Because of its brevity and importance, I shall quote it in full.

> In every judgment there is a concept which holds of many representations, and among them of a given representation that is immediately related to an object. Thus in the judgment, 'all bodies are divisible', the concept of the divisible applies to various other concepts, but is here applied in particular to the concept of body, and this concept again to certain intuitions [or appearances][25] that present themselves to us. These objects, therefore, are mediately represented through the concept of divisibility. Accordingly, all judgments are functions of unity among our representations; instead of an immediate representation, a *higher* representation, which comprises the immediate representation and various others, is used in knowing the object, and thereby much possible knowledge is collected into one.

We see from Kant's example that the judgment involves two concepts, 'body' and 'divisibility', which are related both to each other and to the object judged about, that is, to the complete set of x's thought under the general description contained in the concept 'body'. Of these, the subject concept, 'body', stands in the more direct, though still not immediate, relation to the object. It does not relate to the object *simpliciter* (no concept can do that), but rather to an immediate representation of it. Such an immediate representation is, by definition, an intuition; so the subject concept in Kant's illustration refers directly to the intuition, and only mediately to the object. Roughly put, the intuition provides the sensible content for the judgment, while the concept provides the rule in accordance with which the content is determined. It is precisely by determining this content that the concept is brought into relation with the object. That is why

[24] *Critique of Pure Reason* B 142. If one is to make any sense of the claim that every judgment is objectively valid it is obviously necessary to distinguish between objective validity and truth, as Kant himself does at A 760/B 788. For a discussion of this issue see Gerold Prauss, *Erscheinung bei Kant* (Berlin: Walter de Gruyter, 1971), pp. 86–87, and Rainer Stuhlmann-Laeisz, *Kants Logik* (Berlin: Walter de Gruyter, 1976), pp. 28–53.

[25] Following Paton, op. cit., p. 253 n. 3, Kant's own *Handexemplar* and Raymond Schmidt, I am assuming that the text here should read *'Anschauungen'*, not *'Erscheinungen'*.

Kant characterizes the relation between concept and object as mediate.[26]

The judgment then asserts that the object so determined (the subject of the judgment) is also thought through the predicate 'divisibility'. This constitutes a second determination or conceptualization of the object, one that is mediated by the first. In other words, that which was first thought through and specified by the concept 'body' is now also thought through the "higher" or more general representation 'divisibility'. It is this second determination to which Kant refers when he claims that in a judgment "much knowledge is collected into one." Presumably, the collection or unification effected by this particular judgment is of the x's thought through the concept 'body' with the other x's that may be thought through the concept 'divisibility', e.g., lines and planes. The judgment affirms that every x thought under the former concept is also thought under the latter. Kant's claim that "all judgments are functions of unity among our representations" is intended to underscore the point that every judgment involves a unification or "collection" of representations under a concept, that is, an act of conceptualization.[27]

More detailed accounts of this same conception of judgment are to be found in many of Kant's *Reflexionen.* These accounts are generally intended as introductions to the distinction between analytic and synthetic judgments, but the treatment of the generic features of judgment can be considered independently of that issue. The following is the relevant portion of one of the most important of these *Reflexionen:*

> Every object is known only through predicates which we think or assert of it. Before this, any representations that may be found in us are to be regarded only as material for cognition, not as themselves cognitions. An object therefore is only a something in general which we think to ourselves through certain predicates which constitute its concept. Every judgment therefore contains two predicates which we compare with one another. One of these, which constitutes the given knowledge of the object, is called the logical subject; the other, which is compared with it, is called the predicate. When I say 'a body is divisible' this means that something x, which I know through the predicates that together constitute a concept of body, I also think through the predicate of divisibility.[28]

[26] It should be noted that this interpretation is independent of the resolution of the textual question referred to in the preceding note. This is because 'intuition' in the passage under discussion must be taken to mean 'the intuited', which for Kant is always an appearance. The key point is rather the claim that *within* the judgment the concept is related to a "given representation" that is itself immediately related to the object. This makes intuition, qua representation, part of the content of the judgment.

[27] Cf. Paton, op. cit., pp. 245–48.

[28] *Reflexion* 4634, *Kants gesammelte Schriften,* vol. XVII, pp. 616–17. Similar accounts

The first two sentences of this passage reiterate the previously made point about unconceptualized representations or, more generally, about all representations apart from their function in judgment. Such representations, Kant here suggests, are merely materials for knowledge. This account also helps to explain why Kant characteristically refers to an object, considered apart from any conceptualization of it, as a mere "something in general" or its equivalent. Of more immediate significance, however, is the fact that Kant infers from this that every judgment must have two predicates. Certainly, this claim cannot simply be accepted as it stands. The obvious difficulty is that it applies only to categorical judgments; hypothetical and disjunctive judgments can have many more than two predicates. Nevertheless, since Kant regards these latter forms of judgment as logical compounds of categorical judgments, this is a mere detail that can be safely ignored. The crucial point is that when Kant characterizes concepts as "predicates of possible judgments" he is not limiting their function to that of logical or grammatical predicates. If he were, he could not claim that judgments have more than one predicate. His major contention is that predicates function to determine the very content that is to be judged about. They do this by providing a general description under which this content can be thought. Insofar as a concept fulfills this function it is regarded as a "real" rather than merely as a "logical" predicate. Such a predicate is also called a "determination" (*Bestimmung*). Thus, in his well-known critique of the ontological argument, Kant denies that existence is a real predicate or determination.[29] He does so for the perfectly good reason that it does not add any content to the description of a thing to say that it exists. He does not, however, deny that it is a logical predicate; consequently, even existential judgments can be said to have two predicates.

In the judgment under consideration, the logical subject, 'body', functions as a real predicate. In Kant's own terms, it "constitutes the given knowledge of the object." In other words, it provides the initial description under which the subject = x is to be taken in the judgment. Correlatively, since the judgment is analytic, the predicate 'divisibility' is only a logical predicate; consequently it does not add any further determinations to the subject beyond those already established by the characterization of it as a body. Leaving aside for the moment the whole question of analyticity, we see that the judgment

---

are contained in numerous other *Reflexionen,* especially those in the "Lose Blätter aus dem Duisburgischen Nachlass," vol. XVII, pp. 643–73. This particular *Reflexion* is cited by Paton, op. cit., p. 251 n. 3.

[29] *Critique of Pure Reason,* A 598/B 626ff.

"compares" these predicates with one another and asserts that they pertain to an identical x. It thus asserts that the same (or some, or every) x that is thought through the predicate 'body' is also thought through the predicate 'divisibility'. This is the basic Kantian schema for judgments of the categorical form, whether analytic or synthetic. Since, as previously noted, the other relational forms are logical compounds of categorical judgments, it can be taken as the Kantian schema for judgment in general. From it we can see how deeply Kant's analysis of judgment is rooted in his conception of the discursive nature of human thought.

III

We have seen that discursive knowledge is judgmental and that judgment requires both concepts and sensible intuitions. Only insofar as these two "modes of knowledge" are related to one another in judgment do they in fact function as representations in the full sense. We have also noted, without dwelling on the point, that sensible intuition is not the only (logically) possible kind of intuition. It follows from this that discursive knowing is not the only (logically) possible kind of knowing. In other words, a non-discursive intellect, which cognizes its "objects" by means of a non-sensible, i.e., intellectual, intuition is at least logically possible. Kant terms such a mind 'intuitive'. Consequently, his claim that human knowing is discursive is equivalent to the denial that it is intuitive. This rescues the discursivity thesis from the charge of triviality to which it has seemed to many to be condemned.

Kant's fullest and most suggestive account of the difference between the manner of cognition of an intuitive intellect and that of our own discursive intellect, with its reliance upon sensible intuition for data, is contained in the *Critique of Judgment.*[30] A discursive understanding is there said to operate by means of an "analytic universal." This is the familiar general concept or abstract universal. Such a concept is distinct from the particulars falling under it, and can determine nothing with respect to the way in which these particulars differ from one another. In fact, it is formed precisely by abstracting from these differences. As a result of its mode of origination, an analytic universal can determine particulars only as instances of a kind, and not as unique individuals. Moreover, it can only do even this insofar as the sensible intuition of the particular is subsumed under it. This, of

[30] *Critique of Judgment*, §77, *Kants gesammelte Schriften*, vol. VI, pp. 407–10.

course, occurs through an act of judgment; so analytic universals function as "predicates of possible judgments." Finally, since it requires sensible intuition, an analytic universal can only serve as a vehicle for the cognition of things as they appear.

By contrast, an intuitive intellect represents its object by means of a "synthetic universal," which is another name for an intellectual intuition. Unlike its discursive counterpart, a synthetic universal provides a representation of a whole as a whole: it cognizes its object as a fully determinate, unique individual, rather than merely as an instance of a kind. Thus, to know an object intuitively is to know it directly or through itself, not as thought under some general description. It is also to know it as it is in itself. Although the latter is crucial for the understanding of Kant's overall position, particularly for his conception of a noumenon as the object of an intuitive intellect, for our present purposes the main point is simply that such an intellect has no need to conceptualize the content given to it. In fact, nothing is "given" to it. Its act of intuition is at the same time the creation of the object intuited. It is, therefore, to be described as "archetypal" in contrast to our "ectypal," discursive intellect.

It should be clear from this that the concept of an intuitive intellect is only applicable to God. The contrast between discursive and intuitive knowledge is thus, at bottom, a contrast between the human and the divine or infinite intellect. Kant thought it possible to draw this contrast because we can form a problematic idea of an infinite intellect. The ensuing idea may be empty, but it is at least coherent, and this is enough to establish the logical (although not the real) possibility of such an intellect. The main function of this conception in the *Critique* is to undermine the assumption that our "way of knowing" is the only possible way, and in so doing to drive a "critical" wedge between the designated subjective conditions of human knowledge and conditions of things as they are in themselves, independently of these subjective conditions. In a word, it serves as a heuristic device in support of Kant's idealistic stance. I would also like to suggest, however, that it serves another purpose, albeit one that Kant never makes explicit. This is to provide a model for the conception of knowledge that is shared by all non-critical, i.e., transcendentally realistic, philosophical positions. I have argued elsewhere that the label 'transcendental realism' is applicable to all non-critical positions, and that transcendental realism, in all its forms, is committed to what can be called a "theocentric model of knowledge."[31] This does not mean that

[31] "Kant's Refutation of Realism," *Dialectica* 30, no. 2/3 (1976), pp. 224–53.

the transcendental realist is committed to the absurd view that the human mind is actually an intuitive intellect in the sense here designated. The point is rather that the theocentric conception functions as a normative model to which transcendental realists appeal, either implicitly or explicitly, in their accounts of human knowledge. That is why Kant's main predecessors were not able to provide an adequate analysis of the discursive nature of human thought, which, in turn, made it impossible for them to draw a clear distinction between analytic and synthetic judgments. In what follows, I shall try to illustrate this with respect to both the empiricists and the rationalists.

(A) *The Empiricists:* Of the thinkers usually grouped under this heading, Locke is clearly the one who comes closest to anticipating Kant's claim regarding the discursivity of human knowledge. Unlike Berkeley and Hume, he at least allows that there are general ideas, although he does frequently conflate these ideas with images.[32] Indeed, at first glance, the use to which the mind on Locke's account puts its general ideas seems to be akin to the use to which Kant claims the understanding puts its concepts. Certainly, a Lockean general idea, which is essentially the idea of a sort, can be described as a vehicle whereby "much possible knowledge is collected into one" (A 69/B 93). Nevertheless, a closer look reveals that Lockean general ideas differ significantly in both nature and function from Kantian concepts. Kant himself points to these differences in the well-known passage where he remarks that, whereas Leibniz "*intellectualized appearances,*" Locke, "according to his system of noogony [*Noogonie*] . . . *sensualized* all concepts of the understanding, i.e., interpreted them as nothing more than empirical or abstracted concepts of reflection" (A 271/B 327).

The specific target of Kant's attack here is not so much Locke's tendency to conflate ideas and images as his failure to recognize a set of a priori concepts derived from the very nature of the understanding. Implicit in all of this, however, and certainly suggested by Kant's self-conscious use of the neologism 'noogony', is the claim that Locke failed to recognize the true role of conceptualization in knowledge. The point is that Lockean general ideas are not required for the representation of objects in the way in which concepts, both pure and empirical, are for Kant. In Kantian terms, a Lockean general idea

[32] This point has been noted frequently by critics going back at least as far as Leibniz. For a contemporary and balanced discussion of the issue, in which Locke is compared to Berkeley, see J. L. Mackie, *Problems from Locke* (Oxford: Clarendon Press, 1976), pp. 115ff.

does not function as an *Erkenntnisgrund,* that is, it does not serve as a rule through which an "analytic unity" is produced and the mind is for the first time provided with a determinate representation of an object. On the contrary, since *ex hypothesi* all Lockean general ideas are derived by abstraction from experience, it follows that both their formation and their subsequent use presuppose a fund of pre- or non-conceptual knowledge, which is then further articulated by means of sortal concepts. This primary knowledge is provided by the so-called simple ideas of sensation and reflection, all of which are held to be "adequate," that is, to "perfectly represent those archetypes which the mind supposes them to be taken from."[33] By contrast, our sortal ideas ("complex ideas of substances") are held to be ineluctably partial and one-sided because they are all based upon a limited experience, and are designed to meet our classificatory needs rather than to reflect the real nature of things.[34] For all of these reasons, but particularly because Lockean simple ideas are deemed to be given independently of any conceptualization on the part of the understanding, Locke's conception of knowledge must be said to be intuitive in the Kantian sense rather than discursive.

Given this account of Locke, as seen through Kantian spectacles, it should not be necessary to deal at any length with the other empiricists. Clearly, the paradigm of knowledge for both Berkeley and Hume is the immediate apprehension of given mental contents (impressions or ideas). Consequently, their conceptions of knowledge must be regarded as intuitive in the same sense and for the same reasons as Locke's. In fact, as already noted, these thinkers go beyond Locke in the direction of intuitivity by rejecting abstract general ideas altogether. The closest that they come to the Kantian notion of applying concepts to given data are their crude accounts of fitting ideas to impressions or sensible particulars. Hume even insists that every "idea" is nothing more than a "copy" of a corresponding impression. As such, it is itself something that one can immediately inspect or intuit and, therefore, not at all a concept in the Kantian sense.

(B) *The Rationalists:* The situation with regard to the rationalists is both more complex and more interesting. Although Descartes is notorious for his doctrine of the divine creation of eternal truths, and one can find a perfectly explicit, self-conscious appeal to an intuitive,

[33] Locke, *An Essay concerning Human Understanding,* Bk. II, chap. XXXI, #1.

[34] This theme runs throughout the *Essay.* It is discussed at all those places where Locke contrasts real and nominal essence. See especially Bk. II, chap. XXXI, and Bk. III, chaps. III and VI.

theocentric model of knowledge in Spinoza and Malebranche,[35] the most relevant representative of this tradition for our purposes is Leibniz. The fundamental difference between the Leibnizian and the Kantian conceptions of knowledge is already evident from the fact that for the former the predicate of every true proposition is contained in the concept of the subject (the famous "predicate in notion principle"). As is frequently noted, this makes all propositions, even those expressing contingent truths, analytic in the Kantian sense. Of itself, this precludes the possibility of claiming that Leibniz anticipated the analytic-synthetic distinction.[36]

It is not so obvious, however, that Leibniz denies the discursive nature of human thought, as seems to be suggested by Kant's charge that he "intellectualized appearances" (A 271/B 327). In fact, it has been argued that in spite of certain inconsistencies in his own approach, Leibniz actually anticipated Kant's distinction between concepts and intuition. In support of this claim, it is noted that Leibniz has different criteria for the clarity and distinctness of concepts and perceptions.[37] Moreover, as Margaret Wilson points out, Leibniz, unlike Descartes, was concerned with "the problem of recognizing represented particulars—with concept 'application' or the use of 'kind terms' in the usual sense."[38]

Although this is all quite correct, the fact remains that, when viewed from Kant's perspective, Leibniz still can be said to operate with an intuitive rather than a discursive model of knowledge. This becomes clear if one notes the close connection between Kant's characteriza-

[35] For a discussion of Kant's critique of Spinoza (and Malebranche) on this point see my "Kant's Critique of Spinoza," in *The Philosophy of Baruch Spinoza*, ed. Richard Kennington, Studies in Philosophy and the History of Philosophy 7 (Washington, D.C.: Catholic University of America Press, 1980), pp. 199–228.

[36] In the *New Essays on Human Understanding*, Leibniz does seem to recognize a class of judgments called "disparates" which are exceptions to this principle. These are defined (Bk. IV, chap. II, #1) as "propositions which say that the object of one idea is not the object of another idea; for instance *Warmth is not the same thing as color.*" Leibniz remarks that such propositions can be established with certainty without proof, i.e., reduction to identity. It is not clear, however, whether he regarded them as reducible to identity. The issue is discussed by Margaret Wilson, "On Leibniz's Explication of 'Necessary Truth'," *Studia Leibnitiana Supplementa* 3 (1969), pp. 50–63, and by Beck, "Analytic and Synthetic Judgments before Kant," op. cit., pp. 87–88. My own view is that such judgments (propositions) constitute an anomaly for Leibniz, not that they suggest that he recognized judgments that are synthetic in Kant's sense.

[37] Cf. Robert McRae, *Leibniz: Perception, Apperception, and Thought* (Toronto and Buffalo: University of Toronto Press, 1976), pp. 126–29; Margaret Wilson, "Confused Ideas," in *Essays on the Philosophy of Leibniz*, Rice University Studies in Philosophy (1978), pp. 123–25.

[38] Margaret Wilson, op. cit., p. 126.

tion of a synthetic universal and Leibniz's conception of a complete concept of an individual substance, which is the true starting point of his account of knowledge. By definition, a Leibnizian complete concept completely determines an individual, which is just what Kant claims for the problematic synthetic universal. Admittedly, Leibniz, like Kant, insists that only the divine mind is capable of such a "concept"; but whereas Kant uses the notion of a synthetic universal as a point of contrast to the human (discursive) way of knowing, Leibniz uses it as a norm or model in terms of which human knowledge is analyzed. Moreover, such a use of this conception underlies his whole account of concept application and the recognition of particulars.

This is reflected in the fact that Leibniz regards all general (kind) and relational concepts not only as abstract, but as incomplete.[39] General concepts, for Leibniz as for Kant, are purported to encompass what is common to a number of particulars. The problem is that, in the Leibnizian universe, where, in virtue of its complete concept, every substance is qualitatively as well as numerically distinct from every other, there are no properties that, strictly speaking, are common to two or more substances. There are merely similarities, which are reified into identities by the imagination because of the incapacity of the senses to perceive minute differences. Similarly, Leibniz also maintains that relations such as place, space, and time have no reality apart from the individual relata. In contemplating them in abstraction from their relata, the mind is dealing merely with *entia rationis.*[40] This does not make such concepts into fictions; for these products of the understanding, like general concepts, have some basis in the nature of things. It does, however, entail that they are incapable of serving as vehicles for adequate knowledge, and that they are in principle eliminable from an account of the universe. The *Monadology,* of course, is just such an account.

The same model underlies Leibniz's account of the empirical knowledge of individuals. In opposition to Locke, who held that general ideas are formed by abstraction from the primary sensible knowledge of individuals, Leibniz denies that we have any such sensory knowledge of individuals from which to abstract. Abstraction, for

[39] Leibniz, *New Essays on Human Understanding,* Bk. III, chap. VI, §19, and chap. VII, §1. The point is discussed by McRae, op. cit., pp. 83–89.

[40] Leibniz's main account of this topic is in the Fifth Letter to Clarke, §47. The interpretation adopted here is suggested by Hidé Ishiguro's account of what she terms Leibniz's "nominalist thesis," "Leibniz's Theory of the Ideality of Relations," in *Leibniz: A Collection of Critical Essays,* ed. Harry G. Frankfurt (Garden City, New York: Doubleday and Company, 1972), esp. pp. 200–203.

Leibniz, proceeds from species to genus, not from individual to species. What is taken as the sensory awareness of an individual (a determinate empirical intuition for Kant) is really the confused thought of a kind. This is because for Leibniz "individuality includes infinity, and only he who is capable of comprehending it can have the knowledge of the principle of individuation of this or that thing."[41] Correlatively, since Leibniz views space and time as *entia rationis* rather than as conditions of human sensibility, he denies that they are capable of individuating objects.

By contrast, for Kant such an "intellectualist" position entails the denial of the possibility of the empirical knowledge of individuals and thus of the possibility of synthetic a posteriori judgments. Recall that for Kant particular objects are given in sensible intuition and recognized or thought through concepts. But with his analysis of sensory awareness, which is itself inseparable from his conception of a complete concept (as alone capable of individuating), Leibniz effectively denies both of these points. This, I take it, is the real force of Kant's contention that Leibniz failed to distinguish between sensibility and understanding, and that he regarded sensory awareness as confused thought.[42] It also explains why Leibniz, like Locke (not to mention Berkeley and Hume), was unable to provide an adequate account of the discursive nature of human thought.

IV

We are now in a position to examine Kant's distinction between analytic and synthetic judgments as well as his claim of originality for this distinction. Unfortunately, neither its connection with his theory of judgment nor its originality is readily apparent from the well-known formulations in the Introduction to the *Critique.* Kant there provides two different, but purportedly equivalent, versions of the distinction. According to the first version, analytic judgments are those in which "the predicate B belongs to the subject A, as something which is (covertly) contained in this concept A." Equivalently, they are described as those in which the connection of the predicate with the subject is "thought through identity." Synthetic judgments, by con-

[41] Leibniz, *New Essays on Human Understanding,* Bk. III, chap. III, §6. The point is discussed by McRae, op. cit., p. 75.

[42] Cf. *Critique of Pure Reason,* A 43–44/B 60–61, A 270–72/B 326–28; *On a Discovery, Kants gesammelte Schriften,* vol. VIII, p. 220; *The Kant-Eberhard Controversy,* pp. 78 and 134.

trast, are those in which "B lies outside the concept A, although it does stand in connection with it." The connection between subject and predicate in such judgments is thus said to be "thought without identity" (A 6–7/B 10–11). According to the second version, which follows immediately in the text, the distinction is between merely explicative (analytic) and ampliative (synthetic) judgments. The former, Kant maintains, add "nothing through the predicate to the concept of the subject, merely breaking it up into those constituent concepts that have all along been thought in it, although confusedly." The latter, on the other hand, "add to the concept of the subject a predicate which has not been in any wise thought in it, and which no analysis could possibly extract from it" (A 7/B 11). Only much later in the *Critique* does Kant make explicit what is implicit in his entire discussion, viz., that the law of contradiction is the principle of all analytic judgments.[43]

Far from indicating any great originality, the first version seems to support Eberhard's contention, summarily dismissed by Kant, that the distinction is equivalent to the traditional contrast between identical and non-identical judgments.[44] In addition, it provides no hint as to how syntheticity is to be understood, except as the negation of analyticity. To some extent this latter difficulty is remedied in the second version, where syntheticity, the real locus of Kant's concern, "wears the trousers." Even here, however, Kant does not indicate in what sense and by what means we "extend" our knowledge in synthetic judgments; as a result, the actual basis of the distinction is not made apparent. Moreover, the same can be said about the formulations in the *Prolegomena* and *On a Discovery,* both of which closely parallel the second version in the *Critique.*[45]

A much more helpful account is contained in a generally neglected note in the *Lectures on Logic,* where Kant introduces the contrast between a formal and a material extension of knowledge.[46] The basic idea is that analytic judgments extend knowledge in the former and synthetic judgments in the latter sense. The characterization of analytic judgments as involving a formal extension of knowledge requires a distinction between such judgments and tautologies, which, unfortunately, Kant does not consistently maintain.[47] For our present pur-

[43] *Critique of Pure Reason,* A 150–52/B 189–91.

[44] Cf. *The Kant-Eberhard Controversy,* pp. 37–38.

[45] *Prolegomena,* §2, *Kants gesammelte Schriften,* vol. IV, pp. 266–67. *On a Discovery,* vol. VIII, p. 228; *The Kant-Eberhard Controversy,* p. 141.

[46] *Lectures on Logic,* §36, *Kants gesammelte Schriften,* vol. IX, p. 111.

[47] For example, in *The Progress of Metaphysics, Kants gesammelte Schriften,* vol. XX,

poses, however, the most important aspect of this formulation is that it helps to clarify the connection between the analytic-synthetic distinction and Kant's theory of judgment. As we shall see, this is ultimately because the notion of a material extension of knowledge must be understood in terms of the previously discussed relationship of concept and intuition in a judgment.

Let us first consider how analytic judgments provide a formal extension of knowledge. Such an extension occurs through the clarification or explication of what is merely implicit in a concept. This involves the uncovering of implications of which one may not have been previously aware, but which are derivable by strictly logical means from a given concept. Once again, Kant takes 'All bodies are extended' as his example of an analytic judgment. Moreover, as he does in many of the *Reflexionen* dealing with the topic, but not in the *Critique* itself, he provides a schematic rendering of the judgment which makes his position quite clear. As he succinctly puts it: "To every x to which appertains the concept of body (a + b) appertains also extension (b)."[48] This is the basic formula for an analytic judgment; it shows that in such judgments the predicate (b) is related to the object = x (the subject of the judgment) simply in virtue of the fact that it is already contained (as a mark) in the concept of the subject. Analytic judgments, therefore, have a logical subject, and, as Kant's example indicates, they can also have a real subject; but since the truth or falsity of the judgment can be determined merely by analyzing the concept of the subject, the reference to the object = x is otiose.[49] That is why it is perfectly possible to form analytic judgments about non-existent, even impossible, objects, and why all analytic judgments are known a priori.

In his response to Eberhard, Kant supplements this by introducing what amounts to a distinction between immediately and mediately analytic judgments.[50] 'All bodies are extended' is an instance of the former. It is immediately analytic because 'extension', together with

p. 322, he explicitly distinguishes between analytic judgments, which are grounded in identity, and identical judgments. However, in *Lectures on Logic,* §37, he treats tautologies as a subset of analytic judgments. For a discussion of this issue see H. J. de Vleeschauwer, *La Deduction transcendentale dans l'oeuvre de Kant* (Paris and the Hague: Martinus Nijhoff, 1934–37), vol. III, p. 406.

[48] *Lectures on Logic,* §36, *Kants gesammelte Schriften,* vol. IX, p. 111.

[49] As noted by Beck, "Can Kant's Synthetic Judgments Be Made Analytic?" in *Kant: Disputed Questions,* p. 230. Kant himself makes the point in *Reflexion* 4674, *Kants gesammelte Schriften,* vol. XVII, p. 645, where he remarks that in analytic judgments "Das x fällt weg."

[50] *On a Discovery, Kants gesammelte Schriften,* vol. VIII, pp. 239ff.; *the Kant-Eberhard Controversy,* pp. 49–50, 141ff.

'figure', 'impenetrability', etc., is a mark of the concept of body or, in the scholastic terminology interjected into the debate by Eberhard, part of the "logical essence" of the concept. By contrast, 'All bodies are divisible' is a mediately analytic judgment. The difference stems from the fact that the predicate ('divisibility') is not part of the concept (logical essence) of body, but, instead, of one of its constituent concepts. In other words, it is a mark of a mark. As such, the judgment rests on an inference, and in that respect can be said to extend our knowledge. Kant's main point, however, is that this does not constitute an essential difference. In each case the predicate is derived from the concept of the subject by a process of analysis, and thus on the basis of the principle of contradiction. In each case, then, the extension of our knowledge is merely formal.

It should be clear, even from this cursory account, that Kant's conception of analyticity is of a piece with his basic thesis regarding the discursive nature of human thought. In particular, it rests upon his notion of a concept (analytic universal) as a set of marks (themselves concepts), which are thought together in an "analytic unity," and which can serve as a ground for the recognition of objects. These marks collectively constitute the intension of a concept. One concept is "contained in" another if and only if it is itself either a mark of the concept or a mark of one of its marks. Unlike most contemporary conceptions of analyticity, Kant's is thus thoroughly intensional. As Beck quite correctly points out, it rests upon the doctrine of the fixity of a concept, that is, on the thesis that the marks of a concept can be sufficiently determined (even without an explicit definition) for the purpose of analysis.[51] The notorious difficulties that arise concerning analytic judgments involving empirical concepts such as 'water', which we need not consider here, all stem from the difficulty of sufficiently determining such concepts.[52]

[51] Beck, "Can Kant's Synthetic Judgments Be Made Analytic?" op. cit., p. 231, and "Kant's Theory of Definition," op. cit., p. 225.

[52] Cf. *Critique of Pure Reason* A 728/B 756, where Kant asks: "What useful purpose could be served by defining an empirical concept, such, for instance, as that of water? When we speak of water and its properties, we do not stop short at what is thought in the word 'water' but proceed to experiments." As Beck notes in his comments upon the passage: "Description suffices; definition which aims at being more than nominal is a useless presumption" ("Kant's Theory of Definition," op. cit., p. 223). Kant's point seems to be that judgments involving such empirical concepts are normally not analytic; but if one does explicitly endeavor to make an analytic judgment, i.e., appeal to meanings, one can only appeal to a purely nominal definition: "what is thought in the word." This makes the judgment arbitrary. One is perhaps tempted to say that such judgments about words in contrast to the intension of concepts are empirical claims about linguistic usage. Kant, however, does not seem to have addressed that possibility.

As already noted, a synthetic judgment involves what Kant terms a "material extension" of knowledge. The example of such a judgment given in the *Lectures on Logic* is 'All bodies have attraction'. This is rendered schematically as "For every x to which appertains the concept of body (a + b) appertains also attraction (c)."[53] Like its analytic counterpart, this judgment asserts a connection between the predicate (c) and the subject (x), which is thought through the concept (a + b). Specifically, it asserts that every (x), known under the general description contained in the concept (a + b), also possesses the additional property (c). Unlike its analytic counterpart, however, it asserts this independently of any direct connection between the predicate and the concept of the subject. To be sure, in the judgment the predicate (c) is connected with the subject concept (a + b); but the connection is grounded in, and mediated by, the reference of both to the identical object (x), which serves as the subject of the judgment. It therefore extends our knowledge of x (in this case all x's) in the sense that it provides a determination or property of x that is not already contained in the concept (a + b). This is what is meant by a "material extension."

Kant attempts to explicate this further by suggesting that the synthetic judgment contains a "determination" and the analytic judgment only a "logical predicate."[54] It will be recalled that by the former is meant a real predicate, that is, a property that really pertains to the subject of the judgment, while by the latter is meant a concept that is predicated of the concept of the subject in the judgment. Since Kant maintains both that existential judgments are synthetic and that 'existence' is not a real predicate, this account obviously cannot be accepted as it stands. An existential judgment is synthetic, not because its logical predicate, 'existence', is a real predicate or determination, but rather because its logical subject is one, and the judgment simply asserts the existence of an object corresponding to this subject. Now, it might also seem that in analytic judgments, such as 'All bodies are divisible', the logical predicate, 'divisibility', is likewise a real predicate. After all, it is a property of every x that answers to the general description thought in the concept of body; indeed, this is just what the judgment asserts. Nevertheless, the point is that in the analytic judgment the predicate is related to the subject (x) simply in virtue of the fact that it is already contained (either immediately or mediately) in the concept of this subject. Thus the "reality" of the predicate does

[53] *Lectures on Logic,* §36, *Kants gesammelte Schriften,* vol. IX, p. 111.
[54] Ibid.

not come into consideration in the judgment. In synthetic judgments, however, the reference to the object (x) and, therefore, the reality of the predicate is just the point at issue. Consequently, such judgments make an extra-conceptual claim. That is why the question of how such judgments can be known a priori is so perplexing.

Finally, since it makes an extra-conceptual claim, every synthetic judgment (of theoretical reason) contains a relation of its constituent concepts to intuition. Perhaps the central claim of Kant's theory of knowledge is that this relation is necessary in order to "ground," i.e., make possible, a material extension of knowledge. The reason for this is to be found in the very nature of discursive thought. We have seen that concepts, as general representations, cannot relate directly to objects. The relation must always be mediated by the relation of the concept to another representation, and ultimately to one that is in a mediate relation to the object. Such a representation is an intuition, and its epistemic function is to present the "object," or, better, the material for thinking the object, to the mind. This requirement entails that we can never determine simply by means of an inspection of the constituent marks of a concept (analysis) whether or not the concept is empty, that is, whether or not there are any objects falling under the general description contained in the concept. In the terms of the present discussion, which are those of the dispute with Eberhard rather than of the *Critique,* we cannot determine whether the concept, which always functions as a predicate in a judgment, serves as a real or merely as a logical predicate. This can only be determined by an appeal to intuition; and this is because a judgment which connects a real predicate with an object (a synthetic judgment) does so by relating the predicate to the intuition of the object. Only by this means is a material extension of knowledge possible for a discursive intelligence.[55]

It follows from the above analysis that in order to distinguish between analytic and synthetic judgments one must recognize a class of judgments that involve a material extension of knowledge. This, of itself, precludes both Leibniz and Hume: the former because his "predicate in notion" principle undercuts the contrast between a for-

[55]Cf. Kant's letter to Reinhold, March 12, 1789, *Kants gesammelte Schriften,* vol. XI, p. 38; *The Kant-Eberhard Controversy,* p. 164. The claim that synthetic judgments for Kant involve the predication of concepts of intuitions was first made by Moltke S. Gram, *Kant, Ontology and the A Priori* (Evanston, Ill.: Northwestern University Press, 1968), pp. 65–92, and again in "The Crisis of Syntheticity: The Kant-Eberhard Controversy," *Kant-Studien,* Heft 2 (1980), pp. 155–80.

mal and a material extension of knowledge (it renders all synthetic judgments "mediately analytic"); the latter because he explicitly denies the possibility of a material extension (a posteriori as well as a priori).[56] It also follows that in order to account for the possibility of material extension, one must first recognize the role of sensible intuition *within* judgment. Since Kant's predecessors, both empiricist and rationalist, did not recognize this role, they were not able to account for this possibility. Thus, in spite of the fact that some of them, most notably Crusius, saw that many judgments require an extra-logical grounding or principle, they did not have a clear conception of a synthetic judgment in the Kantian sense. At most, they realized that not all judgments fit the model of analyticity subscribed to by Leibniz. But it is one thing to realize that not all judgments are analytic and quite another to offer an adequate account of those that are not. This, I take it, is why Kant could justifiably claim to have been the first to draw the distinction between analytic and synthetic judgments, while at the same time acknowledging that others came close to arriving at it.

University of California, San Diego

[56] For Kant, at least, this is the result of Hume's claim that custom (not rational inference) is the sole basis for our beliefs regarding "any real existence and matter of fact, beyond the present testimony of our senses, or the records of our memory." In other words, Hume's skeptical attack on the very possibility of synthetic a posteriori judgments precludes acknowledging him as a forerunner of the analytic-synthetic distinction. Here it is important to keep in mind that every judgment for Kant is objectively valid.

3 Kant's Theory of Space as a Form of Intuition

ARTHUR MELNICK

1: *Intuition and Description*

An intuitive representation or an intuition is a singular, immediate representation involving sensation or being affected. Sensation is a literal component of an intuitive representation just as the name 'John' is a literal component of the representation of the term 'the brother of John'. Consider the demonstrative term 'This'. It has as its interpretation or referent that which affects the user of the term. Only an affected being could employ the term to singularly represent, and, indeed, the sense of the term is that its referent is determined in terms of the experiential state of the subject who represents. This does not mean that what is represented by, or the referent of, a use of the demonstrative is an experiential state. It may be, but it need not be. The term 'This' by itself is ontologically neutral, involving no divided reference in Quine's sense. It can be regarded as a schematic name. What it is schematic of, however, will be names such as 'Mama' or 'Betty' which themselves too involve no decisions as to identity or reidentification. Let us call such names "reactive names." The child is taught to employ them only on the condition that he is affected in a certain way. In this sense they are reactions to the way things impinge on the child. If the semantics of a term is determined by the conditions of its proper use, then the semantics of reactive names involves being affected in the proper way. The child should not use 'Mama' if Mama is not present and affecting, at least in so far as 'Mama' is a reactive name. Note once again that only a sensing being could, by the nature of such terms, employ reactive names. They have no meaning for a purely conceptualizing being.

Our intuition, Kant says, is sensible. By this he means that for us singular representation or intuition always *ipso facto* involves being affected. This characterization eliminates both ordinary proper names and definite descriptions as candidates for singular representations, for the sense of such terms does not involve sensation or being affected. It is the contrast between definite descriptions and Kantian singular representations that I shall be interested in. Demonstrative representation involves being affected; it does not involve the representation of being affected. In this way, the term 'This' is distinct from the definite description '(lx) (x is affecting me)'. So, in the case of the child, his use of the term 'Mama' does not involve any recognition on his part that he is being affected in a Mama way. 'Mama', that is, is not equivalent to '(lx) (x is Mama-affecting me)'. Still less is it equivalent to '(lx) (x is a Mama-affective state of mine)' or '(lx) (x is a Mama-sensation)'. Reactive names are not only neutral to questions of identity but, in Kant's terms, undetermined with respect to the logical functions of judgment—in particular to the function of predication. The sense of a definite description, whether used attributively or referentially, involves the idea of an object to satisfy the description. For Kant, the notion of an object is contributed by the understanding and is not a matter of intuition per se. Once again, then, definite descriptions are excluded on this ground as Kantian intuitions, while demonstratives are not.

There is the sort of analysis of demonstratives which would ultimately collapse the distinction between them and definite descriptions and so destroy Kant's notion of singular representation independent of the logical functions of judgment. On this analysis, in the metalanguage one says that the referent of the term 'This' is the object that is present to the user of the term 'This'. If one takes the metalinguistic specification of the referent as a singular term of the metalanguage substitutable for the demonstrative term, then one is claiming that the *use* of demonstratives is eliminable in favor of definite descriptions that merely mention them or mention their being used. By "eliminable" I mean that no referential resources are lost if one eliminates the *use* of demonstrative terms altogether. On Kant's view the semantics of demonstratives is quite different. In effect the role of *saying* in the metalanguage what the referent of the term is, is replaced by the user of the term simply being in a certain affective state. The very sense of such terms involves their reference being completed by a passive state of the representer, and no description of such being the case can make do as far as singular reference goes for simply being in the state. It is the primacy of demonstratives understood in Kant's way vis-à-vis definite descriptions that I now turn to.

The notion of a definite description is correlative with the idea of a domain of potential satisfiers of that description. Even if the description is one which could only be satisfied by one object, the point remains that we need to be able to represent the potential class of entities from which the description "selects" the entity that satisfies it. Descriptions are applied to objects or they are (descriptions) of objects, and we need to be able to represent the domain of potential satisfiers before the descriptions can be used to pick out one from that domain. When one gives the model-theoretic semantics of a definite description, the domain is presumed somehow as given or there or fixed or, better, one is working simply with the mere idea of *a* domain of objects. What the description in the object language designates is relative to what the domain of the object language is. In the metalanguage one has a name (an individual constant D) for the domain of the object language, but D itself is a schematic name (or, looked at from the outside, a free variable). D is the domain of the object language *whatever particular domain that is.* Relative to that domain, then, the description singles out or selects an object as the one *of the domain* that satisfies it. This, however, is not singular reference but the mere form or concept of singular reference unless one can represent the domain of potential satisfiers. One may try to do without individual referring terms at all by analyzing descriptions à la Russell and Quine in terms of existential quantification. The sense of the quantifier itself, however, presupposes rather than establishes what the domain of quantification is. It is as domain-relative as definite descriptions. Until or unless the domain is fixed or determined, the truth of an existential quantification is as relative, variable, or schematic as the reference of a definite description. If the domain is represented as the class of entities which make certain existential quantifications "absolutely" true, then one owes an account of what absolute truth is (as opposed to the mere idea of truth that model theory gives). There seem to be two alternatives. First, one may take 'absolutely true' to mean true in the specific domain of what there is, so that absolute truth simply is the specification of the model-theoretic notion gotten by filling in the schematic D by a name or representation of what there is. On this view the notion of absolute truth depends on and does not precede or constitute reference or representation of what there is. Second, one may take 'absolutely true' as being primitive, so that it is not a specific case of true-in-D. But then the model-theoretic notion of truth (and so the model-theoretic semantics of the existential quantifier) is completely severed from the absolute notions.

The use of a demonstrative or of a reactive name on the other hand is ontologically neutral and does not presuppose a domain of objects for its reference or sense, if the semantics for such terms is completed by the user being in a certain state. It is the very affective situation of the user that interprets the term, not any description of the user or his state. The latter would require a domain of users and states, and the problem of how to singularly represent that domain would arise. The point is that 'This' represents what is before me now and that it does, does not involve selecting from many objects (from a domain) the one that is before me now. Let us go back to the child for a moment. He can learn to react with 'Mama', 'Car', etc. according to the state he's in without any conception of a range of things that his reaction selects from. 'Mama', that is, is not one of the mamas there are, nor is 'Car' one of the cars there are as far as the child's reactions are concerned. The language of reactive names is the first step in building up to the representation of what there is which gives sense and determinacy to the use of both descriptions and quantification. It is crucial as we continue with further steps that at no time do we make use of means of reference or means of statement-making which, like descriptions or quantification, presuppose a domain of objects being given for their sense, since our goal is to see how a domain is first given.

2: *Pointing and In-Purview Ostension*

We can teach the child not only to use reactive names but to accompany their use with appropriate pointing or sweeping gestures. We can ask him, that is, not only to say 'Mama' upon being Mama-affected, but also to outline or circumscribe in an appropriate way upon being so affected. In the case of the schematic name 'This', indeed, we shall demand such accompanying gestures for the term to have any sense at all. These circumscribing gestures are some more reaction by the child, and they together with the reactive name constitute *a* reaction. In this new scheme we are *ipso facto* demanding of the child the accompanying gestures as an integral component of any reaction. In this new language, then, 'Mama' is still a term, but its proper use, and so the semantics of the term, now involves not only being in the proper affective state but also carrying out the proper circumscribing or gesturing activity. This activity of "drawing in the air," so to speak, is one nascent form of what Kant means by spatial construction.

Note that the demanded accompanying activity is not a means of representing shape. There will be reactive shape names like 'Square' and 'Round' in the child's vocabulary. If a black square is presented to him, he may properly react 'Square' and squarely circumscribe. Of course it is true from our point of view that only square-shaped objects are to be squarely circumscribed, but it is *not* true for the child that only the use of shape names is to be accompanied by circumscribing gestures. *Every* name whatsoever is to be accompanied by such gestures. Shape names are just reactions to some more of the qualitative diversity that things present to the child. He learns to differentially react 'Square' versus 'Round' by the two appropriate affective states being qualitatively or sensibly discernible, in much the same way as he learns to differentially react with 'Black' versus 'White'. Round and Square are simply more of the content of what affects him, whereas squarely circumscribing is something the child is called on to *introduce* into the situation. We have not of course given the child any means yet of representing the various styles or kinds of circumscription, so that we certainly have not put him in a position to recognize any more intimate connection between accompanying 'Black' by a square-circumscription than accompanying 'Square' by such a circumscription.

We are asking the child, then, to employ a system of representation which demands that he introduce a new element into a situation in order to represent in accord with that system. We are asking him not only to be affected in an appropriate way but to perform a certain construction. Circumscription, then, is introduced into things by an activity on his part.

The purpose of circumscription and other such motioning gestures is, of course, to direct attention. The child's affective states are not neatly parceled out into an all-black one, then an all-square one, then an all-Mama one. Rather, a complex qualitative diversity is what is in his purview. In teaching him the use of 'Red' as a reactive name, I may ostend or circumscribe in order to focus his attention on what in purview he is to react to. His attention then follows my construction. There are other ways of directing attention besides circumscribing. Most importantly I can take the child and move him. Suppose, for example, I come with a child into a room in which there is a toy car. We may or may not suppose the child already has the use of the specific name 'Car', though we do suppose he is speaking our second language, i.e., that he can make appropriate accompanying gestures for names which he already knows. I take the child by the hand and move with him toward the car, *all the while* saying 'Car' or 'See the car' or 'Oh, what a nice car', and when reaching the car I circumscribe or gesture and say 'Car' again. The car has all the while been in the child's view but perhaps not in the focus of his attention. The motion then does not first bring the car in view any more than circumscribing first brings things in view. Like circumscribing, it is an activity which focuses attention, and indeed in our third language we shall demand of the child that his use of terms like 'Mama' or 'Car' be underlain or buttressed not only by circumscribing, but also by moving or taking appropriate steps as well. We may, if we wish, consider this as just some further gesturing, although with one's feet rather than with one's hands. Indeed, what one is doing is carrying out a spatial construction with one's feet. The child will have mastered this stage when, for example, he leads the parent there and points and says 'Car'. What he is doing, in effect, is focusing the parent's attention. A slight variant of this procedure would be for the child to move by himself and point and expect the parent to follow. Another variant would be for the child to stay where he is and follow in attention the parent's motion toward (and so representation of) Car. In neither of these variants, however, is any component of the in-purview manifold representable without actually physically carrying out foot-by-finger the accompanying construction. For example, the child still can't direct others to something he sees and wants without moving to it himself. Nor can he be directed by others except in so far as they move or carry out the construction. Thus, I couldn't get the child to fetch something for me without moving there myself. So let us take the child and say to him 'We are moving six steps' or let us move for the child and say 'I am moving six steps'. Now note, we don't want the child to get the idea that 'moving six steps' is a reactive name to be applied only when he is affected by or presented with a six-step motion, for the point is for that term to first produce the motion. We might as we move indicate our own motion by finger gestures which in effect sweep out a line cut into six segments until we come to Car. Then, without moving we can *symbolically* repeat those gestures by sweeping out a smaller line cut into six segments and saying 'Car'. If the child repeats those gestures and says 'Car', he is corrected, for what we want him to do is use those gestures as a diagram or blueprint for the actual motion or construction he is to perform. The symbolic gestures pictorially represent or resemble the activity to be performed. Eventually the child learns to initiate the activity in others, and eventually he learns to do it without the aid of the blueprint. At this stage, the canonical form of singular representation is 'Take n steps: α' where 'α' is a reactive name, or 'Take n steps: That (and circumscribe)' where one may not have the use of a reactive name for the indicated component of the manifold.

This scheme of representation should be contrasted with what would be the nascent form for relational or absolute theories of space. On both these theories which Kant would call objectivist, spatial appellations would be to some more content of the manifold. They would just be some more reactive names, so that the child having Car in view would also be taught 'six steps from us' as an appropriate reaction to how he is affected. Spatial appellations would not be prescriptive of what is to be done, but descriptive of how one is affected. So let us consider first the relational theory. If one is to be affected by a certain relation's obtaining, one has to be affected by the relata. If, then, the Car though in purview is not in attention, then 'Car six steps from us' is not a proper reaction on the child's part since he is not being Car-affected. As a reactive name, then, spatial representations would be posterior to being affected by elements of the manifold rather than prior means of getting affected in accordance with activities. The absolutist theory would hold 'six steps from' also to be a reactive name, but unlike the relational theory one that was a reaction to a component of the manifold independent of any other component. Thus 'six steps from' is an appropriate reaction if the child is affected by that much of space whether or not he is Car-affected. This apparent independence, however, is a sham, for suppose a car is six steps from us. Then the child will be 'six steps from'–affected only if he is also Car-affected. The further distinct spatial affections will not enable him to represent components of the manifold that he wouldn't otherwise have been able to represent. If space is part of the content of the manifold, its representation will not enable us to represent any other content of the manifold that we couldn't represent without it. We shall return to the relational and absolute theories when we discuss the singular representation of the absent or the out-of-purview.

Note that the child in learning to give and follow directions will be learning concepts. For example, according to Kant, he will have the concept of magnitude. What is crucial, however, is that the concepts involved are *not* employed as predicates or as descriptions. That would require that he be able to represent a domain of objects to which the predicates apply or which satisfy the descriptions. A conceptual representation, according to Kant, is a spontaneous one. I have the concept of red, e.g., when I can use the term 'red' to represent (or represent by means of the term 'red') even though I am not being redly affected. The spontaneity, that is, is in the use of an appellation. 'Red' as a reactive name is not spontaneously usable but is bound down to the circumstance of being affected red-ly. In this sense, then, the child's use of the phrase 'Take six steps' is not bound down to his being affected in a certain way, but is freely available for his use. Though conceptual or spontaneous in this way, it is not a predicational or descriptive use. It would be absurd to say that the use of the phrase 'Take six steps' presupposes a domain of steps for its sense. This is so even though pluralization, which Quine considers part of the referential apparatus of language, is involved. Consider quantification, also supposedly part of the referential apparatus. I can tell someone he may walk as far as he pleases or extend a line as far as he pleases. This, in turn, can be phrased as 'No matter how far you draw, you may draw further' or 'Each drawing can be extended by some further drawing'. These phrases look very much like universal-existential forms but certainly don't demand for their sense a domain of walks or drawings. The prescriptive use of language for formulating rules connects at least syntactically to expressions of plurality, generality, identity, etc. while defusing, apparently, any referential import of the latter.

3: *Out-of-Purview Singular Representation*

For Kant, space is given as a whole. Points and parts are limits. Now what is given as a whole is the form of intuition. In the in-purview case we have taken the form to be a constructive activity or at least the prescription for such an activity which underlies singular representation of components of the in-purview manifold. Pointing and circumscribing without any moving is just a limiting case of representing, or better, a limiting case of the activity that is an aspect of singularly representing. Contrast this, for example, with a Strawsonian view according to which *this,* or what is here, is immediately representable, but absent objects and absent places are both descriptively (non-immediately) represented. Pointing or exhibiting or showing figures into all reference for Strawson because the tail end, so to speak, of all descriptive reference is demonstration. The canonical form of singular reference for him we may say is '(lx) (ϕx this)', where 'ϕ' is some two-place spatial predicate. The very form of the definite description has a "subject" place, for it is to be read as 'That which is (uniquely) ϕ to this', or 'That which uniquely satisfies "It is ϕ to this" '. What we have in Kant's terms is the bare or mere idea of an object or a referent for the predicate. For Strawson, too, space is the form of reference, but it is the form of descriptive reference. For Kant, on the other hand, the requirement of indicating which objects it is that are to satisfy descriptions is in force for descriptions involving spatial predicates as well as any other predicates.

For Strawson, what is present or in purview is indicated; what is absent is simply described in relation to what is indicated. For Kant, all description presupposes indication, whether of the absent or of the present. For Kant, space is the form of indication, not the form of description. In the in-purview case, to indicate is to direct or focus attention by prescribing a spatial construction. One may say that in effect Strawson's canonical descriptions accomplish the same result, for the representation '(lx) (ϕx this)' tells one how to get into a position to be affected by or to attend to the object represented. Thus, from the fact that '*a* = (lx) (ϕx this)' it follows that if I wanted to find *a,* I should take ϕ steps of such and such magnitude, and that this is so *because a* is ϕ to this. The prescriptions are based on how things are and in this sense are not the original or most basic spatial representations. It does seem the merest platitude to say that one can find *a* by taking ϕ steps because *a* is ϕ steps (or meters) from this or away from here, and it would be a platitude if not for the difficulty that *a* or (lx) (ϕx this) is the mere idea of a reference, and not a reference until the domain of potential satisfiers is indicated. For Kant, too, it is a platitude, but one that goes in the opposite direction. It is not until the descriptive term is identifiable with a singular representation, or is provided with a domain of potential satisfiers by singular representation which involves prescription, that it becomes a determinate reference. It is important to note that the issue is not which descriptions are more fundamental, those that talk of distance as a relation between things or those that talk of possible findings or affections as a result of possible carryings out of activities. Kant's position is not that the canonical form of description is '(lx) (x would be found or would affect if I were to move ϕ steps)'. It is indeed so that '*Take six steps: Car*' would be found if I were to move six steps or would affect car-wise if I were to move six steps. The prescription, however, is involved in indicating what it is that the description in terms of possible compliances is applicable to.

The extension of prescriptions to the out-of-purview requires the concept of magnitude, the pure schema of which according to Kant is number. How the child generalizes his directing ability and ability to be directed to 'Take n steps' for arbitrary n is a question I'm not in a position to answer. It is in effect equivalent to the question of how the child can be trained to count generally rather than to six-count or to seven-count. All that is important for us is that this training does not depend on first getting the child to represent an infinite domain of entities to be counted. What the child is supposed to be learning is a schematic means of prescribing or directing, not a schematic repertoire of descriptions to be applied. All I am claiming is that the problem of how the child learns to extend prescriptions to the out-of-purview is no different than that of how on the Strawsonian model he would learn to use an indefinite number of descriptions. Strawson too would have to claim that he doesn't learn to do that by first learning to refer to indefinitely many objects, since it is those descriptions that are supposed to provide, canonically, reference to objects. Put quite simply, in both cases the generalization of the means of representation is prior to the extension or generalization of representation by that means.

On the absolute theory, spatial terms would be names that form parts of descriptions for referring to things. The canonical form would be something like '(lx) (Atxp)' where 'p' is a name for '30 meters from here'. The only difference from the relational theory is that the canonical spatial descriptions are formed with names rather than two-place predicates. For Kant, the canonical form of singular reference would be 'Take n steps: α' where 'α' is schematic for some reactive name. Note, 'Take n steps' is not a prescription for representing or singularly referring. It is a prescription for finding or being affected or, if you will, a prescription for sensing or obtaining sensation. It is this prescription for sensing that is the representation itself. One has to carry out the prescription in order to sense, but not in order to represent.

Note that this canonical form of representation shares with pointing and circumscribing *simpliciter* the feature of being pre-ontological or not involving divided reference. Ontology is decided by deciding questions of identity. These in turn are decided by deciding when predication is transferable from one singular representation to another, and we have not yet introduced what Kant would call the logical function of subject and predicate. Our system of representation so far has made use only of the mathematical categories, not of the dynamical ones. The former, for Kant, are constitutive of intuition or singular reference; the latter, rather, are involved in objectifying or ontologizing the singular reference provided by the former. The key point is that the scope of singular representation is extended beyond the present or the in-purview independently of introducing identity conditions or predication, for it is such singular representation upon which these logical functions are imposed. On objectivist theories of space, the scope of representation itself is extended beyond the in-purview only in terms of what Quine calls the referential apparatus of language or thought.

4: *Geometry*

Kant has two characterizations of space; it is that which geometry studies as well as the form of singular representation. What I wish to investigate now is in what regard geometry is the study of the form of singular representation. My claim shall be that geometry is the study of when distinct constructions or prescriptions underlie the same singular representation.

Let us first look at the connection between geometry and measurement. A direct measurement is an operation carried out according to the following rule. One takes a unit rod and lays it end over end in a straight direction so many number of times. The notion of 'straight' is defined locally as follows. Suppose the rod is initially situated as AB.

One rotates the rod completely about the point B until it comes back to coincide with its original position. Using a shorter rod one measures the circumference of the circle produced to get, say, C, and then marks off the point from A that is C/2 units.

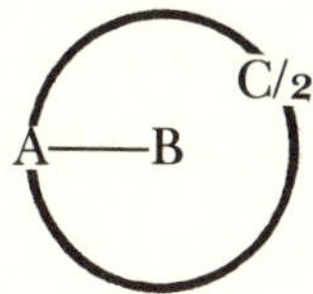

Then laying the rod from B to C/2 is a *straight* extension of the original position of the rod. We also allow direct measurements which change direction or are not straight extensions of the rod position, where the change in direction is likewise defined in terms of the ratio of the new end position of the rod to the total circumference of the appropriate circle. Thus $A_1, \ldots, A_n$ is a direct measuring procedure:

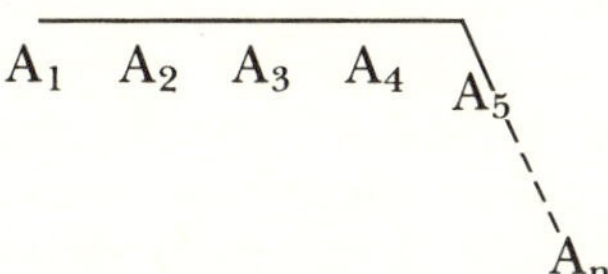

where direction is changed. The totality of direct measuring procedures we take as the domain of the language of geometry. It is taken for granted that it does not matter how fast the procedure is carried out. Different geometrical theories all expressed in the same language correspond to different totalities of coincidences among pairs of direct measurings. A geometrical systematization corresponds simply to deducing all pairs of coincidences from a subclass or basis of coincidences. If, for example, the geometry is Euclidean, one can take as basis all pairs of measurements corresponding to right triangles constructed in accordance with the theorem of Pythagoras. Thus, ABC below

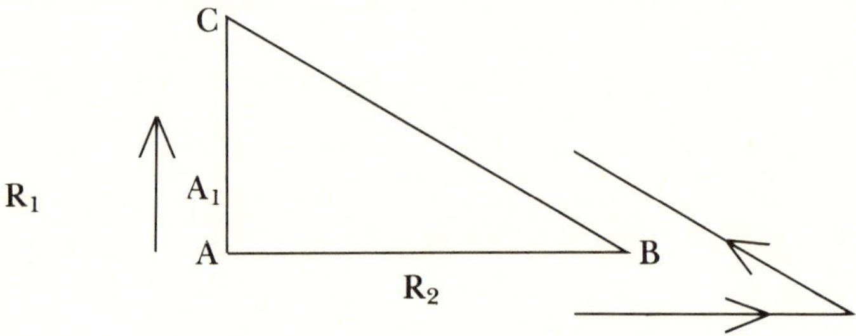

is regarded as a pair of direct measurings according to rules R_1, R_2. The entire procedure is described as follows:

> R_1: (1) Start at A and extend straightly 1,732 times;
> R_2: (2) Go back to A and fix a direction 90° from the original position of the rod (AA_1) and extend straightly 1,000 times, change direction 60° and extend straightly 2,000 times.

In Euclidean geometry measurings according to R_1 and R_2 will coincide. In non-Euclidean geometries, the pair R_1, R_2 will not coincide and so will not form part of the basis. One would then deduce other coincidences from the basis class. For example, in certain non-Euclidean geometries one will deduce that two "parallel" direct measurings meet or even that a one-step direct measuring meets an n-unit direct measuring that straightly extends it (this corresponds to a straight line meeting itself, as on the surface of a sphere). Which geometry holds of the world is empirically determined by carrying out sets of measuring pairs to determine coincidences (and thus the basis set). I present this not as the most elegant or practical representation of geometry, but as one that makes use ultimately only of a common set of local notions or operations.

Note that all the local operations have their counterparts in the situation of the child learning to direct attention. Thus, I may turn the child around before leading him to the car. In the original learning situation also, it does not matter how quickly he steps in following directions. Indeed there is a complete isomorphism between *a* prescription for directing attention and *a* direct measuring. The only difference, so to speak, is that in the former case one uses one's foot as the unit rod. In this regard, the acts prescribed in giving directions are a special case of direct measuring procedures.

Let us recall now the role of spatial prescriptions in singular representation. The canonical form of a singular representation can be put as 'Do R_i: α'. Now consider a child directing a parent to the toy car he wants, via 'Do R_2: Car'.

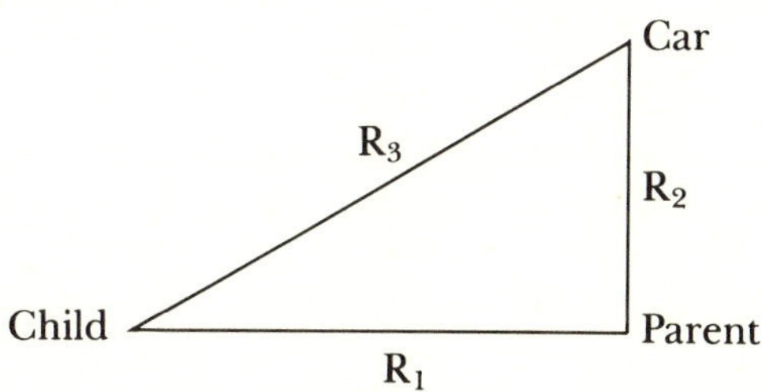

He also learns that in directing others he does not use the same prescription as he would give himself, viz., 'Do R_3: Car', and these are coordinated based on the prescription for finding the parent (R_1). A geometrical statement $R_3 = (R_1 + R_2)$ can thus be interpreted as two prescriptions constituting the same singular representation. The interpretation of geometrical claims then can be carried out in terms of space as a form of intuition. Geometry is the systematic study of the structure of the coordination of singular representation from different points of view and thus is involved at a fundamental level in our representation of things.

The application of some geometry or other to the manifold is as a priori or as necessary as the intersubjectivity of singular representation. Kant would like to conclude from this that which geometry obtains is a priori determinable. This is a mistake one part of whose diagnosis I shall discuss in the following section.

5: *Pure Intuition*

On our interpretation the form of intuition is a prescription or direction for action governed by rules according to the same concepts which constitute the interpretation of geometry. I think that Kant envisaged that one could "follow" such directions or prescriptions in imagination. One could, that is, carry out an *imaginative* act or sequence in accord and just in accord with the prescriptive rule. What this act or sequence is, is a pure shift of attention. Consider first the in-purview case. The teacher points successively to Car, Boat, Plane, where each pointing is a limitation or a cut of a sweeping gesture describing a line. The child follows the hand motions of the teacher by successively shifting and focusing his attention. The 'construction' of a three-times-"cut" line segment is carried out "physically" by the teacher and in imagination by the child. Kant also holds that could be done without the physical gestures, as when I successively survey or attend to Car, Boat, and Plane. It is the shift or "movement" in attention that is the transcendental motion of the subject as opposed to empirical motion of any object (including taking steps or moving one's body). Consider now the out-of-purview case, where the teacher points to what is beyond reach and even beyond view. Thus, suppose the child has the use of the reactive names 'Mama' and 'Wall' and that Mama is in the next room. The teacher points in that direction by sweeping out a line and stopping first and saying 'Wall' and then continuing the sweep (further outstretching the arm so the finger describes a further segment in that direction) and stops a second time and says 'Mama'. The entire motion of the teacher, of course, is in purview. The purport, however, is that the child shift and direct his attention beyond purview. Beyond the wall, anyway, the shift and focus in the attention is 'pure' or isolated from an empirical or affecting or sensory component. The child is, by definition, not Mama-affected by the Mama out of purview, but can (in inner sense) follow in his focusing and shifting the import of the pointing directions beyond sensory affection. This again for Kant would be an imaginative construction. These acts of imagination are the sheer form of ostending or pointing out. Kant holds, I think, that it is these acts themselves that underlie or are the form of singular representation. Singular representation in the in-purview case is a matter not just of being affected (which is sensory and non-representational in itself) but of indicating or ostending appropriately *upon* being affected. Indeed, the imaginative focus-shift can be regarded as a case of indicating to or ostending for oneself. On this interpretation, then, so far what we have is that the canonical form or structure of singular representation is '*Doing* attention shift x: α'. An actually performed act, not a prescription for an act, is a constituent of the singular representation.

If this were how spatial construction functioned as the form of intuition, Kant would still be in trouble over the supposed a priori character of geometry. Even though attention shifts are "immediately" produced in empirical intuiting and so are themselves, so to speak, given (produced) in intuiting, what is not thereby shown to be producible this way is when pairs of incompatible attention shifts coincide. It is only the latter which would a priori verify the coincidence basis set which determines one geometry as opposed to another. This pair of acts would have to be carried out one after the other, and in carrying out a second attention shift I would have to keep the first shift I carried out in focus to see whether the second one ended by meeting it. But that is precisely, it seems to me, what cannot be done if focusing is a matter of concentrating attention one way *as opposed to* another.

One may object that it is enough if I simply keep the first shift in attention rather than specifically focus on it. But what is it to keep a prior imaginative act in attention as I perform a second one? It is one of two things. I might 'record' the product of the first act with pencil and paper. But then I'd be testing (as to meeting) a second act with a *record* of the first act which in the out-of-purview case is *only* a symbolic (not an ostensive, in Kant's sense) record or construction. Now obviously if the second attention shift is (to the) beyond purview, it can't end at the record of the first (which is in purview on paper before me). So it must be that a similar *record* of the second is compared with a record of the first. This corresponds to drawing a geometrical diagram. But the diagram can *only* be symbolic, since what it records are attention shifts that go beyond purview. The coincidence of symbols would show the coincidence of attention shifts only if space were homogeneous with respect to size or magnitude as far as coincidences are concerned. This, however, is a substantive claim that is false in some geometries, and as far as I can see Kant has no theory of how this claim can be established a priori by construction.

Secondly, I might keep the first attention shift *in mind* (as opposed to keeping it in intuitive attention). This is just a matter of my knowing what I have just done, which in turn is just a matter of my knowing the rule according to which I just acted. All that can be kept in mind, besides a symbolic record, is the rule. But then how do I compare a second attention shift with a rule for the previous one? If, instead, we talk of comparing the rules themselves, then we have nothing but the concepts expressing the rules to compare, and since geometry is not analytic, this gives us no means of a priori discernment.

Even if attention shifting is "given" in imagination, coincidences of attention shifting are not thus given, and so geometrical knowledge cannot be obtained by pure construction. A further difficulty is that these attention shifts must be carried out according to rule. The rule has two components at least. One is that one focus and further focus one's attention so many times. The second component is that each refocusing be subsequent to a *unit* shift of attention. There are all sorts of at least prima facie difficulties with the idea of performing a mental act according to rule that Wittgenstein has pointed out. What would it mean to incorrectly perform the act? The issue is *not* what it would mean to find out that one has performed it incorrectly, but rather what it would mean to perform it incorrectly *tout court.* Suppose the rule is 'Take n steps of magnitude m each' (or 'Focus attention n times with each further focus at a unit of size m beyond the preceding one'). How do I purely produce a shift of size m at all, let alone subsequently duplicate it?

Probably, Kant thought of spatial representation in terms of attention shift as well as prescriptions for taking steps, and he probably thought the former was involved in understanding and making the latter prescriptions. Even if this were so, however, that would not provide him with a method of determining a priori coincidences of the latter by the former, for the two reasons we've just discussed. My claim in this paper has been that very little of Kant's account of the relation of spatial representation to singular representation and geometry is lost with the excision of attention shifts, and what Kant thought he gained with them (viz., the a priori knowledge of geometry) can't be had with them anyway.

In particular we can still understand Kant's view that not only is space a pure form of intuition, but this form of intuition is itself isolable as, or given in, a pure intuition. To move and circumscribe is a productive activity which produces what I can be affected by. In this regard, in an intuition, a moving-about-and-being-passively-affected, I am also affected by my own behavior. My own behavior is given to me sensibly. Nevertheless, space is still pure, because I myself produce the constructions which sensibly affect me. This sensitive awareness of my own behavior is, of course, crucial if I am to be sensitive of when I have complied with a prescription to spatially behave. Thus, that space is also given in intuitions is necessary if one is to be able to employ our canonical singular terms.

My spatial behavior is pure in the sense that to take three steps and circumscribe, say, is not constrained by how I am affected. I cannot legitimately react 'Red' except in so far as I am properly affected. There is no such passive constraint on the legitimacy of taking steps and circumscribing. The active or productive behavior I am sensitive of is thus pure. The sensitivity is produced by the behavior; it is not an empirical constraint which first allows it.

6: *Intuition and Infinity*

I have suggested that space is the affection-obtaining activity and as such is neither a relation among entities, nor an entity in its own right. Categories, roughly, apply to phenomena by unifying this activity. We get, for example, as a canonical singular representation the direction or prescription 'Take n steps Circumscribe Be affected React ϕ'. The ordinary demonstrative 'This' can now be regarded as of this canonical form if we equate it with 'Take o steps Circumscribe Be affected'. Such directions or prescriptions are ontologically neutral in that they do not settle issues of identity. It is not that I am directed to be affected by *an* X, where X is an event, an enduring object, a temporal slice, a sensation, or whatever. I am simply directed to be affected in a certain way or style. The mathematical category of quantity (and its schema number) are clearly implicated in our canonical singular representations, as guiding and unifying the otherwise amorphous undirected moving around and being affected. The ontological neutrality of this moving around governed by the mathematical categories simply means that our canonical singular representations are such without being representations of *objects.* In this, our prescriptions differ from definite descriptions which are always of the form 'the entity or object X which is so-and-so'. What I wish to discuss briefly is the bearing of this ontological neutrality on the mathematical antinomy of extent in space.

For Kant the extent of things in space forms neither a finite nor an infinite totality. The exactly wrong conclusion to draw is that therefore the extent of things forms an indefinite totality or, perhaps, a potentially infinite totality, for there is no such thing, nor did Kant think there was. What can be indefinite is the rule for the attaining of appearance. We remarked before that if space is relational or absolute, then singular representation of what is in space will be formed by definite descriptions like '(lx) (x is ϕ meters from this)' or '(lx) (x is at place p_K)'. In either case, as with all definite descriptions, the sense of the representation depends on a domain of potential satisfiers. This domain or collection of objects will have to be either a finite or an infinite totality, since there cannot be indefinite collections or totalities. Thus, if space were relational or absolute (as Kant would say, if space were objective), the extent of what is in space would be either finite or infinite. This point remains, no matter what objects one takes to be in relational or absolute space. Even if these objects are sensations, there cannot be an *indefinite totality* or domain of sensations.

Since Kant thinks the extent of things in space is neither finite nor infinite, and since an extent of *things* cannot form an indefinite totality, the only conclusion to be drawn is that the general representation of the filling of space cannot be or involve a representation of *things* at all. Let us see how this can be so, given our view of what it is for space to be a form of intuition. If we take our singular terms to be of the form 'Take n steps Be affected React ϕ', i.e., a particular direction or prescription to behave and subsequently respond, then a general representation must be a general direction to behave which has as instances or consequences the particular or individual directives. Such a representation I claim would be the unlimited directive to keep on going being affected and reacting ϕ. To keep on going does not mean to finish or complete; it is an incompletable prescription. In this regard it is neither a prescription to perform a finite nor a prescription to perform an infinite task or synthesis. Nor does it require or involve representing "the objects" that one will meet or be affected by. This would be to lapse back into there having to be a finite or infinite totality of objects there to be met with prior to the regress of my behavior. It is simply an indefinite prescription to designate or exhibit, consequentially upon moving. Just as I cannot indicate *this here* except upon actually circumscribing and being affected, so I cannot indicate or exhibit upon moving except as I carry out the prescription. To keep on going is an indefinite prescription to keep moving, all the while circumscribing and reacting.

If we equate 'Take n steps Be affected React ϕ' with the atomic form 'ϕa_n' of quantificational logic, then we can equate the universal '$\forall x \phi x$' with 'Take$_x$ steps freely Be$_x$ affected React ϕ', i.e., with the prescription to keep on taking steps without restriction, and as one does to keep on being affected and reacting ϕ. We can then equate the existential representation '$\exists x \phi x$' with the prescription to keep on taking steps until one reacts ϕ, i.e., with the representation 'Take$_x$ steps until Be$_x$ affected React ϕ'. In this way we get a prescriptive reading of quantificational generality with regard to what is in space, which does not require a domain of objects or entities for its sense, but just the idea of ongoing activities. Thus, we may say that our conception of the world generally does not involve the conception of a totality of objects, whether finite or infinite, at all. It is because space is the form of our exhibitive or demonstrative *activity* that general representation of the spatial, as prescriptive or directive, does not involve objects at all, and so neither a finite nor an infinite totality of objects.

University of Illinois, Urbana-Champaign

4 The Deduction of Causality

JOSÉ BENARDETE

I

That both outer and inner sense (the Kantian idiom comes almost too readily to hand) presuppose causality from the start, has been growing increasingly evident in recent years, though precisely how those results bear on the central nerve of the Kantian program, which I take to consist above all in an effort to execute a transcendental deduction of causality, is only beginning tardily to be understood. I am alluding specifically to two influential papers, the one by H. P. Grice,[1] the other jointly authored by C. B. Martin and Max Deutscher.[2] Grice's paper may be said to show that causality is built into the very concept of outer sense, which is not of course to be confused with mere outer imagination (i.e., hallucination): the distinction is drawn by Kant himself in his footnote to the Refutation of Idealism at B 277. By way of an ironical reply to Hume when he insists that "the simple view of any two objects. . . , however related, can never give us any idea of power," for "this idea arises from the repetition of their union," we are entitled now to say that the simple view of any one object alone, a mere apple say, suffices by itself to yield the idea of causality and *a fortiori* power once we reflect deeply enough on what is involved in an object's being viewed at all.

Much more foundational, however, as regards the Kantian program proves to be the causal theory of memory. Whence the importance of the Martin/Deutscher paper. Inner sense being presumably postulated by Kant above all in order to account for our non-inferential awareness of the passage of time, it can be seen to play a

[1] H. P. Grice, "The Causal Theory of Perception," *Proceedings of the Aristotelian Society*, Supp. Vol. 35 (1961).

[2] C. B. Martin and M. Deutscher, "Remembering," *Philosophical Review* 75 (1966).

role all of a piece with the threefold synthesis and the synthetic unity of apperception (they come to pretty much the same thing), which in their turn are constituted in no small measure by memory. If memory now is conceded to entail causation the transcendental deduction of causality as a necessary condition of (temporal) experience goes through. It is our recognition (apperception) of the passage of time that grounds the deduction. Such recognition requires that some state of affairs obtaining at one time be recognized as being different from (or the same as) a state of affairs obtaining at another time. But any such recognition presupposes at least short-term memory of the earlier time, and with memory entailing causation there are then at any rate some causal episodes.

Strikingly, the deduction of causality can already be found to be in effect anticipated in Hume, who can be shown to be committed to the validity of the argument "I think, therefore there are causal episodes," seeing that in his chapter on personal identity "the true idea of the human mind" comes to sight in terms of "that chain of causes and effects which constitute our self or person." Although the negative import of Hume's doctrine of the self is the more familiar 'I am no more than a mere bundle of perceptions', the positive content of the doctrine lies in the threefold principle of unity (resemblance, causation, and memory) that serves to wrap up the bundle. Proceeding one step further in the argument by appealing to Hume's principle 'No causality without universality', we can extend the argument into its full form to read, "I think, therefore there are causal episodes, therefore there are at least some laws of nature, i.e., exceptionless regularities stretching across all the past and all the future." That Hume could not be expected to rejoice in the argument goes without saying, and yet it is precisely here that the Kantian project can be seen to secure a distinct internal grip on the Humean material. And it is here also, I conjecture, where Hume veers asymptotically close to Kant, that his enigmatic misgivings regarding his doctrine of the self ("this difficulty is too hard for my understanding"), as expressed in the appendix to the *Treatise,* must find their explanation. What precisely is this difficulty that baffles Hume? Well, here is certainly one to consider. One need hardly be an outright Pyrrhonist to wonder if perhaps there are in fact no exceptionless regularities stretching across past and future. But that very modest sort of skepticism commits the Humean to the further doubt as to whether there are any singular causal episodes. Which in turn commits me in my Humean mood to wonder whether I exist at all, even in the fairly exiguous form of a mere bundle of perceptions. That final doubt Hume never entertains.

Having rejected the substantial self of traditional metaphysics, Hume does go one step further toward impugning the ontological status of the self by insisting that the identity across time of all the following—"any mass of matter," persons, animals, plants, rivers, buildings—involves a definite fictitious component. But granting all that, it may be proposed that Hume never doubts his own existence in some modest form or other as a bundle of perceptions, and it is precisely this tacit feature of his thought that he rightly finds incapable of reconciling with the principle that "the mind never perceives any real connection among distinct existences." Although the emphasis in the chapter on personal identity lies very much in a third-person rather than a first-person approach, based on supposing that "we could see clearly into the breast of another and observe that succession of perceptions which constitutes his mind," what I can come upon in my own case can amount to no more than what I can come upon in yours. In the one case as in the other "the train of past perceptions . . . are *felt* to be connected together" thanks to the pervasive resemblances and regularities that obtain among them. But, as we have seen, no matter how massive those regularities from the beginning to the end of my life and yours, they fail to entail our existence. At best they can only render our existence probable. In strict logic Hume ought to conclude just that. Only if those regularities prevail uncontravened throughout the whole universe and into the remote past and future is our own local existence here and now assured.

If the most important chapter of the *Treatise* is the discussion of causality entitled "Of the Idea of Necessary Connection," it is at any rate arguable that the second most important chapter is the one on personal identity, for does not Hume insist that, "no question in philosophy" being "more abstruse than that concerning . . . the nature of the uniting principle which constitutes a person . . . we must have recourse to the most profound metaphysics to give a satisfactory answer to it"?[3] Kant may then be read as undertaking to play the second chapter off against the first in his effort to answer Hume. The unity of apperception being for Kant by no means merely probable on the available evidence, how is it in turn to be understood? We know this much. It has an objective side and a subjective side. On the subjective side that unity is grounded in the threefold synthesis of apprehen-

[3] *Treatise* (ed. Selby-Bigge), Bk. I, Pt. 4, sec. 2, p. 189.

sion, reproduction, and recognition. On the objective side it is no mere natural relation that constitutes it, it is rather an epistemic relation, for it consists above all in (the process of) thinking (about) an object (i.e., intentionality). The pure concept par excellence is the concept of an object, and it is that indeed (as we have learned from Quine) that is tacitly featured in the science of formal logic. The whole 'to which/of which/over which' package comes into play here, for it is the object to which we refer, of which we predicate, and over which we quantify. Take the simple judgment "This pain is increasing in intensity." The object (of reference) is the pain of which increase in intensity is being predicated. If the judgment is to be expressive of knowledge we must be "conscious that what we think," namely, the object, "is the same as what we thought a moment before" (A 103), for an earlier and a later state of the object must be contrasted, which requires a synthesis of recognition and *a fortiori* memory and causality. But, as Hume insisted, no causal episode can be a merely local affair, segregated from the rest of the universe; it has cosmic import that transcends the case at hand. Universal laws (regularities) are thus presupposed.

Read one way, with emphasis on the subjective faculties required for judgment, the argument proves to be a subjective deduction of causality. Read another way, with emphasis on the object itself and the pure concept of identity that is brought to bear on it, the argument is to be seen as an objective deduction. By inviting Kant to help himself to the causal theory of memory we can now dispel his profound ambivalence regarding the subjective deduction (at A xvii). All that incessant cranking and creaking of transcendental machinery going on behind the scenes that Kant presciently feared his critics would deplore as a mere "hypothesis," suitable enough perhaps for the hypothetico-deductive procedures of a positive science of mind but hardly acceptable in pure philosophy, prove finally to be vindicated. The cognitive episode that is expressed by the judgment "This pain is increasing in intensity" is found to be constituted at least in part by a causal episode. But the causal episode as such, and here we simply follow Hume, can never be open to introspection thanks to its transcendent character. No wonder, then, the need for all that talk of transcendental activity generating an a priori synthesis that underlies the manifest exercise of the understanding. Once the causal theory of memory is seen to supply the missing link in the argument a genuine, historical episode of a priori synthesizing discharged behind the scenes can be precisely identified with a causal event and no longer explained away as a conflation of the logical and the genetic.

The very expression "a priori synthesis" (A 118) suggests of course the synthetic a priori, and one can scarcely be expected to resist the temptation to ground the latter in the former. Kant says that the unity of apperception—more exactly, he speaks of the numerical identity across time of our self-consciousness—is a priori certain (A 113). What does he mean? Is it then the contingent proposition that there is in fact (a case of) apperceptive unity that we know to be true on a priori grounds? (Doubtless a somewhat deviant sort of a priori here.) After Saul Kripke the notion of a contingent, a priori proposition cannot be dismissed out of hand. On the strength now of the transcendental deduction of causality that finds the unity of apperception to be enforced by a causal link we may insist that the contingent, synthetic proposition "There are some causal episodes and *a fortiori* some laws of nature" is likewise known to be true on a priori or at any rate quasi–a priori grounds. And it is then that proposition that is seen to enshrine the synthetic a priori and to express the a priori synthesis that grounds all possible (self-conscious, temporal) experience. Such necessity as appertains to the proposition proved to be merely a hypothetical necessity. What is necessarily true is the hypothetical proposition that if there is (self-conscious) experience then there are causal episodes.

II

Although the mnemonic deduction of causality is doubtless more immediately in accord with the Kantian program than any other, a whole family of such deductions has been virtually tumbling into our hands in recent philosophy. Thus one has only to accept Max Deutscher's causal theory of inferring[4] in order to be in a position to argue, "I infer, therefore there are laws of nature." One aspect of mind after another (perceiving, remembering, inferring, etc.) being found to presuppose underlying processes of causation, the deduction of causality in its most general form can be seen to come to this, "There is mind, therefore. . . ." For it is nothing less than an omnibus causal theory of mind that has been coming to a head in our time, albeit in piecemeal fashion. In ringing the changes on the general theme one finds that Wittgenstein's private language argument, widely acknowledged in any case as the most important piece of sustained transcendental argumentation since Kant himself and every bit as tantalizingly inconclusive, must be read in a new way.

[4] M. Deutscher, "A Causal Account of Inferring," *Contemporary Philosophy in Australia*, ed. R. Brown and C. D. Rollins (London, 1969).

The basic question harks back to Hume. If the mind never perceives any real connection among distinct existences, "how do words *refer* to sensations?" (*Phil. In.* I, #244). There are two distinct existences here, this sensation-token (the pain in my foot) and the word-token 'pain' that is presumably being used by me to refer to the sensation-token. "But how is the connexion between the name and the thing set up?" Even more to the point, how can there indeed so much as *be* a (real) connection between the two items that is there for me to recognize as such? Has not Hume shown that no such connection is so much as thinkable? In Kantian terms, how is it possible to think an object? Or, equivalently yet more concretely (in Wittgenstein's idiom), to apply a word to it? Merely to invoke the non-natural relation of meaning ('x means or refers to y') or intentionality serves only to label the puzzle. Notice that the puzzle of intentionality is here being seen in terms not of how we can think what doesn't exist (Brentano) but rather of how we can think what does. The deepest clue to this intentional linkage is found in the causal nexus. And vice versa. 'Only connect' is the watchword. It is only here in the interplay between the two, causality and intentionality, that Hume's demand for real connection can be satisfied with total clarity.

All appeals to 'immediate experience' must of course be ruthlessly eschewed. To say that "I impress on myself the connexion between the sign and the sensation" gets us nowhere, for that "can only mean: this process brings it about that I remember the connexion *right* in the future." 'Brings it about' expresses causality, but even more to the point if I produce a 'pain' token (and this involves 'agent causality') every time I am in pain the (Humean) regularity with which the one item invariably accompanies the other (in my 'diary') cannot be purely accidental if it is indeed the case that the relation of meaning or reference obtains between them. Each sensation-token must cause (must at any rate serve as a causal factor in bringing about) the attendant word-token, which is not by any means to say that the causal process is somehow 'available to consciousness'. Nor will it suffice to suggest, as Donald Davidson has shown,[5] that the pain merely serves as the reason, not the cause, of the 'pain'-token. If the argument "I refer to my pain with the word 'pain', therefore there is a law of nature" proves now to be valid, the validity belongs rather to transcendental than to formal logic. *What* the law of nature might be I do not know. It is a mere caricature to suppose it to be a rule to the effect that whenever I am in pain I say 'pain', though the caricature is not

[5] D. Davidson, "Actions, Reasons and Causes," *Journal of Philosophy* 60 (1963).

without its use as a crude first approximation, as much as to say in the Humean case that windows shatter whenever hit by stones. Thanks above all to its normative character ('correct' and 'incorrect' apply here) the semantic rule "'pain' means pain" can never be identified with any law of nature; it merely presupposes it by way of 'substratum'. Being itself "the faculty of rules," the understanding can thus rest assured that there are laws of nature underlying its own exercise that are there in principle to be discovered by it.

In effect Wittgenstein applies to meaning the same strategy that Hume applies to causality. In the one case as in the other we are inclined to suppose that we have some understanding of what goes on in a purely local phenomenon (this stone's breaking this window, this word-token's referring to this sensation). Exaggerating, I can put the matter as follows. There is nothing going on right here when the stone breaks the window, when 'pain' is used to refer to this pain. Both relations (causal and semantic) are constituted by regularities occurring elsewhere and elsewhen. Of course something *is* going on right here, namely, causing and referring. It is just that 'going on right here' cannot be explicated in the purely atomistic fashion that one supposes: it involves the whole universe.

Whether the private language argument can succeed in its official purpose of establishing that "inner processes stand in need of outward criteria" remains as much of a vexed question as ever. Causality, not publicity: that (it may be argued) is the proper upshot of the private language argument. Because both are modes of objectivity and transcendence it may be that the one (causality) can do the job that Wittgenstein demands of the other (publicity).

III

Ever since Gilbert Ryle's *Concept of Mind* it has been widely accepted that belief in particular and mind in general—mind at any rate in many if not all its modes—involves a definite dispositional component. We are thus invited to argue, "I believe that there is a wall behind and a table in front of me, therefore something is disposed to behave in certain ways in certain conditions." Kant being seen as concerned above all with the necessary conditions of judgment, I propose now the following transcendental sorites. Judgment entails belief, belief entails dispositions, dispositions entail subjunctive contrary-to-fact conditionals, counterfactuals entail causality, causality entails laws of nature. Packed into the "doxastic deduction" may be found almost half the content of contemporary philosophy.

It is the premise above all upon which Ryle would drill his beady eye. "I believe . . .," he would protest, is to be viewed as a mere "avowal," being as such in its performative or quasi-performative role altogether unsuited to serve as the *pied-à-terre* of a demonstration. The point is precisely reminiscent of Kant's insistence that the 'I think' has a purely "logical employment," it can never be used as premise by a philosopher to generate any ontological conclusion whatever. Even simply to argue, "I think, therefore there is something, not nothing," is presumably to be guilty of a paralogism. Is not that in fact the paralogism par excellence against which Kant inveighs in his critique of rational psychology? But isn't Kant's entire Deduction, its only text being scarcely more than the 'I think', itself a piece of rational psychology and, accordingly, shot through with paralogism? Kant at any rate can reply, "You have failed to credit my anti-realism. Once that is acknowledged you will see that my Deduction issues in no properly ontological conclusions." My own battery of deductions being intransigently realist in import, I have no such easy escape from the charge of paralogism. Paralogism, not verificationism. If verificationism does vitiate the more familiar styles of transcendental argumentation, as Barry Stroud charges,[6] I am to be seen as conspicuously exempt from the charge.

One can, however, choose to object to the doxastic deduction as follows. "If belief were what Hume took it to be, a vivid idea, Cartesian certainty regarding it would be readily forthcoming. But to the extent that belief is taken to be dispositional, to that precise extent you are denied privileged access to it, for that something (anything) is disposed to act in certain ways can only be known through familiar empirical, highly fallible inductive procedures. Seeing that you do insist on the dispositional component in belief, you have undercut your right to any Cartesian certainty in its regard. Your premise, then, though doubtless true, fails to be known by you to be true in the Cartesian fashion that your transcendental program requires."

So I am being asked, then, to concede that I merely believe, not know, that I have beliefs? Is it merely inductively probable that I have beliefs? Is *that* what I am expected to believe? But no one who so much as believes that he has beliefs can possibly be mistaken in that belief. Reminiscent of the Cartesian paradox involved in doubting that one doubts, those queries are designed merely to indicate the kind of approach needed at this critical point. There is a good as well as a bad Descartes. The bad Descartes is the Descartes of mentalism

[6] B. Stroud, "Transcendental Arguments," *Journal of Philosophy* 65 (1968).

and immediate experience. The good Descartes is the logical Descartes that comes to mind when we entertain the paradox of doubting that one doubts. This is a very different matter, where the foundations of knowledge are secured by the dialectic of paradox.

The note of paradox may be further accentuated by registering a third objection to the doxastic deduction, based on the challenging work of Fred Dretske.[7] Applicable across the board to every transcendental argument whatever, the Dretskean objection, even while allowing us to know that the premise of our argument is true, on top of conceding that we know the conclusion to follow from the premise, simply refuses to admit that those resources in and of themselves can suffice to propel us over into knowledge of the conclusion's truth. Dretske's eerie denial of epistemic closure is to be welcomed for positively forcing the foundationalist problematic into its proper mode of paradox where Plato's insistence that dialectic on the highest level of the Divided Line requires that we be able "to run the gauntlet of all objections" (*Republic,* VII 534C) (one can only trust that they are not infinite) comes peculiarly into its own. Looking no further, the three objections I have noticed fail to combine in any formidable way, being each incompatible with the other two.

If someone says he is in pain he cannot possibly be mistaken, though he may of course be lying. Impossibility of mistake is thus rightly required of the premise of any transcendental argument. For such arguments being always designed to refute one form of skepticism or another, the skeptic invariably bases his case on the possibility of mistake ("you may be hallucinating").[8] So when I say that I believe (merely believe) that there is a wall behind me the skeptic will not contest my claim, being satisfied that here at any rate I am exempt from every chance of being in error. The doxastic deduction is thus seen to be peculiarly adapted to meet the demands of skepticism.

IV

To say that "causal laws are necessary in the sense that (a) there must be (known) causal laws if there is to be self-consciousness" is one thing, writes Jonathan Bennett, adding that "this, however, is very different from saying that causal laws are necessary in the sense that

[7] F. Dretske, "Epistemic Operators," *Journal of Philosophy* 67 (1970). See also Robert Nozick, *Philosophical Explanations* (Cambridge, Mass., 1981), p. 689.

[8] See P. Butchvarov, *The Concept of Knowledge* (Evanston, 1970), where knowledge is defined as impossibility of mistake.

(b) every causal law expresses some non-empirical kind of necessity." And yet "when Kant says that 'the very concept of cause . . . contains the concept of a necessity of connection with an effect' he is surely making a (b)-type complaint against Hume's analysis of cause," even though "(a) brings against Hume a charge that is compatible with any analysis" of cause—in particular, with Hume's regularity account.[9]

Bennett's challenge is of the first importance, and not merely for Kant scholarship. How it is to be met by the line of transcendental argument sketched in these pages can be brought out most clearly in connection with Mackie's recent effort, in his massive study of causation, to update Hume's analysis of cause with the specific aim of showing how it can accommodate the distinction between nomological regularities that support counterfactuals and purely accidental ones (equally exceptionless) that do not. Current Hume scholarship applauds Mackie's solution as being "stunningly Humean." The trick here is to argue that "a generalization sustains a counterfactual if our reasons—our evidence for embracing the generalization—are not undermined by the supposition of the counterfactual's antecedent."[10] The difference between the two (nomological versus accidental regularities) is thus deemed to have an epistemic rather than ontological character.

It is to be noticed that Mackie's analysis, precisely by insisting that "singular causal statements cannot be true . . . as we ordinarily mean them,"[11] can be readily shown to be incompatible with (to mention but one case) the private language deduction of causality. Starting from the premise that there are occasions when I refer to my ongoing pain using the word 'pain', we conclude that there is a true singular causal statement, namely, the statement that J.B.'s pain was at least in part the cause as well as the reason of his saying 'pain'. The situation here is confessedly fairly droll, seeing that one may well be inclined to protest, "Surely any old causal episode, e.g., fire being extinguished by water, will suffice to refute Mackie." And that of course is in a way correct. But Mackie is satisfied that "statements of singular causal sequence involve in their analysis counterfactual conditionals which . . . state what would have happened not what did happen" by appealing to "possible situations or possible worlds" and "which on the present showing are not capable of being true," though they may be

[9] J. Bennett, *Kant's Analytic* (London, 1966), p. 155.

[10] T. L. Beauchamp and A. Rosenberg, *Hume and the Problem of Causation* (Oxford, 1981), pp. 155, 149.

[11] J. L. Mackie, *The Cement of the Universe* (Oxford, 1974), pp. 54, 229.

"acceptable or unacceptable, well or poorly supported and so on." Very much in the spirit of Hume a "psychological explanation" is called upon at this juncture to account for our counterfactual discourse. Logically, however, 'x caused y' is to be basically analyzed as 'x occurred and y occurred and in the circumstances y would not have occurred if x had not'. x's occurring in those circumstances was thus a necessary condition of y's occurring: absent x, no y. More than that, "the general notion of a cause," allowing for complications, "is of something which is both necessary and sufficient in the circumstances for its effect," though "different parts of this concept," namely, the necessary and sufficient components, "will be stressed in different settings." It is precisely because singular causal statements do express some non-empirical kind of necessity, on Mackie's account, that he despairs of seeing how they can ever be "true in a strict sense." Logical necessity as narrowly construed (in terms of the valid formulas of first-order predicate logic) will not suffice; and though there may be a synthetic a priori kind of necessity involved in color incompatibilities, "nothing in this example helps us to see what could be conjectured about a necessity linking two distinct existences." Mackie concludes that "causal statements, though not themselves true, are surrogates for clusters of statements which can be true."[12]

Well, what about Saul Kripke's 'necessities of origin'? If, on the one hand, this table is not identical with the wood of which it is composed and if, on the other hand, it could not possibly have been made from any other (quantity of) wood, have we not here an intelligible necessity linking two (logically) distinct existences? (Logically distinct not in the sense that either can exist in the absence of the other but in the sense that $6 \neq 7$.) Granted that such a necessity is intelligible in the case where x is the material cause of y (for that is what Kripke's table comes to in Aristotelian terms), what about the case where x is the efficient cause of y? I believe that Mackie would hesitate to say flat out that "nothing in this example," namely, Kripke's table, "helps us to see what could be *conjectured* about a necessity linking two distinct existences" that are related as cause to effect. Conceding that the example doubtless "helps," it can hardly be said to be coercive, and yet it is fair to say that it goes no small distance in taking the sting out of Hume's insistence that "we have no idea of this connection nor even any distinct notion of what we desire to know when we endeavor at a conception of it." A bare (epistemic) possibility of there being a (meta-

[12] Ibid., pp. 54, 55, 37, 49, 216, 230.

physically) necessary link between cause and effect—*that* and no more Kripke's table opens up for us.

I am prepared to follow Mackie all the way up to the point of accepting the following disjunction. Either there are no true singular causal statements or there is a non-empirical kind of necessity actually instantiated in ongoing causal episodes. At this point we are placed in a quandary. Which disjunct to choose? Commonsense realism of the most familiar sort prompts us to reject the first and plump for the second disjunct, simply on the strength of everyday cases where fire is quenched by water. One may even wish to say with David Lewis that "one comes to philosophy already endowed with a stock of opinions" and that "it is not the business of philosophy either to undermine or to try to justify, these pre-existing opinions, to any great extent, but only to discover ways of expanding them into an orderly system."[13] But that cannot be right. For it rules out both Zeno and his critics, the one in his efforts to show that there is no motion, the others in theirs to refute him. The Mackian disjunction is thus seen to enshrine precisely the sort of antinomy upon which so much of philosophy thrives. How, then, to break the deadlock and refute Mackie's anti-realism regarding causation?

Speaking under the cloak of anonymity, one of the early reviewers of the *Treatise* (Hume himself in the *Abstract*) writes, "It is sufficient if I can make the learned world apprehend that there is some difficulty in the case," i.e., causality and necessary connection, and that "whoever solves the difficulty must say something very new and extraordinary—as new as the difficulty itself." I take it to be Kant who has said that something very new and extraordinary. Mind itself in a wide variety of forms, e.g., sense perception, memory, belief, referential discourse, being found to entail that there are true singular causal statements, the Mackian antinomy proves to be resolved in favor of the second disjunct. Our access to the non-empirical kind of necessity involved in causal relations remains, however, very indirect, being vouchsafed us only through the roundabout route of transcendental reasoning. Hume's demand that "we must produce some instance wherein the efficacy is plainly discoverable to the mind" cannot be satisfied on his terms.

Necessity (possibility) has been implicitly divided into three sorts: metaphysical, epistemic, and logical. In this scheme of modal distinctions it is logical *im*possibility that 'wears the trousers'. Something (some state of affairs) is logically impossible in the narrow sense if it

[13] D. Lewis, *Counterfactuals* (Cambridge, 1973), p. 88.

reduces in the last analysis to an outright contradiction, thereby certifying the state of affairs to be absolutely or metaphysically impossible (impossible of obtaining). By parity of reasoning one might suppose, and Humeans have been characteristically prone so to suppose, that if something is logically possible it is then really or metaphysically possible. Not so, as Kant recognizes at B 268/A 221. Something is logically possible if it is not ruled out by logic. But that leaves it open as to whether it might not be ruled out by other considerations (consider here color incompatibilities). By a bit of a trick logical possibility can be profitably viewed as a form of mere epistemic possibility. Confront the goddess of logic with any arbitrary statement and ask her whether it is true. (Being a goddess, she is exempt from the incapacities imposed on us by Church's theorem.) Let her now answer, "Could be," adding *sotto voce,* "as far as I know." The statement, then, by expressing an epistemic possibility for the goddess of logic, is thereby certified as expressing a logical possibility *tout court.* I take it now that though it is logically possible for potassium to fail to ignite in the presence of oxygen that state of affairs is really or metaphysically impossible. Causal necessity is shown to be a mode of metaphysical or absolute necessity by showing that there is nothing else it could be. Notice that though our original paradigm of metaphysical necessity was found in cases of logical necessity we succeeded in prying the one concept loose from the other.

V

States of affairs, possible worlds—these being seen to be platonic entities, presumed to lie outside space and time and as such incapable of entering into causal commerce with us or indeed with anything whatever, how could we possibly come to know of their existence (assuming they do exist)? Injected into recent discussions by Paul Benacerraf with specific reference to the abstract entities of pure mathematics (numbers and sets),[14] the query was soon recognized as having application across the board to all abstract entities, on the crest of the causal theory of knowledge.[15] Another antinomy, then, Quine versus Benacerraf: on the one hand, the powerful considerations in favor of abstract entities associated largely with Quine, on the other, the insidious doubts with which Benacerraf has infected the contem-

[14] P. Benacerraf, "Mathematical Truth," *Journal of Philosophy* 70 (1973), pp. 661–79.

[15] A. Goldman, "A Causal Theory of Knowledge," *Journal of Philosophy* 64 (1967), pp. 357–72.

porary philosopher. Causality being taken to undergird our knowledge of concrete particulars, causality is assumed here to be itself unproblematic, at any rate for the nonce.

Suppose now we can show independently that "statements of singular causal sequence involve in their analysis counterfactual conditionals" and that "these counterfactual conditionals describe possible situations or possible worlds."[16] Accordingly, the hypothetical proposition "If there are true singular statements of causal sequence then there are abstract entities" will emerge for us as a necessary truth. We can then argue as follows. "The stone broke the window, therefore there are abstract entities." Ironically, in some unexpected fashion we thus come to know of abstract entities (that they exist) on the basis of certain causal episodes. The argument is itself irreducibly a posteriori in character.

Not everyone will be convinced by the argument, certainly not one who like Quine or Mackie is deeply disturbed by the concept of causality in its pure, unreconstructed form, feeling perhaps not only that the "notion of cause is out of place in modern physics" but that "the trouble with causation is, as Hume pointed out, that there is no evident way of distinguishing it from invariable succession."[17] In fact such a person, on being persuaded by the causal theory of knowledge, might well emerge as a *metaphysical* skeptic: knowledge is impossible precisely because it presupposes true singular causal statements which in their turn presuppose a non-empirical kind of necessity that cannot be reasonably credited.

It is at this point in the dialectic that a transcendental deduction of platonic objects (not to mention the very possibility of empirical knowledge by way of satisfying our metaphysical skeptic) turns out to be mandatory. How to construct such a deduction will be evident.

Syracuse University

[16] Mackie, op. cit., p. 54.
[17] W. V. Quine, *The Roots of Reference* (La Salle, 1974), pp. 5–6.

5 "Knowing How" and Kant's Theory of Schematism

DANIEL O. DAHLSTROM

A central purpose of Kant's discussion of schematism in the *Critique of Pure Reason* is to teach us how the power of judgment applies pure concepts of the understanding to appearances.[1] This aim has struck more than one critic as pretty absurd, since it seems to suppose an illegitimate distinction between possessing and being able to apply a concept. What can it mean, it is argued, to say that I have a concept if I am not able to use it?[2]

Agreeing on its superfluousness but for a different reason, other critics question the role of the doctrine of schemata following the deduction of the categories. If the transcendental deduction has demonstrated that the categories are a priori applicable to experiences, what need is there for a doctrine of schematism?[3] Disputed by this second line of criticism is a distinction underlying the very structure

[1] Kant, *Kritik der reinen Vernunft* (Hamburg: Meiner, 1971), A 135 = B 174. Hereafter this work is referred to as 'KrV', followed by the pagination of the A and B editions. All quotations from KrV are my translations. All quotations bordered by double quotation marks in the text are phrases or sentences of others, while every mention of words by me is bordered by single quotation marks. For helpful suggestions on revising this paper I am particularly indebted to Professors Lewis White Beck and Antonio S. Cua and to Ulrich Lange.

[2] G. J. Warnock, "Concept and Schematism," *Analysis* 9 (1948–49), p. 80: "If I cannot apply a concept, then I have not got it." J. Bennett, *Kant's Analytic* (Cambridge: Cambridge University Press, 1966), p. 146: "Having a concept involves both being able to use it in 'rules' and under favorable sensory circumstances, to apply it to instances."

[3] H. A. Prichard, *Kant's Theory of Knowledge* (Oxford, 1909), p. 246: "It seems clear that if the first part [the Deduction] is successful, the second [the Schematism] must be unnecessary." Robert P. Wolff, *Kant's Theory of Mental Activity* (Cambridge, Mass.: Harvard University Press, 1969), p. 207: "The artificiality of both the problem and the solution is evident upon reflection. . . . Either appearances can be subsumed under the categories without the aid of schemata, or else they cannot be subsumed at all." T. E. Wilkerson, *Kant's Critique of Pure Reason* (Oxford: Clarendon Press, 1976), p. 94: "The Schematism serves no useful purpose and can in my opinion be ignored without loss."

of Kant's Transcendental Analytic, viz., the distinction between "knowing that" and "knowing how" categories are applicable to experience universally and necessarily.

In the first part of this paper I attempt to show that the first of these criticisms is misdirected and false. As demanded by Kant's own commitment to experimental science, a legitimate distinction can be drawn between possession and applicability of empirical concepts, while the transcendental deduction can be construed as demonstrating their equivalence for the categories.

However, the equivalence of categorial possession and applicability does suggest that after the transcendental deduction the doctrine of schematism is superfluous. Indeed, though inconclusive, there is evidence that Kant shared this view at times. More importantly, this challenge to the necessity of the categories' schematization raises in turn questions about the legitimacy of the categories' deduction and, indeed, about similar metaphysical or transcendental arguments which claim to demonstrate that something is the case without being able to demonstrate how it is. In the final portions of this paper I address these issues, outlining how only a rather unique, philosophical hermeneutic can rescue Kant from this second and potentially fatal line of criticism.

I

Criticism of the chapter on schematism in the *Critique of Pure Reason* is often aimed at a so-called general theory of schematism, understood as encompassing all types of concepts.[4] However, it is far from clear that Kant held a general theory in the sense that for each concept there is some corresponding schema. Indeed, though Kant is mute on this detail, it seems legitimate to assume that schemata for empirical concepts, unlike transcendental schemata, are contingent.

Inasmuch as a schema involves one kind of application of a concept, this last remark suggests a non-equivalence between the possession and applicability of empirical concepts. Since a denial of some senses of such non-equivalence is a key element in much criticism of Kant's theory, the remark demands both clarification and justification. Applicability of a concept can signify an ability to use some expression properly, either in silent soliloquy or with others. This meaning of applicability can be construed as a criterion for external (i.e., non-

[4] Bennett, op. cit., pp. 143–45; T. E. Wilkerson, op. cit., p. 95.

introspective) evidence that one in fact possesses a concept.[5] Though Kant is not particularly interested in such criteria, his theory of concepts and their (possible) schematization is not incompatible with the notion of a criterion provided by this sense of applicability.

However, understanding applicability in this sense, I can certainly be said to possess a concept without being able to recognize an instance of it. Not only children learning a language but students of scientific theory who comprehend the concepts involved in that theory without being able to perform the experiments that yielded those concepts are able to apply concepts in this fashion. Indeed, the working scientist himself fashions hypotheses that may never be corroborated. Such a scientist applies a concept without being able to recognize an instance of the concept.[6]

Kant's theory of schematism is, of course, not concerned with the criteria for evidence of possessing a concept but with the use of a concept in cognition. A schema for an empirical concept is a procedure or method by means of which images are produced in accordance with that concept.[7] Apparently (though the theory neither is nor is intended to be wholly clear on this point), these images are quasi-instances of the concept involved, which both render the concept meaningful and aid in the recognition of real instances or objects—if there be any—falling under the concept. If applicability signifies this ability to recognize an object as an instance of a concept, there is, as testified by the examples in the preceding paragraph, no equivalence between this sort of applicability and possession of an empirical concept.[8] The lack of an equivalence between possession and applicability of an empirical concept is one of the features that distinguish empirical concepts from the categories. Empirical concepts may have accompanying schemata, but these procedures, like the images they yield, are neither universal nor necessary. How you form an image of a concept of economy or a concept of polluted air, if you can be said to have such a procedure at all, need not be the same as my technique for imagining instances of these concepts. If an empirical concept has a schema, the schema, its relation to that concept,

[5] Warnock, op. cit., p. 80: "If I have a gauge, I can sensibly ask how to use it, how to apply it; but to ask how I can apply a concept that I have, is to ask how I can use a word that I know how to use."

[6] See Chipman's example of "bone marrow" in his "Kant's Categories and their Schematism," *Kant-Studien* 63 (1972), pp. 36–50.

[7] KrV, A 141 = B 180.

[8] See my "Thinking, Knowing, and Schematism," forthcoming in *Akten des 5. Internationalen Kant-Kongress* (Mainz, 1981), herausgegeben von Gerhard Funke.

and the very procedure of schematizing are all empirical and contingent.[9]

While possession and applicability in the sense of recognizability are not equivalent for empirical concepts, their equivalence is necessary for pure concepts of the understanding. By demonstrating that categories are a priori conditions of any possible experience, Kant is arguing—even before the account of schematism—for the very thesis some of his critics accuse him of rejecting! To be sure, a category has a function apart from its relation to experience, i.e., a category may be understood as a logical form apart from any application (in the sense of recognition). Yet even as a logical form the category is *applicable.* The purpose of the Transcendental Deduction is to show that categories are "conditions of the possibility of experience and are valid therefore a priori also of all objects of experience."[10] There is no experience that is not already subject to categories and there is no category which is not able to be applied to experience.

If the preceding interpretation is right, then the difference between Kant's account of the categories' deduction and their schematization does not turn on a bifurcation of possession and applicability. Prior to the chapter on schematism, Kant is demonstrating the a priori applicability of categories in general to experience.[11] The particular character of schemata for categories, moreover, makes even more explicit Kant's commitment to the equivalence of categories' possession and their applicability. Since imaginings are contingent and particular, there can be no images corresponding to categories in the way some images correspond to some empirical concepts. A transcendental schema, however, is a transcendental determination of

[9] Heidegger is one of the few commentators to have grasped the full weight of this distinction between categories and empirical concepts in terms of their relations to their respective schemata. See M. Heidegger, *Kant und das Problem der Metaphysik* (Frankfurt am Main: Vittorio Klostermann, 1973), pp. 89–98. In English: *Kant and the Problem of Metaphysics,* trans. James S. Churchill (Bloomington: Indiana University Press, 1965), pp. 97–106.

[10] KrV, B 161: "Folglich steht alle Synthesis, wodurch selbst Wahrnehmung möglich wird, unter den Kategorien, und, da Erfahrung Erkenntnis durch verknüpfte Wahrnehmungen ist, so sind die Kategorien Bedingungen der Möglichkeit der Erfahrung, und gelten also a priori auch von allen Gegenstände der Erfahrung." See also KrV, A 89–90 = B 122.

[11] Dr. Beck has called my attention to an obvious difference between the Deduction and the Schematism. The Transcendental Deduction is not about 'die Kategorien' but about 'Kategorien überhaupt', while the Schematism, like the Metaphysical Deduction, is about specific concepts. In other words, the schematism is not concerned with the procedure *überhaupt* but with finding the *specific* temporal form necessary for *each* category.

time.[12] This determination is, like the images yielded by schemata for empirical concepts, a sort of quasi-instance of the concept, but an a priori instance and the work of the productive imagination. Since time is an a priori form of sensibility and a pure intuition, i.e., a condition of all other intuitions, the categories schematized as time-determinations are necessary and universal conditions of experience.[13] Transcendental schemata, in other words, demonstrate *how* categories are applicable universally and necessarily.

The fact that Kant argues for the equivalence of possession and applicability of categories while rejecting it for empirical concepts is often overlooked by Kant's commentators, though much of the responsibility for the oversight lies with Kant himself. Kant all too casually introduces accounts of schemata for empirical and pure sensible concepts (e.g., the concept of a circle) into his account of schemata for categories. Apparently intended to illuminate the nature of a schematism in general, these insertions fail to make clear the precise sameness and difference among the various types of schemata.

A prime instance of this ambiguity, the effects of which have seriously prejudiced interpretations of the schematism, is Kant's remark that "this schematism of our understanding, in regard to appearances and their mere form, is a hidden art in the depths of the human soul."[14] Numerous commentators cite this remark as evidence of the failure or serious inadequacies of Kant's transcendental project.[15] But is Kant referring to schematism for categories? Perhaps so; after all, he is referring to the mere form of appearances, presumably time, a distinguishing feature of transcendental schemata. But the comment is immediately preceded by two lengthy sentences in which Kant is talking exclusively of schemata for empirical concepts. It seems quite likely that 'this' in the expression "this schematism" refers to the immediately foregoing account of empirical schemata. If so, talk of the

[12] KrV, A 145 = B 184–85: "Die Schemata sind daher nichts als *Zeitbestimmungen* a priori nach Regeln, und diese gehen nach der Ordnung der Kategorien, auf die *Zeitreihe,* den *Zeitinhalt,* die *Zeitordnung,* endlich den *Zeitinbegriff* in Ansehung aller möglichen Gegenstände."

[13] KrV, A 146 = B 185.

[14] KrV, A 141 = B 180–81: "Dieser Schematismus unseres Verstandes, in Ansehung der Erscheinungen und ihrer blossen Form, ist eine verborgene Kunst in den Tiefen der menschlichen Seele, deren wahre Handgriffe wir der Natur schwerlich jemals abraten, und sie unverdeckt vor Augen legen werden."

[15] For example, Bennett, op. cit., p. 142; Gottfried Martin, *Kant's Metaphysics and Theory of Science,* trans. P. G. Lucas (Manchester: Manchester University Press, 1955), p. 82.

"hidden art in the depths of the human soul" might very well be intended to apply solely to schemata for empirical concepts.

The contingency and particularity of schemata for empirical concepts further supports this last interpretation, as does Kant's view of the teachability of the power of judgment in regard to formal and to transcendental logics. In the introduction to the Analytic of Principles (immediately preceding the chapter on schematism) Kant distinguished the power of judgment in formal logic as "a particular talent" that cannot be taught from the power of judgment in a transcendental logic.[16] The power of judgment in a transcendental logic is supposed to be governed by specific and determinable rules, viz., the schemata and the principles of pure understanding, and thus is apparently not to be written off as some inscrutable art.

II

A critic may agree with the interpretation offered in the first part of this paper, viz., that the applicability of categories, far from being in question, is actually presupposed in the chapter on schematism, having been purportedly demonstrated by the transcendental deduction. This same critic may, however, cite that very demonstration as evidence of the schematism chapter's superfluousness. On this view the doctrine of schematism with its appeal to the imagination may be construed as evidence of the truth of Hegel's complaint, revived by Strawson, that the genuine accomplishments of Kant's theoretical philosophy are sabotaged by his commitment to a psychological model of human knowing.[17] As a psychological theory, the account of schema-

[16] KrV, A 133 = B 172: ". . . so zeigt sich, dass zwar der Verstand einer Belehrung und Ausrüstung durch Regeln fähig, Urteilskraft aber ein besonderes Talent sei, welches gar nicht belehrt, sondern nur geübt sein will." KrV, A 133 = B 172n.: "Der Mangel an Urteilskraft ist eigentlich das, was man Dummheit nennt." KrV, A 135 = B 174: "Ob nun aber gleich die *allgemeine Logik* der Urteilskraft keine Vorschriften geben Kann, so ist es doch mit der *transzendentalen* ganz anders bewandt, sogar dass es scheint, die letztere habe es zu ihrem eigentlichen Geschäfte, die Urteilskraft im Gebrauch des reinen Verstandes, durch bestimmte Regeln zu berichtigen und zu sichern."

[17] Hegel, *Vorlesungen über die Geschichte der Philosophie,* III in *Werke in zwanzig Bände,* 20 (Frankfurt am Main: Suhrkamp, 1971), p. 337: "Von der barbarischen Terminologie nicht zu sprechen, bleibt Kant innerhalb der psychologischen Ansicht und empirischen Manier eingeschlossen." Schopenhauer, *Die Welt als Wille und Vorstellung,* Erster Band, Anhang: "Kritik der Kantischen Philosophie" (Wiesbaden: Eberhard Brockhaus, 1949), p. 534: "Kant . . . am Leitfaden der Analogie, für jede Bestimmung unserer empirischen Erkenntnis ein Analogon a priori darzuthun, sich bestrebt, und Dies zuletzt, in den Schematen, sogar auf eine blosse psychologische Tatsache ausdehnt, wobei der anscheinende Tiefsinn und die Schwierigkeit der Darstellung gerade dienen,

tism is certainly out of place in any attempt to demonstrate a priori principles of human cognition.

This objection raises the question of the nature of the distinction between "knowing that" and "knowing how" underlying Kant's division of the Transcendental Analytic into an Analytic of Concepts and an Analytic of Principles. The result of the deduction of the categories (the end of the Analytic of Concepts) is

> that the categories contain, on the side of the understanding, the grounds of
> the possibility of all experience in general. How they make experience possi-
> (1) ble, however, and what fundamental principles of its possibility they supply in
> their application to appearances will be shown in the following chapter on the
> transcendental use of the power of judgment (B 167).

Also, in the introduction to the Transcendental Logic, Kant speaks of transcendental knowledge as that "through which we know that and how specific representations are applied exclusively a priori" (A 56 = B 80). What is the relation between this "knowing that" and "knowing how"? The schematism provides part of the answer to the question of how the categories are a priori applicable to experience. But is this answer superfluous to the argument that the categories are so applicable?

Surprisingly, Kant himself *seems* to answer this question in the affirmative. I say "surprisingly," since I argued in the first part of this paper that schematizing categories, unlike schematizing empirical concepts, is supposed to be necessary, universal, and specifiable (not inscrutable). In a footnote to the preface to the *Metaphysical Foundations of Natural Science* Kant responds to objections that a "clear and adequate" deduction of the system in the *Critique of Pure Reason* is indispensable but lacking. Kant claims not that the deduction demanded is present but that the deduction contained in the *Critique* is sufficient.

> For if it can be proved *that* the categories which reason must make use of in
> all its knowledge have no other use than merely in relation to objects of
> (2) experience . . ., then the answer *how* they make such possible is, to be sure,
> important enough in order to *complete* this deduction where possible, but in
> relation to the chief purpose of the system, viz., the determination of the
> boundary of pure reason, it is in no way necessary, but simply helpful.[18]

---

dem Leser zu verbergen, dass der Inhalt derselben eine ganz unerweisliche und bloss willkürliche Annahme bleibt." P. F. Strawson, *The Bounds of Sense* (London: Methuen and Co., Ltd., 1966), pp. 15–16, 29–31, 266.

[18] Kant, *Metaphysische Anfangsgründe der Naturwissenschaft,* in *Kants Werke,* Akademie Textausgabe, Band IV (Berlin: Walter de Gruyter and Co., 1968), p. 474.

If Kant is referring in this remark to the distinction between "knowing that" and "knowing how" in (1), he seems to be acknowledging the superfluousness of schemata. An answer to the question of how the categories are applicable a priori to experience is perhaps helpful but not necessary to the argument that the categories are so applicable. Yet this interpretation of (2) at the same time seems inconsistent with the character of transcendental schemata (viz., necessary, universal, and specifiable). Is Kant in (2) in fact referring to the distinction between "knowing that" and "knowing how" in (1)? Commentators disagree.

Robert Pippin claims that (2) concerns a "psychological how-question" to be distinguished from the "transcendental how-question."[19] The latter question apparently *must* be answered and thus the doctrine of schematism is necessary. Wolfgang Detel, on the other hand, argues that Kant, in (2), is explicitly referring to the difference between categories' deduction and schematization.[20] The doctrine of schematism supposedly works out the positive content of the categories, but it is not at all necessary for the deduction of the categories. In other words, taking (2) as a reference to the distinction between "knowing that" and "knowing how" in the *Critique of Pure Reason,* one can conclude that Kant thought it possible to know that categories are a priori applicable to experience without knowing how.

There is, apparently, no clearly indisputable interpretation of (2) nor, for that matter, of how Kant viewed the role of the doctrine of the schematism. In support of Detel, it does seem a more straightforward reading of (2) to construe it as referring to the difference between the categories' deduction and schematization. Yet if this is the correct reading of (2), it seems not only to corroborate the charges of psychologism and/or irrelevancy as far as the schematism is concerned, but also to contradict the necessity Kant apparently attaches to schematism for categories. Detel's talk of the schematism as a "working out . . . of the completion" of the categories' deduction simply sidesteps the issue.[21]

Both commentators, however, overlook the crucial words "in relation to the chief purpose of the system" in (2). Kant is claiming that the answer to the 'how' question is not necessary in one respect, viz., determining pure reason's boundary. But this assertion leaves open

[19] Robert Pippin, "The Schematism and Empirical Concepts," *Kant-Studien* 67 (1976), p. 160.

[20] Wolfgang Detel, "Zur Funktion des Schematismus Kapitels in Kants Kritik der reinen Vernunft," *Kant-Studien* 69 (1978), pp. 40–41, 44.

[21] Ibid., pp. 29–37.

the question of the necessity of determining the conditions of the applicability of categories within experience.[22]

Determining what Kant has in mind in (2) is, in any event, far less significant than determining the relation between "knowing that" and "knowing how," both within the framework of Kant's transcendental philosophy and for the theory of knowledge. However, before that issue is addressed, the meaning of "knowing that" and "knowing how" in the present context must be clarified.[23] Knowing that categories are a priori applicable to experience is not knowledge by acquaintance or direct evidence but rather the conclusion to an argument. The understanding of experience by means of categories may be called categorial knowledge. Kant, then, is claiming to know by demonstration (the transcendental deduction) that he is able to know categorially. This knowledge by demonstration is formally presented as independent of the knowledge of how categorial knowledge is possible (the schematism and the system of all principles of pure understanding). From the standpoint of Kant's philosophy, knowing how categorial knowledge is possible can be described in terms of the subject or the object and empirically or transcendentally.[24]

[22] Dr. Beck was instrumental in clarifying this issue for me.

[23] There are *rough* parallels with Russell's distinction between knowledge by acquaintance and knowledge by description, Ryle's distinction between knowing that and knowing how, and Danto's between knowing that and knowing that knowing that, though none of these should be taken as equivalent to Kant's distinction. Bertrand Russell, *The Problems of Philosophy* (New York: Oxford University Press, 1959), pp. 46–59. Gilbert Ryle, *The Concept of Mind* (London: Hutchinson, 1949), pp. 25–61. Arthur Danto, "On Knowing That We Know," in *Epistemology: New Essays in the Theory of Knowledge,* ed. Avrum Stroll (New York: Harper and Row, 1967).

[24] Here a comment is in order on the relation of the doctrine of schematism to what Kant called the "two sides" of the deduction of the categories. The objective side "refers to the objects of pure understanding and is supposed to demonstrate and make intelligible [dartun und begreiflich machen] the objective validity of its concepts a priori." The subjective side considers "the pure understanding itself, in terms of its possibility and the cognitive powers on which it rests, i.e., considers it in a subjective connection." This subjective side is thus an attempt to explain how the human mind is in the position of making use of concepts a priori. In a use of terms closely resembling (2) above and thus adding support to the interpretation that relates (2) to the Transcendental Analytic, Kant describes the objective side as "essential" and the subjective side as "important" but "not essential" (KrV, A xvi–xvii). Given that the objective deduction establishes *that* experience is only possible through categories, the question remains of *how* the human power of knowing is constituted to be able to achieve this a priori knowledge. This I take to be the question of a subjective deduction. Yet one might also ask *how* the categories make experience possible (and thus how the categories have objective validity). This question points to an objective condition a priori beyond the pure concepts of the understanding. The answer to this second and necessary "how" question is given by the doctrine of schematism. Thus I would distinguish two "how questions": (1) subjective and psychological and (2) objective and transcendental.

Returning now to the relation between these types of knowledge, it is clear that a real distinction between knowing that I know and knowing how knowledge of x is possible is commonplace in human experience. I can recognize (i.e., know that I know) that something is a dog by means of a concept (or at least know how to employ 'dog' to identify a dog) without knowing how such knowledge by means of concepts is possible. "Knowing that" and "knowing how" are thus empirically distinguishable in the sense that I experience one sort of knowing without the other. Does the relation between "knowing that" and "knowing how" in the *Critique of Pure Reason* merely reflect this empirical distinction?

At certain levels of analysis (e.g., the *ordo exhibitendi et discendi;* see below) this interpretation of the relation between "knowing that" and "knowing how" may be perfectly acceptable, but it runs the risk of placing Kant's transcendental claims on an empirical footing. Even should there be an acceptable sense of 'knowing' such that I can be said to know that x is a dog without being able to explain how I know, recourse to empirical knowledge or knowledge via empirical concepts does not justify a similar distinction for transcendental knowledge. Kant is not interested so much in knowledge of objects as in knowledge of the type of knowing insofar as this is possible a priori. "I name all knowledge 'transcendental' which concerns itself in general not so much with objects but with our type of knowledge of objects insofar as this is supposed to be possible a priori" (B 25). Perhaps I can know that Fifi is a dog without knowing how I know. Knowledge of this state of affairs—which happens to include a distinction between kinds of a posteriori knowledge—is itself a posteriori. As such this knowledge does not warrant the supposition of such a distinction between similar kinds of a priori knowledge, the concern of transcendental knowledge. I cannot assume that I can know that I know something a priori without knowing a priori how I know. Indeed, even for empirical knowledge, let alone supposed conditions for any possible experience, such a distinction may be tenuous. Am I really entitled to assert that I know Fifi without being able to state to some degree—however slight—how I know her? Would I normally say "I know Fifi is a dog" unless I could add something like "because Fifi *is* a dog, because I saw her, because Fifi has the marks of a canine," and so on?

What I am suggesting, then, is that the relation between "knowing that" and "knowing how" (or between categories' deduction and schematization) is transcendental. By 'transcendental' I mean that each term of the relation, i.e., each type of knowledge, is a ground of the possibility of the other, and that there is some principle making the relation possible a priori. There is some evidence that Kant conceived the relation in this fashion. In the first part of this paper I cited those indications Kant gives that the schemata for categories are necessary, universal, and specifiable. Already in the deduction there is talk of "the transcendental synthesis of the imagination" and determinations of "the inner sense in terms of its form" (B 151; B 155), features that figure prominently in Kant's account of transcendental schemata. In the same context Kant identifies the understanding and the imagination. "It is one and the same spontaneity, which there under the name of the imagination, here of the understanding, brings some unity [*Verbindung*] into the manifold of the intuition" (B 162). Finally, both in the transcendental deduction and in the doctrine of schematism Kant refers to "the unity of apperception" as the ultimate principle of synthetic unity, a unity required for knowing that and how categories are a priori applicable to experience.

III

Although there are indications that the relation between the categories' deduction and schematization is in some sense 'transcendental', the case for this interpretation is far from conclusive. Above all, what needs explaining to establish this interpretation are: (*a*) certain troublesome quotes, especially that footnote to the *Metaphysical Foundations of Natural Science,* (*b*) the precise sense in which the categories' schematization is necessary to their deduction, and (*c*) the status of the chapter on schematism *after* the transcendental deduction of the categories. Each of these items can be construed as evidence of the schematism's superfluousness or of the psychologism underlying (and sabotaging) Kant's transcendental philosophy. Either knowing how the categories are universally and necessarily applicable to experience is irrelevant to knowing that they are or, if such "knowing how" is relevant, transcendental knowledge is dependent on some claims about certain psychological facts (indeed, some rather dubious claims at that). Such is the unkind option Kant's critics find in his account of transcendental schemata.

In the face of this criticism, there remain at least two possible lines of defense of Kant's theory of schematism, though either defense requires something like a philosophical hermeneutic distinguishing different levels of analysis. On one level of analysis the distinction between "knowing that" and "knowing how" may be granted, while at another level denied. To close this particular hermeneutic circle the interpreter of Kant's theory of schematism and thus of the entire

Transcendental Analytic must take a stand on a central issue at the nexus of metaphysics and epistemology.

A defender of Kant's theory might agree that the specific contents of the chapter on schematism are indeed superfluous, but argue that some sort of schematism is nonetheless necessary. This reading of Kant's theory of schematism would explain not only the passage from the *Metaphysical Foundations of Natural Science* but also Kant's talk of the "boring analysis" of what is required for a transcendental schema and his description of the latter as "the phenomenon or the sensible concept of an object, in agreement with the category" (A 142 = B 181; A 146 = B 186). In other words, a schematization of categories is in general necessary and so much is demonstrated by the transcendental deduction, but the particular schematization of a category may be specifiable in a variety of ways, no one of which is known to be necessary for that demonstration. (To be sure, as a transcendental determination of time, a schema for a category is necessary *for* experience to be possible, but this necessity does not preclude the possibility of another sort of schema for the same category.) Moreover, specifying how the categories are a priori applicable to experience amounts to providing a categorial determination of time as a transcendental condition, and hence is neither psychological nor empirical. Yet further specification of time in terms of categories is not necessary to establish that some such specification occurs.

According to this interpretation, a distinction between knowing that and knowing how categories are a priori applicable is legitimate with respect to the knower (*ordo cognoscendi*) although the specific but unknown principles of the categories' applicability are in fact (*ordo essendi*) operative. In other words, the categories are schematized in specific ways, i.e., are temporally specific conditions of any possible experience, regardless of whether those specific ways are able to be indicated.

While there is a great deal of plausibility to this interpretation, it not only runs counter to Kant's own apparent claims for the transcendental schematisms, but also rests on a highly problematic thesis. According to this thesis, which I label "the metaphysical thesis of nonspecifiable necessity," the necessity of certain general features (or conditions) of experience can be demonstrated without being able to demonstrate the specific ways these general features (or conditions) are necessary (or that a specific way outlined is the only and necessary specification). The legitimacy of this thesis seems to depend on the legitimacy of distinguishing something like an *ordo essendi* from an *ordo cognoscendi.* The articulation and defense of such a distinction within the framework of what Kant means by "transcendental" is obviously a highly complicated affair. While it appears plausible enough to distinguish knowing on an empirical plane from the essential order of things, it is not so easy to distinguish transcendental knowledge from that order. Kant's *ordo essendi,* if I may be permitted the odd expression, is transcendentally constituted. In other words, conditions of the possibility of real experience are also cognitive principles, i.e., principles of knowing that experience. What sort of cogency is there to an argument that a certain principle is a condition of the possibility of real experience if the way in which that principle conditions experience cannot be specified with necessity? Is it legitimate to claim that one knows that one knows if one cannot account for how one knows that one knows? Moreover, as noted in the first part of this paper, Kant appears (in the *Critique of Pure Reason* anyway) to consider it a task of transcendental philosophy to demonstrate in clearly specifiable ways how the categories are universal and necessary conditions of any possible experience. There is no place for stupidity in the application of transcendental logic.[25]

There is another possible line of defense. Kant may be understood as invoking the distinction between "knowing that" and "knowing how" for the reader in the *ordo exhibitendi et discendi* while denying that distinction absolutely. To justify this interpretation the quote from the *Metaphysical Foundations of Natural Science* would have to be understood, as Pippin conceives it, as referring solely to a "psychological how-question." In Kant's mind, knowledge of categories' schematization is a necessary condition for their deduction, but it appears after the deduction because Kant considered this order the most suitable for *presenting* his argument and *educating* his readers. The advantage of this interpretation is that it preserves the transcendentally necessary character Kant appears to assign to specific schematizations of the categories.[26]

[25] See note 16 above. Also, KrV A 135 = B 174–75: "Es hat aber die Transzendental-Philosophie das Eigentümliche: dass sie ausser der Regel (oder vielmehr der allgemeinen Bedingung zu Regeln) die in dem reinen Begriffe des Verstandes gegeben wird, zugleich a priori den Fall anzeigen kann, worauf sie angewandt werden sollen." KrV, A 136 = B 175: ". . . sie [die Transzendental-Philosophie] muss zugleich die Bedingungen, unter welchen Gegenstände in Uebereinstimmung mit jenen Begriffen gegeben werden können, in allgemeinen aber hinreichenden Kennzeichen darlegen, . . ."

[26] Indeed, given Kant's account of the regulative employment of ideas at the end of the *Critique of Pure Reason,* it is to be expected that there is a necessary and reciprocal sort of unity to the sorts of knowing that form the backbone of the Transcendental Analytic.

Yet the difficulties with this second line of defense are also formidable. How does one establish the difference between the *ordo exhibitendi et discendi* and the *ordo cognoscendi,* especially when an interpretation of a given text or sentence is to be assigned to one level rather than another? Can the footnote to the *Metaphysical Foundations of Natural Science* be so glibly dismissed as unrelated to the distinction between "knowing that" and "knowing how" in the *Critique of Pure Reason*? Above all, even assuming these queries can be satisfactorily answered, do we have any reason to suppose that the transcendental schemata, i.e., the time-determinations of the categories, are the necessary specifications of how categories are a priori applicable? Are other specifications possible, and, if so, why are they to be dismissed in favor of the schematizing Kant indicates? (Walsh, for example, has suggested reversing the temporal order in the schematization of causality, thereby rendering the category of causality teleological.)[27] Perhaps most significant in regard to this challenge is the lack of any extended discussion or argument on Kant's part attempting to establish that his schematisms are the only possible or are the necessary principles of how categories are a priori applicable.

CONCLUSION

Though neither defense of Kant's theory of schematism as presented in the preceding pages is compelling and unobjectionable, together they demonstrate a need for a unique, philosophical hermeneutic. This hermeneutic must sort out the possible levels on which Kant intended the distinction between knowing that and knowing how categorial knowledge is possible. This direction of research is fraught with difficulties but is necessary if the meaning of the schematism and thereby the structure of Kant's argument in the Transcendental Analytic is to be determined. The possibility of refuting or defending Kant's transcendental project presupposes this understanding.

This hermeneutic is, moreover, eminently philosophical because it forces the interpreter to make a case for a relation between knowing that and knowing how in regard to transcendental or metaphysical knowledge in general. A transcendental philosophy aims at demonstrating that there exist certain conditions for the possibility of any

[27] W. H. Walsh, "Schematism," in *Kant: A Collection of Critical Essays,* ed. Robert P. Wolff (Garden City, New York: Doubleday and Co., 1967), pp. 86–87.

experience, that these conditions are categories possessed by human understanding, and that thus there is universal and necessary knowledge of experience. Must the transcendental philosopher or a post-Kantian metaphysician be able also to demonstrate how the categories condition experience and how this knowledge is possible?

Catholic University of America

6 On Kant's Socratism

RICHARD L. VELKLEY

I. The most important epoch of Greek philosophy finally began with Socrates. It was he who gave an entirely new *practical* direction to the philosophic spirit and to all speculation. He stands almost alone among men as the one whose conduct came closest to *the idea of a wise man.*[1]

II. But, above all, there is the inestimable benefit [of a systematic metaphysics, constructed in conformity with a critique of pure reason], that all objections to morality and religion will be forever silenced, and this in Socratic fashion, namely, by the clearest proof of the ignorance of the objectors.[2]

III. Without in the least teaching common reason anything new, we need only to draw its attention to its own principle, in the manner of Socrates, thus showing that neither science nor philosophy is needed in order to know what one has to do in order to be honest and good, and even wise and virtuous.[3]

IV. The mere theoretician, or as Socrates calls him, the *philodoxus,* strives only after speculative knowledge, without caring how much his knowledge contributes to the ultimate end of human reason. . . .[4]

I

We have not been as interested in Kant's Socratism as we should be. Lest this assertion strike us as excessively Kantian, it should be noted that the implied imperative is hypothetical, not categorical. Restated:

[1]Immanuel Kant, *Logic* (G. B. Jäsche edition, 1800), trans. R. S. Hartman and W. Schwartz (Indianapolis and New York, 1974), p. 34, and the original in *Kants gesammelte Schriften* (Berlin and New York, 1902–), IX, p. 29 (henceforth *KGS*). I would like to acknowledge the support of the Earhart Foundation which made possible the initial phase of research for this essay.

[2]*Critique of Pure Reason,* trans. Norman Kemp Smith (New York, 1965), B xxxi (henceforth *CPR*).

[3]*Foundations of the Metaphysics of Morals,* trans. Lewis White Beck (Indianapolis and New York, 1959), p. 20; *KGS* IV, p. 404.

[4]*Logic,* op. cit., p. 28, and *KGS* IX, p. 24.

if our aim is to understand Kant's philosophic aim as he himself understood it, and if Kant understood his aim as somehow Socratic, then it should be our concern to gain insight into the nature of his Socratism. That Kant is somehow a Socratic has almost the status of a commonplace of scholarship and even of popular rumor. The evidence is overwhelming, if a few easily made historical assumptions are allowed. Among modern philosophers, Kant is the philosopher who breathed new life into the "categories" of Aristotle in his theoretical philosophy, and into the "ideas" of Plato in his practical philosophy as well as in the "regulative" doctrines of the theoretical. Kant is surely a Socratic of sorts on the assumption that Plato and Aristotle are Socratics, and Kant assumed this much.[5] Kant sees Socrates as beginning "the most important epoch of Greek philosophy" (see quotation I above), and Kant sees himself as inaugurating a wholly new epoch in philosophy; he is a *Socrates redivivus,* or so it has been said more than once.[6] The new life given to "categories" and "ideas" would perhaps not be necessary for making the case. That which Kant sees as central to Socrates, the emphasis on the practical, is repeated by Kant with his own doctrine of "primacy of the practical."

Just as readily as this last point is admitted, it is then dismissed as inconsequential for a philosophical reading of Kant's works. Socratism is pervasive in these works only in the way that something like "moral tone" or "moral fervor," placed on a plane only somewhat above literary style, is pervasive. Socratism cannot be seen as a substantive issue unless Kant's emphasis on the practical, found in all the writings, can be seen as substantive. Only then is it not a matter of *Weltanschauung.* Of course, it will be hard to get past viewing it as such when even the heart of ancient Socratism (or Platonism) is relegated to *Weltanschauung* by much current scholarship and philosophy.

Kant's Socratism, on a conventional *Weltanschauung* construal, amounts only to this: we can give the name "Socratism" to that area of Kant's philosophy where "belief" or "faith," rationally purified by "criticism," is given equal rights with or even a certain priority to

[5] Ibid., op. cit., p. 34, and *KGS* IX, pp. 29–30.

[6] Consider the remark of Herder quoted by Gerhard Funke in *Die Aufklärung* (Einleitung, "Das Sokratische Jahrhundert"), p. 13 (Stuttgart, 1963): "Ich will . . . ihn [Kant] seiner Absicht nach Sokrates nennen und seiner Philosophie den Fortgang dieser seiner Absicht wünschen, dass nämlich, etc." For some discussions of Kant's reading of ancient philosophy see the following: K. Düsing, "Das Problem des höchsten Gutes in Kants praktischer Philosophie," *Kant-Studien* 62 (1971), pp. 5–42; J. Schmucker, *Die Ursprünge der Ethik Kants* (Meisenheim, 1961), pp. 307ff.; M. Wundt, *Kant als Metaphysiker* (Stuttgart, 1924), pp. 153–78.

knowledge (see quotation II above). In this way Kant allows himself and other men to satisfy some part of themselves that will always be left stranded on the dry shoals of the primary argumentation of the *Critique of Pure Reason,* while only the latter is truly of interest to the philosopher qua philosopher.

Kant did not see the matter in this way, and it is worth our while to see why. The primary argumentation of the said *Critique* must reveal this to be so. The central and guiding question of the *Critique* is whether and how metaphysics can become a science with recognized methods and results.[7] Metaphysics is seen as pure reason's attempt to answer questions which it propounds to itself, where both the questions and the answers are not established with the help of something called "experience." Metaphysics as a natural disposition to raise and to try to answer such questions (*metaphysica naturalis*) is a factual, universal feature of human reason. Thus "in all men . . . there has always existed and will always continue to exist some kind of metaphysics."[8] Metaphysics as disposition is not a discovery credited to individuals, but philosophy as "cognition *in abstracto*" is credited to the Greeks, and even to certain individuals among them.[9] Since we cannot credit any philosophers with the discovery of metaphysics, not Thales and not Parmenides, the highest honors must go to whoever discovered the truest form of philosophizing; this happens to be Socrates. But metaphysics is the primary ground and problem that carries philosophy along; Socrates is not simply an ethical teacher, but the philosopher who uncovers the correct way (or approaches the correct way) of stating the question *about* metaphysics. One might say that Socrates was the first to have an insight into the connection between metaphysics, when it becomes a concern of "science," or of "the learned," and the practical concerns of man.[10]

Our questions now are these: (1) whether and how Kant's way of seeing "the problem of metaphysics" is a repetition of the Socratic way; (2) whether and how this Socratism conditions or is a premise of the primary "critical" argumentation of Kant's work. Let us note in advance with regard to (1) that we shall discover that Kant's Socratism is not a repetition, but a transformation; it is wholly modern and unlike any version of Socratism in the ancient schools. As Kant stands to Plato (via the new doctrine of "ideas"), so he also stands to Socrates,

[7] *CPR,* B xiv–xv, xxii.
[8] Ibid., B 21; cf. A 852–53/B 880–81.
[9] *Logic,* op. cit., pp. 31ff., and *KGS* IX, pp. 27ff.
[10] Cf. Aristotle, *Metaphysics* 987b1ff.

as a philosopher who claims to understand his predecessor "better than he has understood himself."[11]

II

The investigation must first confront Kant's very evident assertions about the wholly non-traditional and *eo ipso* non-Socratic features of his enterprise. No previous philosophy has attempted a "critique of reason" as the necessary propaedeutic to metaphysics.[12] An examination of the sources, extent, and limits of rational knowledge must precede the attempt to extend our knowledge into the first causes and principles of being. In the past (and in accordance with a "natural" tendency of our reason), thinkers have built their "speculative structures" first, and only afterwards inquired "whether the foundations are reliable."[13] Thus the critique of the pure rational faculties "is a perfectly new science, of which no one has ever even thought, the very idea of which was unknown," although Hume came closest to the idea.[14] Surely Kant knows of previous modern attempts to define "the limits of reason," but the novelty of which he is proud is the formulation of the hitherto-unknown question: "How are a priori synthetic judgments possible?" The whole "problem of reason" is contained in this question, the key question of the critical propaedeutic.[15] And on this question Kant erects his self-estimation of superiority to antiquity: "If it had occurred to any of the ancients even to raise this question, this by itself would, up to our time, have been a powerful influence against all systems of pure reason, and would have saved us so many of those vain attempts, which have been blindly undertaken without knowledge of what it is that requires to be done."[16] Only when we know whether and to what extent reason can have a priori knowledge which goes beyond mere "analysis" of concepts, and which "synthetically" extends knowledge, will we be able to determine whether metaphysics as science (i.e., as a body of a priori synthetic knowledge) is possible.[17]

For our purposes, we must examine a few Kantian assumptions that

[11] *CPR*, A 314/B 370.

[12] Ibid., A 11/B 25ff., A 841/B 869.

[13] Ibid., A 5/B 9.

[14] *Prolegomena to Any Future Metaphysics*, trans. L. W. Beck (Indianapolis and New York, 1950), pp. 9–10 and *KGS* IV, pp. 261–62.

[15] *CPR*, B 19ff., B 73.

[16] Ibid., A 10.

[17] Ibid., B 18.

are contained in this account of "the problem of reason." To apply the Kantian question of "possibility" to Kant himself, we should ask: What assumptions make it possible for him to formulate the "problem" in this way? We must limit ourselves to issues that more directly impinge on the theme of Socratism. It helps us to note that Kant modeled the new science, the critical propaedeutic, on what he thought to be an existing and completed science: logic. The core of the new science is a new logic: transcendental logic. The traditional logic, which is "general" and is concerned with the "rules of all thought" as these apply to any object, is "to all appearances a closed and completed body of doctrine," and since Aristotle's time has been unable to "retrace" or "advance a single step."[18] Logic is susceptible of completion, for its subject matter is simply the understanding itself; the understanding can give a complete inventory of its own operations, which are the content of the logical doctrine, but through an *inspectio mentis* it cannot oversee the nature and extent of objects given to it from without.[19] "Common logic itself supplies an example, how all the simple acts of reason can be enumerated completely and systematically."[20] Kant conceived a final solution to the problems of metaphysics to be possible, by means of an analogy between reason's self-knowledge of its "pure" logical employment and such self-knowledge as it might acquire of its pure employment in metaphysics. Reason can fully know its own powers, and thus "it must be possible for reason to attain certainty whether we know or do not know the objects of metaphysics," and thus to know the "limits" of its powers.[21] The problems of metaphysics must be viewed as arising from entirely within reason, for they "are imposed upon it by its own nature, not by the nature of things which are distinct from it."[22] The completed propaedeutic to metaphysics will in truth then finish the chief part of the work of reason in metaphysics, what remains being only the "analysis" of the basic concepts of metaphysics, discovered by the new science, which "marks out the whole plan" of metaphysics.[23] The completability of metaphysics, foreshadowed in the completed propaedeutic, brings it into alliance with the completed logic of tradition: "There are but few sciences that can come into a permanent state beyond which they undergo no further change. To these belong logic, and also metaphysics."[24]

[18] Ibid., B viii.
[19] Ibid., B ix.
[20] Ibid., A xiv.
[21] Ibid., B 22.
[22] Ibid., B 23.
[23] Ibid., B xxii and A 11/B 24ff.
[24] *Logic*, op. cit., p. 23, and *KGS* IX, p. 20; also B ix and B xxiv in *CPR*.

The question about a priori synthetic judgments is the key question of the "transcendental" logic which decides in wholly a priori fashion the possible extension (a priori) of reason into knowledge of objects. The completability of metaphysics is grounded in the carrying out of this project in the new logic. Now it is a question whether any of the ancient Socratics conceived of metaphysics as completable science. It is safe to say that none of them regarded any form of logic as the highest and most decisive science. Aristotle, for example, does not include logic (or syllogistic, or "analysis") among the theoretical sciences at all.[25] We recall that Kant claims to leave the Aristotelian logic intact, as to its content, while improving the orderliness of its presentation and derivation. The new transcendental logic, whose principal judgments and categories are derived from those of general logic, only supplements, and does not modify or replace, the logic of tradition. But to conceive of any logic as the highest science is quite un-Aristotelian, and what is more, is related to the character of *formality* which Kant ascribes to traditional logic.

When the question of logical formality was already controversial well over a century ago, Kant was often regarded as the founder of modern "formal" logic. ("Christian Wolff ist noch der Ansicht, dass die Gründe der Logik aus der Ontologie und Psychologie stammen und die Logik nur für den Gang des Studiums diesen Wissenschaften vorangehe. Erst in Kant's kritischer Philosophie, in welcher die Unterscheidung von Materie und Form durchgreift, bildet sich die formale Logik scharf heraus und eigentlich steht und fällt sie mit Kant.")[26] The logic of tradition which Kant calls "general" abstracts from all content of knowledge, in his opinion. It is a logic which relates indifferently to experiential or merely thinkable objects. Transcendental logic is also abstractive and formal although limited to experiential objects, in that it ignores all "empirical" content of knowledge, and treats only the laws of understanding as these relate to a "pure" content (the "pure sensibility" of space and time).[27] The new logic legislates the structure of this content, and therewith legislates the formal requirements of "possible experience." In this decisive respect, the new logic is still formal.

Kant underlines this formality by insisting that no logic, of whatever kind, is an *organon* of the sciences. Logic is not a body of princi-

[25] *Metaphysics* E, chap. 1; K, chap. 6; see I. M. Bocheński, *Ancient Formal Logic* (Amsterdam, 1963), p. 25.

[26] F. A. Trendelenburg, *Logische Untersuchungen* (Hildesheim, 1964), vol. I, p. 15; cf. H. Sluga, *Gottlob Frege* (Boston, 1980), pp. 12, 49–54.

[27] *CPR,* A 55–57/B 79–82.

ples of demonstration suited to extending human knowledge, as it was in a dominant strand of tradition. In Kant's view, an *organon* presupposes particular knowledge of the subject matter of the science served by it, and the generality of all logic precludes any association with a special science.[28] (Kant implies that Aristotle's logic is compromised by such association. Yet, if he disagrees with Aristotle, it is on a matter of the "interpretation" of logic, which in no way for Kant affects the validity of formal rules discovered by the ancient.)[29] This apparent demotion of logic tends to conceal the real elevation of its position within the whole of "reason," for "logic is to be considered as the basis of all other sciences and the propaedeutic of all use of the understanding."[30] While not an *organon,* logic is indeed a *canon* of the correct use of the understanding, empirical and pure; it can be called a "critique of cognition" which brings the understanding "into agreement with itself."[31] The understanding can determine the conditions of its own internal consistency only because it is able to abstract from "content." And logic, being thus determinable in autonomous fashion, without "particular" knowledge of any features of nature, the world, or first causes, can serve as propaedeutic to all sciences (but not as instrument of them).

One should contrast with this the Aristotelian view that there is an "ontological" study of the first principles of demonstration which belongs properly to the inquiries of first philosophy, the study of being qua being. Even the principle of contradiction is ultimately not "formal." Knowledge of such principles is certainly presupposed by first philosophy, but is not the basis or "foundation" of the latter (nor, equally, is logic "derived" from first causes). Such principles can indeed be autonomously apprehended by human reason without knowledge of being qua being; this does not entail that such principles exist autonomously of being qua being.[32] The principles of demonstration are grasped prior to the first causes, but they point towards

[28] *Logic,* op. cit., p. 15, and *KGS* IX, p. 13.

[29] *CPR,* A 81/B 107. It is open to question whether Aristotle himself conceived of "logic" as *organon,* a term applied by later Peripatetics and central to disputes of the later schools (i.e., as to whether logic is *organon* to philosophy, a part of philosophy, or both). See C. von Prantl, *Geschichte der Logik im Abendlande* (Leipzig, 1855), vol. I, pp. 89, 136–37, 345, 532ff. Adamson states emphatically that Aristotle did not regard the logical doctrines as the "common introduction to the whole system of sciences," but this denial is compatible with the conception of an *organon.* See R. Adamson, *A Short History of Logic* (Edinburgh and London, 1911), pp. 32 and 38.

[30] *Logic,* op. cit., loc. cit. in n. 28 above.

[31] Ibid., pp. 15–16 and 23 (*KGS* IX, pp. 13–14, 20) and *CPR* A 53/B 77, A 60–61/B 84–86.

[32] Aristotle, *Metaphysics* 982a25–b12, 995b7–11, 996b25–97a16, 1005b2ff.

reflection on them. They are instrumental to the reflection on them; the logical doctrines are the *organon* of *philosophy.* Accordingly, one can show that historically the Aristotelian doctrines of the syllogism emerged from "dialectic": from the dialogical practices intended to enhance the soul's capacity for philosophical discovery. As such, Aristotelian logic forms an integral part of a pedagogical task of habituation, and is inseparable from a conception of the soul (as having its *telos* in inquiry) which is quite alien to Kant.[33]

On any reading of Kant, transcendental logic relates not to inquiry and the soul's fulfillment therein, but to something called "experience," for this logic can be called the "logic of experience." It shares with "general logic" the characters of autonomy, formality, and completability. Unlike "general logic," which we employ for analysis of concepts, transcendental logic is presupposed in all our experience of objects. The account of experience which emerges from the articulation of this logic is inevitably as autonomous of "first causes" as is the logic itself. The logical categories can refer to nothing in itself, but only to the manner in which something is given under the conditions of the human mind's receptivity. (By contrast, "experience" can never be "autonomous" in the Socratic view, but the "universals" implicit in the phenomena point towards the first causes beyond the phenomena.) This point can be expressed in another way: as underlying any and every "possible experience," the transcendental logic cannot be limited to an "instrumental" function, employed by conscious agents for certain purposes. Rather, it is an automatic or "blind" function of the soul.[34] The "universality" which precludes instrumentality also makes thinkable the notion of a self-sufficient "science" of the principles of this logic. In the view of the Aristotelians, to repeat, logic is not a theoretical science but the instrument to science. As such, it cannot possibly be inherent in, or presupposed in, all experience. The latter is indeed based on "blind" and unconscious processes, but these are hardly "logical," or certainly not wholly so.[35] Thus from a Socratic

[33] E. Kapp, *Greek Foundations of Traditional Logic* (New York, 1942), passim.

[34] *CPR,* A 78/B 103.

[35] Thus there is an Aristotelian tradition, whose sources are primarily *Metaphysics* A, 980b25ff., and *Posterior Analytics* B, 99b15ff., holding that the formation of experience consists in a natural "occult" anticipation of universals which cannot be wholly perspicuous to analysis. Cf. E. Gilson, *History of Christian Philosophy in the Middle Ages* (New York, 1955), on Avicenna (logic presupposes the formation of universals but cannot account for the process), p. 192, and on Ockham (*Natura occulte operatur in universalibus*), p. 495. In Kant's view, the basis of experience is not the anticipation of universals but the construction of "objects" through judgments, where "objects" are viewed in the light of the modern non-generic "scientific" universals (homogeneous space and time, etc.). This approach makes a wholly perspicuous analysis of experience seem possible, per-

(or Aristotelian) standpoint, to speak of a "logic of experience" is to conflate what is "first for us" with what is higher, with the principles of discursive thinking which "intend" the first causes of the mere phenomena of experience.

Ancient logical thinking is a bridge between the indemonstrable starting points in experience and the discovery of the highest causes (which are also indemonstrable, being the highest premises of all argumentation). It aids in the articulation of the true natural whole which lies behind the phenomenal articulation of things into kinds and classes. The bridge between the phenomena and the causes is not a science which determines the character of the *termini.* But such is the character of "transcendental logic"; it serves both to articulate the universal and necessary logical structure of experience and to delimit the "possible" with respect to metaphysics. That is, it has a dual function as the unconscious "logic of experience" and the "propaedeutic to metaphysics" which is articulated by the philosopher. Logic has a comprehensiveness undreamed of by any ancient philosopher. This comprehensiveness depends on the power of reason to "legislate" both experience and first philosophy. But reason legislates what is universal and necessary; "experience" so legislated takes on the character of what can be universal and necessary, or a particular notion of the "logical" predominates in experience. A homogenizing of experience is the result; the "whatness" or the kind-character of things, which is the starting point in the "phenomena" of ancient philosophical analysis, cannot be the starting point of a Kantian analysis, which seeks knowledge of the "rules" of experience. Instead, the modern mathematical natural sciences provide a better notion of how one can find a priori (universal and necessary) rules of experience.[36] The logic of experience is a logic of the "pure" sciences, as well; it will show how these are "possible," transcendentally.[37]

The "transcendental logic" appears to combine the uncombinable: a "logic" of unconscious processes involved in forming "experience" (the "transcendental synthesis") and a philosophical inquiry which determines the possibility of metaphysics as science. This ambiguity

---

haps for the first time in the history of philosophy. Such analysis can become part of "logic," where "logic" now includes "the logic of phenomenal reality or valid construction," to use an expression of Felix Grayeff. The transcendental logic does not presuppose any mode of being which is extra-logical, other than "intuition" which is ontologically neutral with respect to things in themselves.

[36] For the contrast of ancient (Socratic) and modern (Cartesian and Spinozist) modes of philosophical analysis, see R. Kennington, "Analytic and Synthetic Methods in Spinoza's *Ethics,*" in *The Philosophy of Baruch Spinoza,* ed. R. Kennington (Washington, D.C., 1980), pp. 309ff.

[37] *CPR,* B 20.

lies at the heart of the project. "Experience" itself must determine the ground and nature of metaphysics; it must act as a "limit" upon the uncritical adventures of speculative reason; the "logic" making experience possible (thus somehow always active within it) also establishes the whole scope of theoretical inquiry. It may appear that Kant's stipulation of this dual function of his new "logic" is arbitrary. Where can we find the compelling reason for beginning where Kant does—not with the "phenomena" as they present themselves, but with an analysis of the "faculty of the understanding," in order to arrive at a "logic of experience"?[38] The reasons for this decision must be sought in Kant's reflections upon the need for "criticism" of all metaphysics of first causes.

Before proceeding, we must take note of another basic ambiguity, one related to that just mentioned. "Metaphysics" has more than one status or form. It has the "pre-scientific" form of the natural impulse to raise metaphysical questions; it can also become "philosophical" and "scientific," insofar as the reasoning inspired by the "disposition" to metaphysics proceeds "*in abstracto.*" Metaphysics as speculative inquiry into first causes is in fact the abortive, "dialectical" form of the "scientific" metaphysics; it is the form of metaphysics to be criticized. True "scientific" metaphysics and the natural metaphysical disposition have this in common: neither is a pretended body of a priori knowledge about first causes. The natural disposition to metaphysics finds its true satisfaction in "faith" or in the postulations which support morality. "Scientific" metaphysics of the "critical" sort, through discrediting speculative doctrines about first causes, "justifies" the non-theoretical character of the "disposition." True scientific metaphysics is a "propaedeutic" chiefly to the "practical metaphysics" of moral faith. Hence the "propaedeutical," critical inquiry is often called "metaphysics," somewhat confusingly by Kant, since *no other* theoretical knowledge exists which could have that name.

III

We seem to be at the furthest remove from ancient Socratism, with Kant's transcendental "logic of experience." Surprisingly, Kant would have us see that the Socratic element in his thinking is located in the propaedeutical function ascribed to this logic. One begins to understand this complex state of affairs by taking note of the insufficiency

[38] Ibid., A 65–66/B 90–91: "By 'analytic of concepts' I [understand] . . . the hitherto rarely attempted *dissection of the faculty of the understanding itself* . . ."; cf. A 247/B 303.

of strictly theoretical grounds in accounting for the propaedeutic. The point at which to begin is the characterization of metaphysics itself, the *telos* of the whole critical inquiry, and the "true philosophy."[39] Metaphysics, as "natural disposition," has a practical origin and *telos.* This must be borne in mind when reading the opening lines of the first of the *Critique*'s prefaces: metaphysics and its "natural dialectic," as the "fate" of human reason, define the starting point of the critical inquiry. The term "fate" has the connotations of both ineluctability and universality: the questions of metaphysics are fated to arise for all men, as they "can never be indifferent to our human nature."[40] The claim of metaphysics to be "queen of the sciences" appears to have its legitimate base in the practical urgency of the natural questions at its core: whether the world has a beginning or exists from eternity, the nature of the soul, the nature and existence of free causation, the nature of the supreme cause of the world. These questions more directly concern the "interests of humanity,"[41] where the word "humanity" has moral force, than any other questions; for their solution "the mathematician would gladly exchange the whole of his science."[42] The non-skeptical solutions to these questions "are so many foundation stones of morals and religion," and thus speculative metaphysics "promises a secure foundation for our highest expectations in respect of those ultimate ends towards which all the endeavours of reason must ultimately converge."[43] All the interests of reason are *combined* in the three questions: "What can I know? What ought I to do? What may I hope?"[44]

This account of metaphysics provides an architectonic principle for all of reason, and a definition of philosophy, a definition which is Socratic in Kant's estimation. All metaphysics issues in the practical "ideas" of God, freedom, and immortality, the supports of morality, and "the whole equipment of reason" is determined by nature to find the solution to metaphysical problems.[45] In other words, the whole of reason is naturally (not contingently, or conventionally) determined towards the discovery of the foundations of morality, or the elaboration of the theoretical grounds which support the hopes of rational morality for the attainment of its ends in the world. Here the critical propaedeutic finds its *telos:* its task is "to level the ground [of reason]

[39] *Logic,* op. cit., p. 37, and *KGS* IX, p. 32.
[40] *CPR,* A x.
[41] Ibid., B xxxii.
[42] Ibid., A 463/B 491.
[43] Ibid., A 466/B 494, A 463/B 491.
[44] Ibid., A 804–5/B 832–33.
[45] Ibid., B 395, A 800/B 828.

and to render it sufficiently secure for moral edifices."[46] The critical propaedeutic (with its "logic") is unintelligible without this reference to the moral teleology of reason.

That all rationality must be related to a highest organizing *telos,* moral in nature, was recognized by the ancients, who rightly defined philosophy as the "teleology of human reason."[47] And Kant surely here means the ancient post-Socratics, who "in the use of the term 'philosopher' meant especially the moralist."[48] They thought of philosophy as especially concerned with arriving at scientific knowledge of the "highest good" (the achievement of the ends of morality within the natural world),[49] and in this they were correct, Kant insists. "In moral philosophy we have not advanced beyond the ancients."[50]

The supremacy of the practical *telos* within philosophy and reason as such has a special consequence: the philosopher is "the lawgiver of human reason"; he legislates the systematic unity of reason, i.e., its subordination to a single organizing principle.[51] Thus Kant can equate reason's demand for "systematic unity" with its highest "practical" demand: the demand for "purposive unity" among the aspects of rationality is "founded in the will's own essential nature."[52] To say that philosophy is essentially systematic, and to say that it is essentially practical or legislative, are to say the same. Only that which *gives* systematic unity properly *has* such unity itself: philosophy alone "gives systematic unity to all other sciences" and for this reason it is "the only science which has systematic coherence in the proper sense."[53] But to endow science with systematic unity is the deed of legislative-practical reason; this same reason will both demand and effect the completion of metaphysics as science.[54] If certain natural questions of reason must remain unanswered, reason cannot be a true "whole." The requirement that wholeness be attained thus makes necessary the "completion" of metaphysics. Among other evidences of "good fortune" or natural benevolence in the constitution of human reason, we have the completability of logical thought as a doctrine, which provides the clue for the systematic account of the transcendental principles of

[46] Ibid., A 319/B 376.

[47] Ibid., A 839–40/B 867–68: ". . . philosophy is the science of the relation of all knowledge to the essential ends of human reason . . ."; also *Logic,* op. cit., p. 28, and *KGS* IX, p. 24.

[48] *CPR,* A 840/B 868.

[49] *Critique of Practical Reason,* Bk. II, chap. 1.

[50] *Logic,* op. cit., p. 37, and *KGS* IX, p. 32.

[51] *Vide supra,* nn. 46, 47.

[52] *CPR,* A 817/B 845.

[53] *Logic,* op. cit., p. 28, and *KGS* IX, p. 24.

[54] *CPR,* A xiii–xiv.

theoretical reason. Of course, the unity of logic is not itself grounded in a legislative "will"; but surely the employment of logic in the "setting of limits" is a legislative act.[55] This setting of limits alone permits reason to harmonize its theoretical concerns with its ultimate organizing practical ends.

Kant underscores the practical character of this legislative setting of limits with language about its "negative" import for speculative reason. The critique's (or propaedeutic's) primary use is negative:[56] "It is therefore the first and most important task of philosophy to deprive metaphysics, once and for all, of its injurious influence, by attacking its errors at their very source";[57] the critique's "utility, in speculation, ought properly to be negative, not to extend, but only to clarify reason, and keep it free from errors."[58] The attainment of the highest moral end is seriously endangered by the "injurious" dialectic of metaphysics, hence elimination of metaphysical error must take precedence over pursuit of knowledge unfettered by practical considerations.

Thus when one asks the question of Kant: What faculty undertakes the critique of reason? one must expect him to answer: Reason itself, as guided or self-compelled by the combination of its practical demand for systematic wholeness (the realization of moral freedom in the "moral world") and its experience of frustration in the pursuit of knowledge for the sake of this aim. The "logic of experience" which is "blind" and certainly not an "instrument" in the synthesis of ordinary experience, becomes a consciously elaborated doctrine in the hands of the philosopher (and other men enlightened by the philosopher), a doctrine which serves the disciplinary ends of practical reason ("all philosophy of pure reason . . . serves not as an *organon* for the extension but as a discipline for the limitation of pure reason . . .").[59] This is evident in the centerpiece of the critical argumentation: the "transcendental deduction" of the legitimate a priori employment of the categories. By placing restrictions upon the possible employment of the categories, and by showing that the categories lose objective validity (or the power to articulate a "possible experience") if referred to the merely thinkable realm of "unconditioned" entities, Kant intends to show that no "first cause" (monad, world-whole, or trans-temporal being) is a possible object of experience.[60] The deduction points to the

[55] Ibid., B 22.
[56] Ibid., B xxiv.
[57] Ibid., B xxxi.
[58] Ibid., B 25.
[59] Ibid., A 795/B 823.
[60] Ibid., A 277–78/B 333–34, B 148–49.

demarcation between phenomenal experience and noumenal thinkable or postulable objects. And this demarcation is the most necessary deed of the philosopher; it is "the most urgent but also the most difficult task, of which the *philodoxus,* however, takes no notice."[61] (See quotation IV above.)

Kant makes plain enough to all readers of his works that for the theoretical aims of science, and for the pragmatic (as distinct from practical-moral) aims of ordinary experience, such a transcendental deduction is quite gratuitous. The deduction does not rescue the sciences from skeptical demolition, through securing their "foundations."[62] Kant did not have to establish the validity of the "pure" sciences which make a priori experiential judgments. The *quid juris* question as regards the categories is a question of propriety (to what are they entitled?) and not a question of *quid facti* (do they apply to experience a priori?). The deduction establishes a limit on what qualifies as "universal and necessary" knowledge, but not the fact of such knowledge. The pure sciences of modern physics and mathematics "rest upon a secure foundation."[63] "Pure mathematics and pure science of nature had, for their own safety and security, no need of such a deduction as we have made of both. . . . Both sciences, therefore, stood in need of this enquiry, not for themselves, but for the sake of another science: metaphysics."[64] The establishing of the "limit" or *quid juris* is the stipulation that these pure sciences are in fact the *sole* theoretical sciences which "extend" knowledge, and that they provide a *criterion* for possible extension of knowledge, which speculative metaphysics fails to meet.[65] Thus the critical use of the sciences in the deduction has less regard for the "internal teleology" of these sciences, than for the critical employment of them in the propaedeutic, which has the practical end of reason (metaphysics) in view.

Thus transcendental logic is not only a logic of experience, but a logic of experience interpreted from the standpoint of the modern "pure" sciences—something frequently remarked upon, especially in Husserlian phenomenological criticisms of Kant's apparent neglect of pre-scientific experience. The matter might be put as follows: Vertically this logic abstracts from metaphysical first causes; horizontally, it claims to be coextensive with all experience, not merely with scientific

[61] *Logic,* op. cit., p. 29, and *KGS* IX, p. 25.

[62] Cf. the persuasive arguments of G. Brittan, *Kant's Theory of Science* (Princeton, 1978), pp. 122–31.

[63] *CPR,* A xi.; cf. B x–xiv, B 4–5, B 20–21, B 128, B 147.

[64] *Prolegomena,* op. cit., p. 75, and *KGS* IV, p. 327.

[65] *CPR,* B xvff.

natural law and the unification of the system of natural laws. One might say that the vertical abstraction had already been sought by several of Kant's modern predecessors, in their accounts of reason's "limits." But these philosophers remained content with, or felt compelled to accept, a certain ineradicable differentiation between "opinion" or common experience and philosophical knowledge. One might say they disclosed, and did not bridge over, a "gap" between the scientific account of nature, inclusive of man, and our pre-scientific sense of the whole. Kant sought definitive closure of this gap, and in the phenomenological assessment, he did so through wholesale sacrifice of the pre-scientific. Yet phenomenology itself remains under Kant's spell, for it continues to uphold the primacy of the Kantian "transcendental" turn to the "conditions of experience"; theoretical philosophy can have no higher theme than "ordinary experience." The investigation of causes has been handed over to the modern natural sciences. Phenomenology is not always aware of the Kantian motivation for the "turn" it perpetuates, which we can restate: the horizontal grounding of experience in the new logic is an essential step in the vertical critique of the metaphysics of first causes, this critique being indispensable on "practical" grounds. The "scientific" critique of speculative thought becomes buttressed by the demonstration to "ordinary experience" that it is subject to the strictures of the critique. Kant is here moved by considerations of the universality of the concern with metaphysics, and the injurious influence upon universal "practical" principles exerted by unresolved dialectical argument. He is at all points attentive to a "life-world" that includes more than science; it includes the questions of metaphysics, regarded as "natural" to all men and as bearing directly on their moral self-understanding. Such questions are "first for us," as moral beings; the critique of the speculative reason which has failed to assist us practically, *becomes* "first for us"; therewith, the canon of knowledge which shares an abstraction from first causes with modern natural science becomes a methodological starting point.

IV

We are now in a position to point to the special character of Kant's Socratism with greater force and accuracy. Kant in a sense renewed the Socratic account of philosophy as being essentially directed towards knowledge of ultimate ends (the good, the *summum bonum*). But such Socratism does not distinguish Kant from other modern philosophers with a "theodicean" dimension to their thinking. It is better to say that Kant's Socratism asserts that the metaphysical elaboration of the good fails to differentiate the philosopher from common opinion as regards highest ends. Earlier modern thinkers had already placed all human activity on the plane of passion, or had already begun to undermine the difference between the true rational good and a merely apparent good of passion. Kant instead unites all mankind on the plane of the "natural metaphysical" interest, which is satisfied not speculatively, but only through the "practical" achievement of a "moral world." As regards the good, the highest end, common "moral belief" is the surest guide to its nature—it is the ground of the true non-speculative "metaphysics," insofar as moral belief leads unerringly to the highest organizing *telos* of all rational activity. Thus ". . . in matters which concern all men without distinction nature is not guilty of any partial distribution of gifts, and . . . in regard to the essential ends of human nature the highest philosophy cannot advance further than is possible under the guidance which nature has bestowed upon the most ordinary understanding."[66] This Socratism is antipodal to Platonic Socratism, whose heart and core is the distinctively philosophical critique of common moral belief and opinion, which critique liberates the soul from these "conventional" fetters. It seems that Kant's Socratism is an inversion of Plato's: the former demonstrates the commonness of the highest *telos,* thus refuting the philosophers who speak of the necessity of leaving the "cave" of opinion for the natural light of truth. (See quotation III above.)

Kant's new Socrates undertakes a reversal of the metaphysical tradition, a tradition which had been untrue to the practical and skeptical spirit of ancient Socratism.[67] Nonetheless not even the ancient Socrates had subordinated metaphysics to a universal *telos,* or to the interests of humanity, a deficiency which runs parallel to the ancient failure to perceive the requirements of a scientific metaphysics. Yet Kant never speaks of this defect in the ancient Socrates; for him the metaphor of "Socrates" is sufficiently malleable to stand for the new enterprise. Kant sees himself as completing the work which had begun in antiquity, while believing that this project had only been dimly perceived or anticipated in antiquity. The errors of any ancient form of Socratism are merely the imperfect graspings of untutored wisdom, not the well-articulated arguments of an equal. In other words, Kant's high regard for Socrates barely conceals his sharing in the

[66] Ibid., A 831/B 859.

[67] Cf. G. Tonelli, "Kant und die antiken Skeptiker," in *Studien zu Kants philosophischer Entwicklung,* ed. H. Heimsoeth, D. Henrich, and G. Tonelli (Hildesheim, 1967), especially p. 118, nn. 32 and 37. Also *KGS* XXIV ("Blomberg Logic"), par. 178, p. 212.

fundamental condescension towards all antiquity on the part of the modern doctrine of philosophic "progress." Such progress (as contrasted with technical or other forms of progress) is essentially the elimination of the distinction between philosophic and non-philosophic reason, i.e., it is the attainment of wisdom by the whole species. For if philosophy is essentially a way of life that begins anew with each philosopher, and its *telos* is to be found in that life, or the activity of the mind made possible in that life, then philosophy is not essentially progressive. In Kant's view, the ancients cannot be faulted for failing to know that philosophy is essentially progressive. The ancient belief in the "nature" of the philosopher and the distinction between this "nature" and other "natures" could only express a naive standpoint with respect to nature in general.[68]

It is the new Socrates of Kant who declares that the proper use of metaphysics (theoretical reason) is "criticism," which "serves to remove obstacles in the way of religion and virtue" through a critique of speculation, "and which has more to do with dispensing than with

[68] Cf. *Critique of Practical Reason,* Bk. II, chap. 2, sec. 5: Ancient philosophical virtue (i.e., the virtue of the philosopher) rests on an error common to all of the Greek schools, namely, the reliance on the merely natural use of man's powers, including here the "heroism of the sage" or the natural character distinguishing the philosopher as such. In other terms, the ancient error is that of supposing that philosophic autonomy is attainable without the subordination of the philosopher's own use of reason to "universal maxims." The ancient philosopher regards his nature as able to achieve autonomy through the employment of natural "gifts" unique to himself or his like. But in Kant's account, nature is not "nature" except where subject to universal "laws." Yet philosophy is not merely another natural phenomenon; rather it is law-giving itself. But in that case, no natural kind can claim to be a philosophical kind. Philosophy, as essentially a doctrine of "ends," is an account of how ends are achieved through rational legislation; legislation is, however, universal in scope. Philosophy can be concerned only with universal ends, therefore. This central aspect of Kant's thinking is the aspect which leads most directly to Kant's concern with "history." The philosophic legislation of universal ends is not yet a "fact," achieved by the species, insofar as the achievement depends upon the universal comprehension and implementation of certain doctrines, i.e., the "critical" doctrines. Accordingly, the philosopher's own reason is not satisfied by the present condition of reason in the species; he cannot achieve his own "autonomy" independently of "history," or independently of the progress of the whole species towards true autonomy. "In man . . . those natural capacities which are directed to the use of his reason are to be fully developed only in the race, not in the individual" ("Second Thesis" of "Idea for a Universal History from a Cosmopolitan Point of View," trans. L. W. Beck, *On History* [Indianapolis and New York, 1963], p. 13). From Kant's standpoint, there is not available to us an account of the human soul (e.g., as able to contemplate an eternal order) which could justify the "individualism" of the ancient philosophers. Obversely, that ancient individualism seems to have rested at least in part on failure to see that reason "acknowledges no limits to its projects," i.e., it acknowledges no natural limits imposed by an immutable order. On the contrary, all order issues from reason itself, and reason's one knowable limit is its inability to discover any order (or being, or first cause) which exists independently of its own "legislation."

7 On the Moral Foundations of Kant's *Rechtslehre*

ROBERT B. PIPPIN

I

In section 40 of *A Theory of Justice,* John Rawls wisely notes that it is a mistake to view Kant's ethics with undue emphasis on the problems of the generality and universality of the moral law, that Kant's moral theory "as a whole" must always be kept in mind, and that this latter goal requires attention to the later writings on politics, religion, and teleology.[1] It is certainly true that any fair inspection of the texts considered by Kant to be parts of his practical philosophy does reveal that he by no means regarded that philosophy as exhausted by the problem of the single, pure criterion by which the permissibility of individual actions could be judged. He obviously believed that he could produce a rich, rationally defensible theory of morals (*Sitten*) as well as a theory of morality, and Rawls is certainly right to suggest that we distort and cannot properly assess Kant's view of the foundations of this whole if we neglect to look to the "building" that these foundations were to support.

However, it is also fair to note that the chief reason commentators have concentrated so heavily on the logical problems of universalizability and moral judgment has not been willful neglect of the rest of Kant's moral theory, but because it has never been clear how to put all the parts together. It is at least clear what problems must be faced in Kant's formulation of the categorical imperative, but it is far from clear how one is to understand the relation between Kant's foundational theory of morality and his philosophy of history, of religion, of law, of politics, of virtue, of education, of beauty, and of teleology, all of which are explicitly said to be parts, in sometimes various senses, of the practical or moral theory.

[1] John Rawls, *A Theory of Justice* (Cambridge: Harvard University Press, 1971), p. 251.

In short, when one attempts to follow Kant from his pure moral theory to his account of applied moral practice, it is often hard to isolate what is essential to the moral theory, either as a direct consequence of the moral law itself, or, apparently, a necessary condition of its application in human life, and what is mere speculation *am Rande,* marginalia of no central importance to the core of the moral theory. Kant's account of what it is to live an actual life "worthy" of happiness just seems to range wildly over issues like justice and revolution, immortality and God, contracts between husbands and wives, the moral claims of taste, belief in progress, all the way to a discussion of why wigmakers should be allowed to vote, but not barbers.

However, there is one issue that is, I want to argue here, a paradigm instance of at least the kind of relation Kant envisaged between the supreme moral law and the derived duties of human practice, an issue that may help to reveal the general form of that relation and thus the general shape of Kant's whole moral theory. That issue is Kant's derivation of specifically political duties. Primarily, this derivation is explained and defended in the first part of the *Metaphysics of Morals,* the "Metaphysical Elements of Justice," although important aspects of his account also appear in such essays as "On the Common Saying: That May Be True in Theory but It Does Not Apply in Practice," and "Perpetual Peace."

This issue in particular is the first and most important one to be confronted in any attempt to find the single thread that may run through the entirety of Kant's moral theory. For, when one turns to the work which best exhibits Kant's understanding of the relation between moral theory in general and a derived system of specific duties, one confronts first of all the fact that that system is in two, quite distinct parts. It has taken commentators some effort, not always successful, to understand just how these two parts are to be differentiated, but it is undeniable that any interpretation of Kant's whole moral theory must begin by noting this duality between duties of "justice" and duties of "virtue," between a *Rechtslehre* and a *Tugendlehre.* Kant's whole understanding of the implications of obeying the moral law begins with this fact, this division between the specifically legal duties we owe others and the different ethical duties we owe ourselves and others.

This basic distinction is important for a number of philosophic as well as hermeneutic reasons. As an issue in political theory, what Kant's architectonic commits him to is a claim that is, I believe, his most important contribution to political theory (although he obviously shares credit with Rousseau): that political duties are a subset of moral duties.[2] This means that the bonds which tie us to others in civil society (and which thereby legitimate public authority) are distinctly moral bonds, rationally derivable from our general moral obligations to others.[3] They thus do not depend on any voluntary act, whether it be consent, tacit consent, or hypothetical consent (what I would choose if I were a hypothetical contractor in a fair, ideal choice situation), nor on "fair play" considerations derived from acceptance of benefits, nor from considerations of gratitude to others, and certainly not from any rational calculation of maximum utility. Although he would not use the term this way, Kant's claim is that there is what many contemporaries would recognize as a "natural duty of justice." Or, to put the point a different way, for Kant there is a *moral duty to enter civil society* (where Kant means by civil society "the rule of law"), and thus a moral warrant to coerce any who refuse. Even in a natural society of benevolent agents, who vote unanimously to remain in their state of nature, such a duty and warrant holds unequivocally.[4]

Now, of course, many so-called contract theories also presuppose a moral premise: that one ought to keep one's promises. But what I mean to stress here is that Kant does not explain political obligation exclusively in terms of this promise-keeping duty. Rather, he argues that there is an original, moral duty to collaborate with others in a state, a duty *to* promise, if you like.[5] Roughly, it is this claim which sets

[2]Cf. sec. IV of the Introduction to Pt. I of the *Metaphysics of Morals, The Metaphysical Elements of Justice,* trans. John Ladd (Indianapolis: Bobbs-Merrill, 1965), pp. 21–30 (hereafter, references to this edition are abbreviated as *MEJ,* and are followed by the page number of the Prussian Academy edition, vol. VI, abbreviated as *PrAk*); *PrAk,* pp. 221–28.

[3]Obviously, a large problem looms for any such moral approach to political theory. Given the universal demands of moral obligation, how could one ever use a moral foundation to legitimate allegiance to a specific civil society? Would not one be bound, if one is, to *all* just regimes? To avoid this, it would seem that one would have to introduce empirical issues into any discussion of the locus of one's political duties. Contrary to the usual interpretation of Kant's formalism, I shall argue that that is just what he does. Cf. the discussion by A. John Simmons, *Moral Principles and Political Obligations* (Princeton: Princeton University Press, 1979), chap. VI, and his reference to the received view of Kant, p. 199.

[4]*MEJ,* pp. 71–72; *PrAk,* pp. 307–8.

[5]Kant, in fact, would agree with Hume's famous criticisms of the "contractarian" tradition (assuming that there is one). Cf. Jeffrie Murphy, "Hume and Kant on the Social Contract," *Philosophical Studies* 33 (1978), pp. 65–79. For a clear statement by Kant of his position, see the essay "That May Be True in Theory but It Does Not Apply in Practice," trans. H. B. Nisbett, in *Kant's Political Writings,* ed. H. Reiss (Cambridge: Cambridge University Press, 1970), p. 73 (hereafter *TP,* followed by *PrAk,* vol. VIII, page numbers), *PrAk,* p. 289; and a helpful exposition by Manfred Riedel in "Herrschaft und Gesellschaft: Zum Legitimationsproblem des Politischen in der Philosophie," reprinted in *Materialen zu Kants Rechtsphilosophie,* ed. Zwi Batscha (Frankfurt: Suhrkamp, 1976), pp. 125–48, esp. p. 135.

up the problem at issue in this essay—assuming we do have, say, a duty to "respect others as ends in themselves," why is it a consequence of that duty that I collaborate in a *Rechtsstaat*?[6]

Now, of course, even at this initial stage, there are further reasons to be wary of this claim. After all, the central problem in modern political philosophy has been and continues to be that concerning the basis for the use of state power to limit the liberty of others. In this context, it is understandable that one might be wary of crowning state power with some moral halo, of claiming that use of such power is warranted as a way of enforcing externally binding moral rules. That wariness stems from the suspicion that such moral claims are either too abstract, too controversial, or especially, too liable to the abuses of self-righteousness, moral arrogance, or self-serving rationalizations, to serve this role. We are on the verge of turning the state into a paternalistic moral busybody with this view of duty and coercion, the objectors warn, and would be far better advised to begin with the clearest safeguard against such abuses: perhaps the supreme liberal maxim—*volenti non fit iniuria,* no injury can be done to the willing.

However, by noting the obvious architectonic fact that, for Kant, political duties, and thereby the authority of law, could be derived from a general moral basis, we are in no danger of interpreting him as some traditional natural law theorist, subject to the potential objections raised above.[7] For the second feature of Kant's political theory

[6] Of course, in other contexts, Kant distinguishes *between* legality and morality. But in this context, we can see that this is still a distinction between *kinds* of duties. The former are duties (part of our moral obligation) which can be said to exist and indeed to be fulfilled independent of any subject's motives. And, on the other hand, it is still true that we are morally bound to adopt justice as our end, but having or not having that as our end is not relevant to whether the act is (legally) just. A like answer could be given to someone who might object to this approach by asking how this notion of a "moral foundation" could possibly be appropriate in Kant, given his famous claim in "Perpetual Peace" that a race of intelligent devils could form what he explicitly calls a *just* state. Again, though, far from excluding a "moral foundation," such a hyperbolic claim just focuses attention on the *nature* of the Kantian view of political duty. That is, what Kant means to stress by this claim is that a state *is* just (if it is), has a certain moral authority, in a way that is independent of any *specific* ends desired by its citizens. He only means to insist that this moral authority can be said to exist even if allegiance to the state does not *actually* derive from pursuit of any moral ideal, even if devils simply realize that allegiance to the form of a *Rechtsstaat* is the most efficient means to satisfy their demonic desires. Such an association *is* not just *because* these devils contracted to obey it, or *because* it is efficient, and can be said to be just, to conform to our universal, juridical duties to others, regardless of the fact that its citizens happen to be devils. Kant himself seems to have discovered the importance of the difference between *Recht* and *Tugend* around the end of the 1760s and beginning of the 1770s, while formulating his differences with Baumgarten's *Initia Philosophiae Practicae Primae.*

[7] Admittedly, there is some controversy about Kant's relation to the tradition, especially in some recent German literature. The issues involved are complicated by some

that makes him directly relevant to many contemporary controversies is his claim to be able to show that the range of legitimate coercion by the state is precisely definable, and by no means ranges over all our moral duties to others. Indeed, as we shall see, that is the major force of the distinction between a *Rechtslehre* and a *Tugendlehre,* and indeed, or so I want to argue, Kant's second important contribution to political theory. There are only certain duties to others that we can, may, and ought to *compel* others to fulfill.

What is most important about this delineation is that it will, if successful, provide a firm basis for understanding an often-used notion in political thought—a right. For Kant, to specify a special class of duties to others, fulfillment of which may be compelled, is to specify those duties owed to others *by right,* as opposed to those owed, but not by right. Of course, in one sense, if A is duty-bound to B in some way, B has a "right" to expect fulfillment of that duty by A. But for Kant, this claim only goes so far as to mean: "It is all right (or morally justifiable) for B to expect fulfillment by A." But it is a much stronger sense that, for Kant, is politically relevant, the sense in which B has a right to *demand* fulfillment by A, and to call on the law to guarantee such fulfillment. It is this sense that Kant promises to give us in his *Rechtslehre,* and to do so, or so I shall interpret him, not (directly) *because* A in some way consented or promised to perform the act for B, but because of the moral duties anyone owes anyone else.

We can now see that the approach Kant takes will continually face two large problems. The first involves a clarification of what we might call Kant's "moral interest" in the state in the first place. After all, suppose one could rationally distinguish a special class of duties that exist and, given their special, formal characteristics, can be said to be fulfilled independent of motives—"legal" duties. That, by itself, would only entail that as an individual, *I* have a duty to treat others "justly." And, again as an individual, *I* could attempt to fulfill that obligation in a thoroughly repressive, unjust regime, even though the consequences of my actions might be disastrous. All Kant does (in the body of the *Rechtslehre* itself) to get us from these individual duties to *political* obligation is to present a brief, inadequate argument that justice is "analytically united with the authorization to use coercion."[8]

---

profound changes, apparently, in Kant's views on politics. I've only the space here to note that I find compelling Werner Busch's case for a genuinely "critical" *Rechtsphilosophie,* in his book *Die Entstehung der kantischen Rechtsphilosophie* (Berlin: de Gruyter, 1979) as opposed to the claims of Christian Ritter and Josef Schmucker. Cf. also the clear explanation of the difference between Kant and Aquinas by Alan Donagan in *The Theory of Morality* (Chicago: University of Chicago Press, 1977), p. 64.

[8] *MEJ,* pp. 35–36; *PrAk,* p. 231.

However, that argument in section D of the *Rechtslehre* only establishes (if it can be said to establish anything) that punishment is consistent with the duty of justice; it does not establish that the coercive rule of law is a moral requirement. That is, he does not establish the stronger thesis that he elsewhere explicitly states—that we have a *duty* to "collaborate" in civil society, to institute, obey, and support a certain rule of law. We need to find his support for that stronger thesis.

And, secondly, we need to try to reconstruct his reasons for treating only some duties to others as political duties. That is, I shall claim that, in the "ideal case" at the center of most political philosophies, (i) Kant will try to prove that showing a state to be just depends on being able to show that the state's legal force or coercion is used to insure fulfillment of certain duties to others, which duties are duties at all only within a moral framework that specifies in general what duties are owed others and why; but that (ii) for Kant those duties which justify coercion are a special, delimitable class, separate from ethical duties to others which do not warrant coercion and fulfillment of which it would be *unjust* to coerce. These juridical duties are those and only those for which others may claim corresponding rights. (As in: I have a right to be free from the murderous and larcenous acts of my fellow citizens, but no *right* to demand benevolence or esteem from them.)

I note immediately two qualifications on the scope of this project. First, from the fact that a state falls far short of this ideal, or approximates it not at all, nothing immediately follows about what I am duty-bound to do, or even, all things considered, what I ought to do. It is a fact that Kant himself thought that even in the latter extreme case I am still duty-bound to obey the law (there is no "right of revolution"), but that is a separate issue and one I shall not discuss.[9] Second, the general characterization given above of justice is very abstract. As it stands it concerns only the state's role in protecting the "one natural right"—freedom.[10] There are also various "acquired rights," and corresponding duties, and in the course of our inquiry, more will have to be said about what kinds of rights can be justly acquired and how.

[9]Several claims, while interconnected, must be kept distinct here. Kant's position commits him to claiming (1) that I have a duty to enter civil society and not leave it, (2) that a just state can be defined as one that best accords with the reasons behind (1), and (3) that I have an obligation to promote and support just institutions. For reasons we shall investigate, (1) is ranked higher in importance than (3) for Kant, but the moral force of both claims stems from a common source. Thus (1) and (3) are not the inconsistent pair critics of Kant on revolution often take them to be.

[10]*MEJ*, p. 43 ("There is only one innate right"); *PrAk*, p. 237. Cf. also H. L. A. Hart, "Are There Any Natural Rights?" *Philosophical Review* 64 (1955).

However, since I have also claimed that how Kant derives his notion of juridical duties might provide a clue to the shape of his whole system of morality, the task at hand now is to turn to the *Rechtslehre* and examine how this derivation is attempted.

II

In the first subdivision of the *Rechtslehre*[11] (A. "Was die Rechtslehre sei") Kant begins with a distinction stressed often throughout the opening pages, although it is far too broad for what he has in mind. "The sum of those laws for which outer legislation [*äussere Gesetzgebung*] is possible is called jurisprudence (*ius*)."[12] He had earlier stressed that the only kind of "legislation" possible for ethical duties was "internal." This difference in the types of possible legislation corresponds to a difference in the types of restraint possible in each case. "Right" actions continue to be right even if performed under external restraint, such as fear of punishment; "good" actions can only be good if the restraint is "inner," if the agent restrains himself out of respect for the moral law, and not fear of "external" consequences.

This distinction does not get us very far unless we can find a clear sense of just which actions "can" be externally legislated, which remain "right" even when externally coerced. In terms of legislative possibility alone, we "can" prohibit almost anything. Kant must mean "can be externally legislated" in a qualified sense; indeed the "can" must be qualified somehow by "in conformity with the moral law," here interpreted to mean "in conformity with the freedom of each." If this qualification can be defended, then Kant's several other descriptions of the distinction will have more force. It will, for example, help us to understand just *what* duties we can be said to have to others that bind independent of any motive we may adopt, versus our duties to pursue other ends or develop certain attitudes. And, in turn, we shall then be able, perhaps, to appreciate why, for the former class, external coercion is morally legitimate (not just possible), whereas for the latter class, external coercion is not just impossible but morally illegitimate. (The former would be those duties correlated with en-

[11] Much could be gained, prior to an examination of the text, by considering what is involved in each of the terms defining this domain of Kant's practical philosophy, a "Metaphysische Anfangsgründe der Rechtslehre," although such a consideration must lie outside the scope of this study. See Mary Gregor's helpful discussion in *Laws of Freedom* (New York: Barnes and Noble, 1963), pp. 1–33.

[12] *MEJ*, p. 33; *PrAk*, p. 229.

forceable "rights," the latter would be those duties not so correlated.)

Now, obviously, Kant has in mind here something like a list of "basic" or "fundamental" duties, a set of duties based on the very notion of a free agent—duties which, when violated, directly contradict the very notion of any agent acting freely. However, just where the move from the special nature of these duties to a political context occurs, and how the duties are to be defined, are both, oddly, given their centrality in Kant's *Rechtslehre,* hard to find. For the most part it is with regard to this distinction between duties to *act* in certain ways versus duties to *pursue* certain ends that Kant tries, however briefly, to spell out this latter division. He uses the distinction to point out either that juridical duties are "narrow" duties, duties to perform or forbear from specific actions, with no judgmental "leeway" for the agent, and are to be contrasted with ethical, "broad" duties to pursue certain ends, duties which always leave such interpretive leeway; or, preserving a distinction from the *Grundlegung* that occasionally seems identical to the narrow/broad distinction, that juridical duties are "perfect" duties (with the exception of perfect duties to oneself), ethical duties are "imperfect."[13] This distinction is grounded, in turn, on the different ways in which the impermissibility of such duties is explained and defended. Juridical duties of action in some way directly contradict the moral law; they involve what one commentator has called a "contradiction in conception."[14] To do *A,* if *B,* if this claim is right, and *A* is to be legally impermissible, can not pass the "law of nature" universalization test. Ethical duties, on the other hand, involve a "contradiction in willing," or can only be shown to involve a contradiction by showing how an agent could not consistently will that everyone adopt some end or policy. The maxim in question for such duties must be to do *A,* if *B,* in order to pursue *C.*

Finally, in one of the only passages in the *Rechtslehre* which specify the differences in some detail, Kant points out that the duties of justice can be said to be binding only with respect to actions that externally influence others, that this influence must be considered in terms of the *will* of the other agent, not his needs or desires (which are the concerns of ethical duties), and third, that this external relation of wills is to be considered only formally, that is, only with respect to the formal consistency of such actions and, again, not with regard to the ends pursued by the agents. With all of the above in view, we have

[13] Kant makes use of the perfect/imperfect terminology at *MEJ,* p. 46; *PrAk,* pp. 239–41.

[14] Onora Nell, *Acting on Principle* (New York: Columbia University Press, 1975). I discuss her interpretation extensively in Section III below.

Kant's statement of the "universal principle of justice" (*Allgemeines Prinzip des Rechts*): "Any action is just that itself, or in its maxim, is such that the freedom of the will of each can coexist with anyone's freedom according to a universal law."[15]

So far, however, these distinctions, some of which coincide, some of which are identical, some of which follow from others, just give us a kind of shopping list of alternatives to try out: capable of external legislation and coercion, versus capable only of internal legislation and restraint; duties formulated with respect to actions only, versus duties to pursue certain ends; duties owed by right, versus those not so owed; duties for which external coercion is not only possible but morally legitimate, versus those for which coercion is impossible and illegitimate; narrow and perfect duties versus broad and imperfect duties; and finally, duties which affect the will (or liberty) of others, which effect is considered formally, with regard to a possible contradiction in conception, versus those duties to others which affect their needs or desires, with regard to a possible "contradiction in willing" some end or policy.

However, if we keep in mind what has been provisionally identified here as the core of Kant's doctrine of justice, that political duties must be understood as a subset of moral duties, but a limited, coercible subset, then the basic problem at the root of all the above distinctions is clear. Since the critical foundation of moral theory proclaims that there is one supreme moral law, understanding the above distinctions comes down to understanding just why *applying* this law generates these two sets of duties. If the relation between the *Metaphysics of Morals* and the categorical imperative can be made out, we should be able to understand the moral legitimacy of law in its enforcing of specific duties, and why they are these specific duties. Obviously, for Kant, to understand why an action or the pursuit of a policy is morally impermissible is to understand why either violates the central prescription of the moral law, and, or so one hopes, perhaps understanding the different *kinds* of violation will give us our distinction between juridical and ethical duties, between what ought to be a matter of public legislation and what ought not to be.

III

Commentators have addressed this issue in different ways. Of major concern, in commentaries on both the *Grundlegung* and the

[15] *MEJ*, p. 35; *PrAk*, p. 230.

Metaphysics of Morals, has been whether *anything* specific can be said to be impermissible according to the standard of the categorical imperative. This problem has been so prominent in the literature that a good deal less attention has been paid to the issue central to the *Rechtslehre:* whether certain acts can be said to be impermissible in a distinct way, a way which explains and grounds the moral authority of public coercion. In those few discussions that tackle both problems, two distinct approaches can be found.

On the one hand, one can try to support Kant's claim that the categorical imperative itself, in what one might call its strictest formulation, can be used to generate specific duties, and the twofold division found in the *Metaphysics of Morals.*[16] (By the "strictest" formulation, I mean the second formulation given in the *Grundlegung:* "Act as though the maxim of your action were by your will to become a universal law of nature.")[17] On the other hand, others have argued that no system of duties, let alone the division in the *Metaphysics of Morals,* can be understood except by appeal to a derivative form of the moral law, one with more "content," if you will, already expressed in it. The most popular candidate for this version has of course always been the third "version" of the moral law in the *Grundlegung:* "Act so that you treat humanity, whether in your own person or in that of another, always as an end and never as a means only."[18] We need to see, then, if either of these approaches can be used to justify the foundational divisions of the *Metaphysics of Morals.*

Kant himself, of course, has frustratingly little to say about the details of either approach, but a recent commentator has taken up what is the least popular of the two, the first, and tried to defend it in as rigorous a way as possible. Onora Nell, in her book *Acting on Principle,*[19] argues that once we take seriously Kant's insistence that the impermissibility of certain maxims is based on a direct *self*-contradiction, visible when the universal "law of nature" corresponding to that maxim is produced, we shall have a clear criterion for showing the special contradictoriness of all violations of duties of justice. What I think she does not show is how that criterion can be used to tell us precisely, or even generally, *which* duties are duties of justice and so subject to legitimate coercion.

[16] Most of Kant's early formulations of the *Recht/Tugend* distinction seem to rely on this strict or legalistic formulation. See *MEJ,* pp. 14–21; *PrAk,* pp. 214–21.

[17] I. Kant, *Foundations of the Metaphysics of Morals,* trans. L. W. Beck (Indianapolis: Bobbs-Merrill, 1959), p. 39 (references hereafter to *F,* followed by the *PrAk,* vol. IV, page numbers); *PrAk,* p. 422.

[18] *F,* p. 47; *PrAk,* p. 429.

[19] Nell, *Acting.* I shall be discussing chapters four and five of this book.

She begins, appropriately, with Kant's clearest statement of the two ways in which the moral law may be violated:

> We must be able to will that a maxim of our action become a universal law: this is the canon of the moral estimation of our action generally. Some actions are of such a nature that their maxim cannot even be *thought* as a universal law of nature without contradiction, far from it being possible that one could will that it be such. In others this internal impossibility is not found, though it is still impossible to *will* that their maxim should be raised to the universality of a law of nature, because such a will would contradict itself. We easily see that the former maxim conflicts with the stricter or narrower (imprescriptible) duty, the latter with broader (meritorious) duty.[20]

She then notes that this distinction between ways of testing for contradiction gives us exactly the distinction between maxims of justice and maxims of virtue,[21] and proposes to defend Kant's use of the former "contradiction in conception" test.

In doing so, she points out that the universalizability test can properly be used, not directly on a practical maxim, but on a putative "natural law" which is the "*typic*" of the maxim.[22] That is, for a maxim like (*a*) To . . . if ———, we consider whether its "typified counterpart" (*a*′) Everyone will . . . if ———, introduces a self-contradiction.[23] And that consideration is, of course, where all the classical problems arise. In trying to work out a clear test of universalizability which does not end up either permitting or condemning too much, the influential English-language commentaries (e.g., Paton and Beck) claim that, in testing whether a maxim's counterpart could be a law of nature, we must have recourse to a notion of a lawlike harmony of natural *ends*. And, finally, this test will have to invoke the notion of human nature as a rational end in itself if we are even to discover which maxims are permissible for us. The ambitiousness of Nell's project is to reject this "teleological" notion of natural law in favor of a stricter test of self-contradiction. Aside from textual support, she does this for what is quite a good reason:

> Further, if purposiveness is to be introduced into every explanation of the role of typifying practical principles, then we may be at a loss to see what differentiates maxims that cannot be conceived as universal laws of nature (and so cannot be maxims of justice) from maxims that merely cannot be

[20] *F*, p. 41; *PrAk*, p. 424.

[21] Nell, *Acting*, p. 61.

[22] Compare Kant's discussion of the "typic" in his *Critique of Practical Reason*, trans. L. W. Beck (Indianapolis: Bobbs-Merrill, 1958), p. 70 (hereafter *CPrR*, followed by the page number of the Prussian Academy edition, vol. V, abbreviated as *PrAk*); *PrAk*, p. 68.

[23] The reason for this use of an analogous natural law is stated clearly by Kant, *CPrR*, p. 70; *PrAk*, p. 68.

willed as universal laws of nature (and so cannot be maxims of any sort of duty).[24]

All of which obviously commits her to showing how this distinction can be made out, under the "stricter" interpretation. (We shall examine in a moment whether the "teleological" approach can successfully account for the basic division of the *Metaphysics of Morals.*)

Her strategy, in essence, is to follow the rough outline of the approach taken by Kemp and Dietrichson,[25] but to modify it so as to make clearer that Kant wants his criterion to test for the *internal* consistency of a possible natural law, not, for example, its inconsistency with assorted empirical facts. We thus do not want to show the impermissibility of false promising by showing that a *consequence* of false promising, given the empirical truth that humans remember and learn from the past, is to make the institution of promising impossible. Rather, she argues, in most of his famous formulations of the contradiction-in-conception test, Kant stresses that the contradiction is between my intention to act on a maxim (and thus also my willing the relevant means and foreseeable consequences) and the possible intention that the counterpart natural law *be* a natural law. *I* cannot, *at the same time* (without contradiction) intend to promise falsely *and* intend that it be a natural law that everyone falsely promise. If I intend to promise falsely, I must assume that all the relevant circumstances within which that act could be successful obtain, and, given that, *I* could not also will exactly the contrary situation.

Nell then deals with how her criterion could deal with problem cases always raised for any strict version of the universalizability test (e.g., maxims like "I will give presents, but not accept them," which should be permissible but might seem to be logically non-universalizable),[26] and goes on to show how her version of the test easily deals with our moral intuitions about bank robbery, embezzling, and the like. However, even though she later insists again that the results of the "test" Kant suggests in his "universal principle of justice" "are the same as those of the contradiction in conception test as interpreted here,"[27] she nowhere tries to work this out in any detail. She even claims at one point, without elaboration or defense, that in the

[24] Nell, *Acting*, p. 65.

[25] J. Kemp, "Kant's Examples of the Categorical Imperative," *Philosophical Quarterly* 8 (1958), and P. Dietrichson, "When Is a Maxim Universalizable?" *Kant-Studien* 55 (1964).

[26] She does this, successfully I think, by showing a way in which such maxims would test, as we should expect, as permissible, neither obligatory nor forbidden. Nell, *Acting*, pp. 76ff.

[27] Ibid., p. 72.

Rechtslehre "Kant is never . . . engaged in deriving individual duties of justice from the Categorical Imperative or directly from the Universal Principle of Justice."[28] If that is so, it is hard to see what relevance the principle of justice has at all to the Doctrine of Justice. Nell just never asks what relevance failing her universalizability test has to *justice.*

Apart from this neglect, there are several other problems with her approach. The most serious is that her interpretation can yield a precise and clear test only at the cost of a loose and potentially *ad hoc* interpretation of an agent's "true intentions." If I intend to play soccer on Saturday morning, on Nell's interpretation, I must assume that all the relevant circumstances which make this possible obtain. But if that is so, then I cannot at the same time intend that there be a natural law such that everyone will play soccer on Saturday mornings. If the latter held, obviously, there would be no room to play, apart from other, potentially disastrous social consequences. A moralistic Kantian might then conclude that soccer playing is forbidden; it is possible only by "exempting" yourself, in a supposedly classically immoral way, from what is possible for all. Obviously, we would want to argue in response that the agent's *true* intention is not to play soccer "come what may," no matter what. If he were fanatically committed to playing, regardless of other overriding duties, commitments, fair distribution of playing time, etc., we might then indeed be willing to say his maxim is forbidden. So, we claim, his true intention is to play soccer if . . ., and here we can fill in some relevant provisos which then make it consistent for him to hold this intention simultaneously with the intention to will that it be a natural law that everyone will play soccer if. . . .

But this all commits us to a potentially quite complex *further* "test" for determining just what an agent's true intentions are. Nell insists on "honesty" in reporting or describing intentions, but never gives an explanation of how to determine honesty, or what relation such a determination should have to law, or a way to avoid worries about the kind of *ad hoc* gerrymandering possible above. (To be fair, she does raise her own objections about this issue in her last two chapters.)

More to the present point, however, it is by no means clear that all acts forbidden by this test *do* coincide with what Kant would consider forbidden by public law. To take the obvious example: it is true, subject to a solution to the problems raised above, that false promising is clearly forbidden on Nell's interpretation. But it is by no means clear that *all* acts of false promising are thereby to be considered *unjust,* in

[28] Ibid., p. 80.

the relevant legal sense, however clearly immoral they may be. (The account she begins with, Dietrichson's, obscures this point by discussing a kind of false promising that is simply intuitively close to our sense of a legally relevant false promising—false promising "to get oneself out of financial difficulties.")[29] Given Nell's identification of all maxims which fail the universalization test with violations of duties of justice, and given Kant's clear insistence that the right of coercion to prevent all violations of duties of justice follows directly from the concept of justice itself, we are left precisely with the "moral busybody" state worried about in Part I, a state which makes *any* false promise, or even more extravagantly, any *lie,* a criminal offense. I see no evidence that Kant would regard this consequence as desirable, and no discussion by Nell to show just how it is avoidable. In sum, while Nell's version of the distinction between a "contradiction in conception" and a "contradiction in willing" is relatively clear and straightforward, and can show at least one way in which different kinds of moral impermissibility can be made out, the contradiction-in-conception test is far too broad, both in itself (given the problem of "intentions"), and with respect to our central problem: which obligations to others are duties of justice?

But there is a clear lesson to be learned from such problems, and it is, I think, the same one that has led many commentators to Kant's alternate formulation of the moral law. Namely, since it is clear that the major problem in using Kant's stricter version of "a possible natural law" is in deciding what could or could not be such a non-self-contradictory law, one needs to go behind that legalistic criterion and examine *why* Kant is so insistent on this kind of generality. To do so is to see him trying to clarify his view of the root "irrationality" of all immoral acts, that they all presuppose for myself a kind of rational agency which is inconsistently denied to those who are equally fully capable of such agency. That is, it is to find a richer moral criterion, the notion of man as a rational end in itself. Can *this* moral criterion be used to connect Kant's moral with his political theory?

IV

Those who have recently commented on Kant's moral theory, especially Murphy and Aune, certainly think so.[30] They attempt to show

[29] Ibid., pp. 66–67.

[30] Jeffrie G. Murphy, *Kant: The Philosophy of Right* (London: Macmillan, 1970); Bruce Aune, *Kant's Theory of Morals* (Princeton: Princeton University Press, 1979).

that, however many difficulties one eventually encounters, there is little chance of defending Kant unless one admits that the only way to explain what counts as a "possible law of nature" is to introduce the teleological notion of a "harmony of ends." The use of law as a test of moral rightness is thus not a test of consistency (or, as in Nell, consistent intentions) but a test of a possible harmony of agents consistently pursuing their goals, with each agent assumed to be an "end in itself." However, to understand the importance of relying on the criterion of "treating humanity as an end in itself" as a way of defining the morally right (especially in its legally relevant sense), we need to step back a bit and consider again Kant's project in political philosophy.

It is obvious that Kant wants to argue for a liberal defense of the state's coercive power (although as I have already argued, he does so on essentially moral grounds): that the only legitimate interference with the free activity of citizens is that which can be shown to secure or protect freedom. But what one always wants to know from any theorist who proposes such a view, including Kant, is how that definition can be defended, and what it entails—what "protecting freedom" amounts to. As we have seen, when Kant is interpreted to be answering the former question with some appropriate *moral* answer (based on a general theory of our duties to others) we can understand very little of that answer if we understand it just in terms of "acting consistently" or "rationally." Rather, Kant's concern with these "tests" clearly stems from his *prior* fundamental commitment to autonomy as that which alone renders man worthy of respect and dignity, and respect for which we "owe" others. Of course, one then wants to know just how Kant goes from his metaethical reflections on any possible moral system directly to *this* supreme moral precept, and the details of this move, especially since they involve a full defense of Kant's understanding of teleology, are notoriously obscure. But it is, I think, at least clear that Kant defends the liberal criterion above *because* he thinks we have a moral duty to respect others as rational ends in themselves, where that means respecting their autonomy. Because of this interpretation of the moral law in human life, that for human beings acting rationally and consistently is acting consistently *with* the possibility of others acting rationally and so autonomously, we can get a clearer sense, in these terms, of the distinction at the heart of the *Metaphysics of Morals.* Respect for another's autonomy thus entails that we may not interfere with another's pursuit of his goals, so long as that pursuit does not, when considered universally, conflict with the possibility of all others retaining their essential end, that which they must be assumed to want protected if they pursue any end at all—

their rational nature, their ability to determine their own course in life. Duties of virtue, on the other hand, are duties to help *promote* others' (and our own) ends, or at least those ends Kant thinks (somehow) are necessarily "tied" to human nature as an end in itself, "happiness" and "perfection" or "culture."

But all of this is, of course, just a crude sketch. At first glance, it might seem to provide us with just a different vocabulary for what we have been discussing all along, and still to involve many of the same problems. But, initially, the new description gets us much closer, I believe, to the spirit of Kant's whole moral system. *Given* (to avoid controversy for the moment) a moral duty to treat others as ends in themselves, where this means respecting their autonomy, we have a duty of justice not to interfere with the free activity of others, as well as an obligation to interfere when another acts in such a way as to be inconsistent with respect for the autonomy of others.[31] Given also that we could not will freely to pursue any end without the cooperation of others, or without the development of our own talents, and given that we could not respect autonomy, either our own or others', without doing what is required as a means to accomplish what we set ourselves to do, we have a "duty of virtue" to help promote the happiness of others (their achieving their goals) and our own perfection.[32] This dual set of duties, expressed in this way, as an extension of respect for humans as ends in themselves, does appear to set out most clearly what Kant is after at the core of his practical philosophy.

Of course, several metaphysical and metaethical issues are immediately raised by this account, but for our purposes, since this is not an essay on Kant's moral theory, what is most important is coming to terms with what is involved in respecting another's autonomy. It is clear that Kant wants his argument to show that a duty of justice can be "narrowly" or "perfectly" determined because it involves an end no one could consistently sacrifice or compromise—his liberty or autonomy. Because of this moral ideal, and because it can be so strictly determined (no one could be presumed not to want this end protected), Kant seems at places to think that this kind of reasoning is sufficient to justify a *Rechtsstaat,* a legal institution the function of which is to protect such liberty, or to insure non-interference with this

[31] To be sure, since this interference itself must occur consistent with the equal freedom of each, it must be pursued in a procedurally fair way. Or: only the state may be the agent of interference. Cf. Murphy's clear contrast between Locke and Kant on the "right to punish," *Kant,* pp. 113–27.

[32] I don't pretend that this is a derivation of Kant's two supreme virtues; it is only a sketch of his argument in the *Tugendlehre.*

necessarily presupposed end in itself of human life. On the other hand, while there are what Kant also calls (somewhat confusingly) "essential ends" which we must also suppose as necessarily involved in any autonomous pursuit, there is no way universally to prescribe how these ends are to be actually pursued, and no defensible way to compel others actually to promote them. Again, these ends, the subject matter of the *Tugendlehre,* involve how I develop my own talents (or "perfect myself") and how I cooperate with others in achieving any goal (or "happiness").

Now, this basic distinction between *Recht* and *Tugend* is admittedly still obscure, but it at least allows us to see how much weight rests on a full explanation of just what is involved in securing the one, necessary "end in itself," autonomy.

For it is obvious that we are not morally bound never to interfere with the free activity of others, as if we are to stroll by rapists, muggers, and murderers out of respect for their freedom. It would be absurd to do so in the same way that it would be absurd to tolerate, out of a sense of duty to tolerate, brutal intolerance. Also, someone might claim that many actions of ours do restrict, impede, frustrate, limit, and perhaps even deny the free activity of others, without any prima facie moral problem. Economic competition, ownership of private property, various authority relationships, etc. would all be relevant examples of interference with the liberty of others that one might claim ought to be legally permissible. Thus, we need to know more precisely when this overriding respect for autonomy demands non-interference and when interference. More precisely, given this new moral test, the question becomes: what *counts* as an action which does not involve treating another as an end in itself? (We should note the parallel problem in the *Tugendlehre:* what counts as being unable to *will* to adopt a policy because such a *willing* would be inconsistent with treating others as ends in themselves?)

One way to achieve this clarification, the way taken by both the commentators mentioned above, is to invoke a more detailed concept of the "essential" ends of humanity. That is, we know thus far that a just action is one which leaves secured, or insures the security of, the freedom of others. But not their freedom to do anything. We might then further qualify the duty of justice by claiming that we must then secure the freedom of agents only to pursue the *essential* ends of humanity, or to pursue ends which are in no way inconsistent with the pursuit of these ends. We would not be requiring the pursuit of those ends, nor specifying in any way exactly how they are to be pursued. But Kant does think that he can show that (i) autonomy is an end in itself and (ii) even when acting consistently with respect for autonomy, an agent can still not be presumed to be *able* to seek *any* material end unless that agent is able to develop his own talents, and *able* to pursue his own happiness or collaboration with others. So if our question is: *what* free activity must be secured? we can answer: the pursuit of these essential ends. Thus we get Jeffrie Murphy's reconstruction of Kant's criterion of just (or right) action.

> X is a right action if and only if the maxim of X would not, if a universal law, interfere with the freedom of any individual rational being to pursue his own ends in action *so long as these ends do not include the denial of freedom to others to pursue their essential ends—happiness and perfection.*[33]

Murphy is quite clear later that this qualification is to function in the relevant political or legal sense at issue throughout our preceding discussion. As he asks: "How are we to know when an abuse of freedom is severe enough to justify intervention?" And later he answers directly that "these ends (happiness and perfection) allow us to define a real violation of freedom."[34] Of course, if this is so, we face the difficult problem of proving that these *are* the essential ends of humanity, a case that would have to involve quite a complex defense of teleology and essentialism itself before it could be taken seriously. Bruce Aune, who in his recent book adopts, with slight differences, Murphy's teleological answer to the "qualification" problem sketched above, argues persuasively that there is no morally neutral way to define these ends, and thus no way to apply the end-in-itself formula in the way Kant intended.[35]

However, it is at least roughly clear how an appeal to these ends is to function in the crucial "ranking" problem now before us. In the first place, as Murphy points out, Kant's whole approach, in a way typical of classical liberalism, throws the burden of proof on anyone arguing *for* interference with the activity of others. Now we can see that what I must show in such cases is that another's acts interfere with my pursuit of, or (in a way that will cause problems shortly) my ability to pursue, an essential end. Thus, I cannot claim that I have a right to demand that others dress neatly or uniformly because sloppy dress so upsets me that I cannot pursue my own ends. We place a strong burden of proof on such a person to show why being free from disgust at sloppy dress is *essential* to the pursuit of human happiness. Obviously, it is not, in a way quite different from cases where another,

[33] Murphy, *Kant*, p. 103.
[34] Ibid., p. 108.
[35] Aune, *Kant's Theory*, p. 121.

by stealing my possessions, beating or murdering me, cheating me or prohibiting me from educating myself, does deprive me of something essential in the pursuit of my happiness. He deprives me of my life, or the food, wealth, shelter, and security necessary to maintain life, or the means to develop my talents so as to improve the kind of life I live—all of which can be said to be essentially involved in the pursuit of any specific goal.

Before examining the problems this account creates, it is important to stress its appeal and force. Murphy states this appeal well and succinctly at one point.

> What we need, obviously, is some way to bring the ideal of pure morality to bear on the concrete empirical contingencies of the human situation. For what is finally rational to do surely depends, at least in part, on the sort of creatures we are.[36]

Further, while there is little direct textual evidence for the reconstruction offered by Murphy, there is much indirect evidence, especially in the *Lecture on Ethics,* that Kant took the notion of these essential ends far more seriously than he often lets on.[37] And, finally, it is also instructive that Kant was forced to include this teleological criterion in his political philosophy at all. It is a fact that renders the standard strict textbook divisions between Kant and, say, Aristotle (or even Hegel and Marx) more than a little suspect.

However, noting this last fact just begins to highlight all the difficulties that must now be addressed. Ironically, Kant, by introducing this "Aristotelian" component, immediately introduces the classic problem with such an account. Murphy admits that Kant nowhere argues that, from the fact that these are our essential ends, it follows that they are therefore of *moral* significance. Even if one were to try to state the essentiality of these ends along lines which preserved Kant's insistence that only a "will" can be "good," that problem would still have to be faced. That is, even if one argued that these are not "natural" ends, but ends I could not but *choose,* the inference to some claim about their moral status needs more development than Kant provides. And, of course, as indicated earlier, it is by no means clear why these two are our essential ends, or even more broadly, exactly what the whole status of teleology is in Kant's architectonic.

However, given the interpretation of Kant I want to develop shortly, there are more revealing and interesting problems in Murphy's approach. Recall that all along we have been searching for the

[36] Murphy, *Kant,* p. 88.
[37] Cf. Murphy's presentation of this evidence, *Kant,* p. 98.

moral foundation of legal coercion or authority in the first place. We have been looking for an explanation not just of what I am obliged to *do* with respect to others, but of on what basis I can be said to be obliged to support the rule of law, which coerces others to do or forbear from doing. Secondly, we have been searching, within Kant's general moral context, for the scope of the state's authority: in Kant, for the ground of the *Recht/Tugend* distinction. Helpful as his account is, I don't believe Murphy's interpretation gets us any closer to answering these questions.

He himself points out that Kant's brief argument that law analytically contains the authority (*Befugnis*) to compel is not supported by any specific moral argument in Kant. Murphy goes on to suggest that a justification of such authority might be made directly "from the Categorical Imperative." He asks, "Could the maxim 'Permit the abuse of freedom' be a universal law?" and claims that it could not because "as a finite rational creature, I necessarily desire that others not interfere with my freedom."[38] Here we can already see that Murphy's notion of some "essential" facts about human nature has already entered the argument. It may be true that I "necessarily desire that others not interfere with my freedom," or, as he says later, that "I would want others to come to my aid in the event of someone attempting to deprive me of my rights as a man,"[39] but the most *this* could establish is that I have a duty of *virtue* to assist others when their freedom is being interfered with (I could not consistently *will* that abuses of freedom go unchecked). If it were a law of nature that abuses of freedom are permitted, the most that could be said is what Murphy does say, "one would have no security,"[40] and it is still unclear why I have a moral obligation to insure that this does not happen. Even in such chaos, as Kant often points out, I am unequivocally obliged to obey the moral law, and still "can." We clearly need an additional premise before we can move from the categorical imperative to our duty to collaborate in a state, and I shall try to supply one in a moment.

Also, it can still be asked whether, if certain ends can be established as essential, and if the moral relevance of that fact can be defended, such a fact can function as a criterion to define "serious" injuries to freedom in the politically relevant sense. In part this question is connected with the former. Even if we can establish that some injuries to

[38] Murphy, *Kant,* p. 95.
[39] Ibid.
[40] Ibid.

another's freedom are more serious than others, or deny his essential ends, we still need to show just why that is politically relevant and other, less serious but still immoral injuries are not. We can say that it would be "odd" to admit that such serious injuries are "wrong" and "not do anything about it," but why exactly we should do something and what we should do are still left open. Moreover, in part, this question asks if the "essential ends" criterion does in fact establish the *Recht/Tugend* distinction itself. To see this, consider how many classical problems involved in defining an injury to freedom are still left open by this criterion. If I may not directly interfere with another's pursuit of his essential ends (and may be forcibly prevented from doing so), may I indirectly interfere by impeding his *ability* to pursue those ends? That is, *on the same basis* that I use to claim that another's property may not be stolen (that it would make impossible any pursuit of happiness if he were continually insecure in his possessions) might I not also claim that it is impermissible to acquire so much property that I make it effectively impossible for another to acquire the means to pursue *his own* happiness? I realize that what has come to be a central issue in political theory is at stake here, "negative" versus "positive" freedom, but all I want to suggest here is that such an issue is raised immediately and not resolved by the "essential ends" form of reasoning. Indeed, as far as I can see, we are still left with the danger, even with these qualifications defined in terms of the ends of humanity, of a "moral busybody state," or exactly what Kant's grand division in the *Metaphysics of Morals* is to allow us to avoid. For example, the maxim of selfish acts, when considered as a universal law, would certainly *interfere* with the freedom of individuals in the sense that such acts work to deny (effectively) others the means to pursue their own happiness, an essential end of humanity, according to Murphy's interpretation. Public sarcasm or vulgarity, if considered universally, as general practices of a society, also seem to injure directly another's free pursuit of happiness. Of course, Kant wants to consider all such duties in the *Tugendlehre,* and to discuss the way in which they violate our duty to treat others as ends in themselves in terms, not of the acts themselves, but of willing the acts. And he also is completely silent about injuries to the essential ends of humanity throughout the *Rechtslehre,* implying, I think, that the treatment in the *Tugendlehre* is the *only* relevant way respect for autonomy can be connected with these ends. If we leave the situation as Murphy does, I cannot see why acts of avarice or even disrespect should not be said to be "serious" injuries to freedom. We know that individuals ought to be allowed to pursue their ends fully, so long as, to quote Murphy again, "these ends do not include the denial of freedom to others to pursue their essential ends—happiness and perfection." The examples cited above, though, force a further qualification question: what counts as the "*denial* of freedom to others"? How seriously must my avarice affect someone for "interference" with the freedom of another to have the means to pursue his happiness, or for "frustration" of that freedom, to count as a "denial"? Murphy begins to discuss this issue by discussing whether homosexual acts can be said to injure my freedom to pursue my ends without disgust, but that case is too easy, as is the sloppy dress case earlier. He does not explain why, on his own criterion, in more obvious cases involving direct effect on the freedom of others like avarice, one should not warrant, say, "Silas Marner laws" prohibiting selfishness and rewarding or even demanding beneficence.

V

However, as indicated earlier, construing Kant's derivation of duties of justice from the moral law as a derivation from the duty to treat others as ends in themselves looks far too promising an interpretation to give up. It looks quite a plausible interpretation of the *Metaphysics of Morals* to suggest that treating others as such ends involves refraining from interfering with their autonomy (or conversely, insuring that the autonomy of each be secured from injury), as well as developing our own talents and assisting others to achieve their goals. The end-in-itself formula also still looks like a promising way to explain why this distinction in types of duties corresponds to that between "legally enforceable" versus "ethically binding, but not legally enforceable." We can make this distinction by showing that while we *can* prohibit (or indirectly prohibit, through fear of punishment) *actions* which are incompatible with autonomy, we cannot (logically cannot) compel the adoption of ends or a policy to help others or develop our talents, and so these latter duties, while they are derivable from the end-in-itself formula, must be left outside the realm of law.[41] All of this seems quite close to Kant's intentions, and, as far as it goes, quite sound. Our problem has continually been to understand how Kant wants to defend a derivation of a class of duties which not only *can* be enforced, but ought to be, and we have suggested that we must settle that issue first before we can begin to understand which duties belong in this

[41] Kant regularly points out that an agent coerced to pursue some goal or policy cannot be said to have adopted such an end in the morally relevant sense.

class. The "essential ends of humanity" qualification, while on the right track, did not do that, and so we need an alternative, if we wish to preserve the general schema sketched above.

I believe that Kant has provided us with this alternative, and that the strategy involved therein is more defensible than those surveyed above. Kant himself, in what is his first mature public statement of his initial *Rechtslehre* (the 1793 theory-practice essay) gives us a clear indication of this alternative. In a context where Kant is discussing the basic issue we are interested in, the relation between moral and political theory, he says the following:

And the necessity of an ultimate end posited by pure reason and comprehending the totality of all ends within a single principle (i.e. a world in which the highest possible good can be realized with our collaboration) is a necessity experienced by an unselfish will as it rises beyond mere obedience to formal laws and creates as its own object the highest good. The idea of the totality of all ends is a peculiar kind of determinant for the will. For it basically implies that *if* we stand in a moral relationship to things in the world around us, we must everywhere obey the moral law; *and to this is added the further duty of working with all our power to ensure that the state of affairs described above* (*i.e. a world conforming to the highest moral ends*) *will actually exist* [my emphasis].[42]

Kant seems to be saying here that we can understand our political obligation (and, thus, conversely, the state's authority) in terms of this "further duty" to pursue or work to ensure the "highest good" (*summum bonum*). And it should not be surprising that Kant would mention this duty to pursue the highest good as part of his derivation of specific, human duties. Five years earlier, in the second *Critique,* he went even further in insisting on the importance of the duty to pursue this end:

But these truths do not imply that virtue is the entire and perfect good as the object of the faculty of desire of rational finite beings. For this, happiness is also required, and indeed not merely in the partial eyes of a person who makes himself his end but even in the judgment of an impartial reason, which impartially regards persons in the world as ends in themselves.[43]

He even writes, though not without some inconsistency with other passages,

Since, now, the furthering of the highest good . . . is an a priori necessary object of our will and is inseparably related to the moral law, the impossibility of the highest good must prove the impossibility of the moral law also. If, therefore, the highest good is impossible according to practical rules, then the

[42] *TP,* p. 65; *PrAk,* p. 280.
[43] *CPrR,* p. 114; *PrAk,* p. 110.

moral law which commands that it be furthered must be fantastic, directed to empty, imaginary ends, and consequently inherently false.[44]

However, before trying to show the relevance of this claim to the political context, and before examining the textual evidence to support such a claim for its relevance, it must be admitted that the claim itself is problematic. Indeed commentators have long been puzzled by such passages. The idea of the highest good, it has been argued, might be relevant in Kant's philosophy of religion, or of history. There, given Kant's rather strained argument for the "primacy of practical reason," reason might be said to require us to hope, or expect, or "think" that there is such a highest good, all as a "practical condition" for continuous moral activity. It is the notion that we are required to *do* something to promote this end that has caused the puzzlement. In the first place, as with the often-criticized notion of "postulates" of practical reason, such a claim seems to introduce a concern with happiness directly into reflection on moral obligation, and, as every sophomore exposed to the *Grundlegung* knows, such an introduction sounds decidedly un-Kantian. Secondly, a famous criticism by Lewis White Beck charges that this purported duty is actually vacuous. Beck asks:

For suppose I do all in my power—which is all my moral decree can demand of me—to promote the highest good, what am I to do? Simply act out of respect for the law, which I already knew. I can do absolutely nothing else toward apportioning happiness in accordance with desert—that is the task of a moral governor of the universe, not of a laborer in the vineyard.[45]

[44] *CPrR*, p. 118; *PrAk*, p. 114.

[45] Lewis White Beck, *A Commentary on Kant's Critique of Practical Reason* (Chicago: University of Chicago Press, 1960), pp. 244–45. There are a number of responses to Beck's criticism. Perhaps the most well known are John Silber's articles, "The Importance of the Highest Good in Kant's Ethics," *Ethics* 73 (1962–63), pp. 179–97, and "Kant's Conception of the Highest Good as Immanent and Transcendent," *Philosophical Review* 68 (1959), pp. 469–92. I agree with the general structure of Silber's reconstruction, as when, in the former article, he writes, "It is the need of a human will for an object that forces Kant to this consideration of ends and to the extension of the law beyond its own limits alone to the condition of man." But I disagree with his neglect of the *Metaphysics of Morals* (as a way of finding out just what this "extension" involves and why), and thus believe he leaves far too vague his final conclusion, that we are "to strive for the realization of happiness in proportion to virtue in the lives of all men" (p. 195). Likewise, in the latter article, although Silber defends well the general relevance of the highest good to Kant's thesis, he again leaves unclarified just what we are supposed to do and why. (There is also no discussion here of the difference between the derived duties of *Recht* and *Tugend*.) The same problem (what am I to do, even if there is a further, immanent duty to pursue the highest good?) is even more apparent in Y. Yovel's book, *Kant and the Philosophy of History* (Princeton: Princeton University Press, 1980), pp. 104–5, 172, 189.

It is, I think, instructive that Beck argues that the task of promoting the highest good is to be assigned to a "governor." In fact, I want to argue, not only is our duty to promote the highest good not vacuous in Kant, but the "content" of that duty directly involves our "governing" our *own* universe, our "collaboration" (a word Kant often uses when mentioning our duty to promote the highest good) in instituting and supporting a *Rechtsstaat.* Basically, what I want to claim is that once we understand why Kant thought that our duty to obey the moral law entails a moral interest in the coincidence of virtue and happiness, we can then understand how specifically political duties can be said to fulfill *that,* if you like, "secondary" or derived obligation.

Recall again that there are two initial problems with Kant's more extravagant statement about our duty to pursue the highest good. The first is, given Kant's famous insistence on the unconditioned nature of moral obligation, how he can go on to posit a moral interest in the coincidence of virtue and happiness; and, secondly, why such an interest should involve the state. The first problem can be solved if we pay attention to what Kant says about the *necessity,* in any action, of what he calls a "material" end, or, loosely, an interest in happiness. For example, in the second *Critique,* he writes:

> Now it is certainly undeniable that every volition must have an object and therefore a material; but the material cannot be supposed for this reason to be the determining ground and condition of the maxim.[46]

He goes on in *Religion within the Limits of Reason Alone* to write:

> But although for its own sake morality needs no representation of an end which must precede the determining of the will, it is quite possible that it is necessarily related to such an end, taken not as the ground but as the [sum or] inevitable consequences of maxims adopted as conformable to that end. . . . It is true therefore, that morality requires no end for right conduct. Yet an end does arise out of morality; for how the question, *What is to result from this right conduct of ours?* is to be answered, and towards what, as an end—even granted that it may not be *wholly* subject to our control—we might *direct our actions* and abstentions so as at best to be in harmony with the end: these cannot possibly be matters of indifference to reason [last two emphases mine].[47]

It is, of course, obvious in the above that Kant still insists that in a morally worthy action this end not determine the will. But if we, and Kant, remained with this insistence, then, to use now the relevant example, the moral status of political life would be hard if not impos-

[46] *CPrR,* p. 34; *PrAk,* p. 34.

[47] I. Kant, *Religion within the Limits of Reason Alone,* trans. T. M. Greene and H. H. Hudson (New York: Harper, 1960), p. 4; *PrAk,* vol. VI, pp. 4–5.

sible to assess. Our moral attention would be limited solely to assessing whether we were obeying the moral law or not, and it would, I think, be most unclear what our duty would be if it turned out that many other individuals were *not.* In that case, *I* might still be able to obey the moral law, and while I might strongly disapprove of the wholesale moral chaos going on around me, and might be most unhappy about the disasters that befall me as the one honest man in town, I would have no *moral* basis for any action other than my own continuing obedience.

Rather, I suggest, it is because Kant realizes that we *cannot* be indifferent to our pursuit of our own ends (or happiness) and to the consequences of the social practices of others, that he argues that respect for the moral law itself (the only true incentive), when thought together with the necessary characteristics of volition, generates a secondary "duty of justice," a duty which involves not only our own individual respect for the freedom of others, but allegiance to a legal institution which compels that respect from others. Again, the core of this argument is that, while, in any one act of volition, I *can* remain effectively indifferent to my material end (which I nonetheless still desire), I cannot *continually* remain indifferent to being able to achieve my ends in concert with others achieving theirs, all subject to the condition that no one violate the moral law in doing so. (That is, I *cannot* simply obey the moral law, without having some interest that my pursuit of my own ends is not thereby endangered or frustrated.)[48] If I tried to argue that way, to remain content with being some perpetually tragic moral hero, indifferent to his own ends, *only* concerned with doing the right thing, I would in effect be denying, or at best ignoring, what Kant takes it we have just admitted: that each action necessarily presupposes a *material* end. In other words, as Kant pointed out to Garve, not only am I not forever condemned to excluding consideration of my happiness in my pursuit to be "worthy" of it, but I *cannot* be indifferent to the possibility of a coincidence of happiness and moral worth.[49] What I am claiming here is that this

[48] The modality issue here is complex and insufficiently discussed by Kant. I *can* always simply do the right thing according to Kant (the right remains the "supremum bonum" in Kant, the condition of all other value). But *once* that is admitted, I cannot ignore my empirical nature, or leave wholly unconsidered the possible coincidence of happiness and virtue. My interest in moral worth must lead to an interest in whether or not pursuit of this worthiness is Sisyphean.

[49] "Nor had I omitted to point out at the same time that man is not thereby expected to *renounce* his natural aim of attaining happiness as soon as the question of following his duty arises; for like any finite rational being, he *simply cannot do so*" (my emphasis). *TP,* p. 64; *PrAk,* p. 278.

impossibility is what is most of all at work in Kant's transition from morality to politics.

Now, of course, this transition is not yet effected, and the argument itself still has to be spelled out in more detail, but the basic form of Kant's argument for what he had called, in the 1793 theory-practice essay, the "further duty" to promote the highest good should be clear. Assuming that I have a duty to respect others as ends in themselves, then, Kant is arguing, I cannot be indifferent to others *not being* so treated, to their being treated as means in the pursuit of material ends. This, though, does not mean that I must attempt to coerce others to give up their pursuit of those ends, in order to insure this respect. I know, for one thing, that such a pursuit *cannot* be given up. In other words, I have the "further duty" of creating a situation where such a moral ideal of autonomy is "actualized," and I know that one of the conditions of any such actualization is pursuit of happiness. And, I believe, Kant thinks a "state" can most effectively insure that obedience to the law coincide with the possible pursuit of happiness; or stated negatively, that I and others are not "victims" or "means" for others just because we respect autonomy, and do not lie, cheat, rob, or embezzle.

Now clearly, nothing in his argument claims that the state or any agency must actually *bring about* happiness. Kant realizes that no one can create happiness any more than one can create "internal" or truly moral obedience to the law. But my moral interest in a just polity is, I think, best explained in Kant by means of this *summum bonum* form of reasoning. Also, it is clear, just from the architectonic division of the *Metaphysics of Morals,* that Kant does not think that *all* moral duties to others are the subject of legislative coercion. He must defend only a restricted set of "minimal" or "essential" duties to others as so subject. If we look now at Kant's entire system of moral duty, reconstructed in the way I have suggested, we can see clearly where this restriction becomes most important.

(I) Given Kant's "critical" demonstration of the possibility of morality, he grounds all moral obligation on reason, so interpreted in the practical realm that it virtually means autonomy (in the literal sense of self-legislation). (II) The law relevant to such self-legislation can only be the categorical imperative. (III) The "typic" of the moral law for human beings is a "law of nature," understood as a harmony of beings pursuing their ends, where human agents are ends in themselves. (IV) Our obligation to treat other rational beings as ends in themselves entails a further obligation—to do what we can do to establish the most favorable conditions under which others are treated as ends in themselves. This obligation stems from the impossibility of continual indifference to achieving our material ends, consistent with the moral law and with others achieving their material ends (happiness). (V) When we specify what we *can* do to fulfill (IV), we find two types of obligations: (*a*) to collaborate in civil society by prohibiting actions, which, considered universally, would render impossible any agent pursuing his own ends in conformity with the moral law (i.e., with respect for agents as ends in themselves), and (*b*) doing what we can as individuals actually to promote and aid others achieving their ends, and the development of our talents.

Clearly, within this overview, one wants to know how to use this duty to pursue the highest good to help make out the distinction between (IV*a*) and (IV*b*). But before addressing that issue, I also want to stress the textual evidence for using this approach. Its role is even apparent in passages where Kant seems to contradict it—where he sounds his most "rigoristic." For example, in the 1793 theory-practice essay, he writes:

> But the whole concept of an external right is derived entirely from the concept of *freedom* in the mutual external relationships of human beings, and has nothing to do with the end which all men have by nature (i.e. the aim of achieving happiness) or with the recognised means of achieving this end.[50]

Or, even more directly, "No generally valid principle of legislation can be based on happiness."[51] But in these passages, Kant is arguing against an attempt to legislate in order to promote some particular view of "what makes men happy." He is not discounting the relevance of a concern for happiness, in a theoretical sense, to our interest in politics. Again, without this relevance, given only our moral duty to respect others as ends in themselves, political institutions would, at best, be consistent with that duty, not required by it, as the *Rechtslehre* teaches. Indeed, just after the last quotation, Kant writes,

> The doctrine that *salus publica suprema civitatis lex est* retains its value and authority undiminished, but the public welfare which demands *first* consideration lies precisely in that legal constitution which guarantees everyone his freedom within the law, so that each remains free to seek his happiness in whatever way he thinks best, so long as he does not violate the lawful freedom and rights of his fellow subjects at large.[52]

Such a claim seems to me perfectly consistent with the interpretation presented here of our duty to promote the highest good.

[50] *TP*, p. 73; *PrAk*, p. 289.
[51] *TP*, p. 80; *PrAk*, p. 298.
[52] Ibid.

Moreover, at several places in the body of the *Rechtslehre* itself, Kant's own formulations frequently echo just this form of reasoning about the "conditions" for autonomy. Most clearly, in section 41, he writes, "A juridical state of affairs is a relationship among human beings that involves the conditions under which alone every man *is able to enjoy his right*."[53] Passages like these confirm that, in deliberating about the structure of political institutions, we are deliberating not only about the normative issue of right, but, to a larger extent than is often realized in discussions of Kant, about the empirical conditions which allow the *exercise* of rights.

It is undeniably true, though, that when Kant speaks most directly about the "practical conditions" of the moral law being respected, he mentions either the religion postulates, or his conjectural philosophy of history (i.e., what we ought to believe in order to "keep faith" with the law). Such remarks, unfortunately, not only cloud the picture concerning Kant's reasoning about the highest good, they introduce a good deal of tension into that theory. (If the existence of a benevolent deity and the immortality of the soul can be practically established, then my necessary interest in happiness is *fully* reconciled with my striving for moral worth, no *practicum absurdum* issue need arise, and as in Beck's criticism, there is nothing for me to do to promote the highest good. The "governor" of the vineyard will see to it, ultimately.)[54] Even with this problem admitted, though, it is most important to stress that even in these contexts, the general form of practical reasoning at work in all Kant's moral philosophy is visible. To cite the two most important elements stressed here: (i) that obedience to the moral law entails more than doing the right thing in any individual action, but that such duties themselves are duties only because of general duty to respect a certain *ideal* of human autonomy, an ideal we

[53] *MEJ*, p. 69; *PrAk*, pp. 305–6. Cf. also Kant's note, *Reflexion* 6631, *PrAk*, vol. XIX, p. 119: "Principium formale identitis in moralibus. Materiale: felicitas publica." I am thus disagreeing with the interpretation presented by Klaus Düsing in his "Das Problem des höchsten Gutes in Kants praktischer Philosophie," *Kant-Studien* 62 (1971), pp. 5–42, although this article in general is an invaluable guide to the range of different uses to which Kant put his "highest good" doctrine. See also the lucid discussion by Otfried Höffe, "Recht und Moral: Ein kantischer Problemaufriss," *Neue Hefte für Philosophie* 17 (1979), pp. 1–34. Höffe approaches this problem by pointing out how Kant mediates the traditional opposition between the natural right and positivist traditions, agreeing that *Recht* and *Moral* do not coincide (and that *Recht* requires compulsion), but insisting on the necessity, nonetheless, of a normative foundation for *Recht*. Like so many commentators, however, Höffe leaves unexplained how this distinction is to be defended, and what in particular follows from it.

[54] See Alan Wood, *Kant's Moral Religion* (Ithaca: Cornell University Press, 1970), pp. 1–99, especially pp. 25–33, for a fuller discussion of the moral foundations of Kant's philosophy of religion.

cannot take seriously without also acting to promote it, to see to it that it is respected; and (ii) that the central issue at stake in doing what we can to promote that ideal is reconciling it with desire for our *happiness.* Kant just wandered a bit, all over his moral map, as he tried to come up with either arguments that would make this ideal theoretically reconcilable with our empirical nature, or more specific duties tied to this general obligation to promote the ideal of autonomy.

As final textual support, I would also argue that, without this component being taken seriously as part of Kant's political reflections, there is no way, aside from armchair psychologizing, to explain why the theorist who perhaps most radically defended the absolutely inalienable, moral character of rights, should have been such a cautious *reformist,* such a resolute anti-revolutionary. Our first derived duty is to be *in* civil society, for Kant, the minimum *empirical* condition for any protection of rights. As we shall see, just how the pursuit of material ends and the protection of human autonomy as an end in itself can be reconciled is remarkably wide open in Kant (all much to the irritation of later *Kantian* political theorists like Gentz and Rehburg, some of whom tried to develop a theory of human nature to pin this down more concretely).[55] But, for the moment, all I can claim here is that this interpretation at least systematically explains this prudential reformism in Kant.

VI

But, while this reconstruction of the moral foundation of political duty differs from the others presented here, it still faces the "ranking" problem involved in the *Recht/Tugend* distinction. We have at last seen that for Kant our obligation to the state stems from our obligation to *insure* respect for the freedom of all, and we know that, for human beings, the crucial consideration in such insuring is allowing the possibility of the pursuit of happiness, coincident with respect for others as ends in themselves. We now want to know what formal principles of a state *do* insure this, as opposed to what we as individuals must do privately in respecting the autonomy of others, and in furthering their being so respected.

That is, we still have to ask about more specific actions "ranked" close together as all violations of the moral law, but still significantly different. What makes my use of another as a means in one context

[55] Cf. *Über Theorie und Praxis,* ed. Dieter Henrich (Frankfurt: Suhrkamp, 1967), especially the introduction by Henrich, "Über den Sinn vernunftigen Handelns im Staat."

unjust and so prohibitable (like violating the provisions of a contract), in another "merely" immoral (like withering sarcasm or greed), and in others morally neutral (as when I gleefully exploit my opponent's backhand in tennis, knowing that it embarrasses him and that I am using him only as a means for my own pleasure)? These questions are quite involved and go to the heart of many contemporary disputes about such issues as the relative "rank" of market freedoms versus the freedom to develop distinctly "human potential." But the interpretation offered here at least gives us a clear Kantian way to approach them (although I am not sure that it gives us a way to resolve them). Given what has here been identified as the foundation of the duty of justice, what we must show, in order to show that an act that treats others as means is unjust, is that the act (or maxim) when considered universally would make a civil society of autonomous agents *impossible.* It would thereby violate the *fundamental* duty of justice—to enter and remain in civil society, the one clear empirical condition for insuring that human autonomy is minimally respected. Such acts could be shown to be different from treating others as means in ways that make achieving their (and our) goals difficult (but not impossible) and which thus I could not rationally *will* to universalize. (This distinction also corresponds to what *can* be prohibited, actions—versus what cannot, goals or objects of the will.) More precisely, this ranking principle includes prohibitions against acts which make the *continued* existence of civil society impossible, such as the use of the institution of private property to exploit and destroy natural resources.

To be sure, it might seem that we still do not have a clear criterion by which to define *which* acts would, if permitted, render a civil society of autonomous agents impossible. In clear cases it is not hard to see how the pursuit of any material end would be impossible if cheating on contracts or robbery were allowed, or how the very ground of the duty to enter civil society in the first place would be contradicted if institutions like slavery were allowed. Given that no one could pursue *any* plan of life without life, some security in the means necessary to pursue his ends, and sufficient freedom from authority to form such a plan and act on it, and given that the whole point of civil society is to allow or make possible pursuit of such ends, in uniformity with the moral requirement to respect others' freedom to do likewise, a civil society which made such a coincidence impossible would be incoherent, from Kant's point of view.[56]

[56] This reasoning about ranking is similar to one suggested, but not used, by Rawls in *A Theory of Justice,* p. 42. At least in this book, Rawls prefers a ranking principle more in

However, to come finally to the most difficult questions, can anything more specific be said about these "conditions"? What *are* the externally legislatable (and only externally legislatable) means necessary to secure individual pursuit of happiness consistent with respect for autonomy? Kant is notoriously brief in answering this question in the *Metaphysics of Morals.* With respect to "private law," he deals mostly with property rights; in the section on public law, he briefly argues for the separation of powers, a vague version of republicanism, and the necessity that citizens be free, equal, and independent; he denies the right of revolution, and discusses public welfare, public offices, the right to punish, and some issues in international relations. It would take far more space than I have left here to attempt to assess whether Kant's discussion of all of these issues can be defended along the general lines suggested here. I want to close by discussing one of them—property rights—as a way of raising a serious problem remaining in Kant's account. A full "Kantian theory of institutions" will have to await a future discussion.

I have been arguing that, while there is a fundamental connection between Kant's moral and political theory, there is also an important principle demarcating each realm. That is, political duties are just those moral duties to others that it is not only permissible but obligatory to compel. Said another way, political sanctions involve only the protection of rights. I have further argued, incorporating some of Kant's brief remarks on external legislation and perfect duties, that the criterion that defines which duties ought to be compelled must involve Kant's argument about our "further duty" to promote the highest good—that is, to prohibit those actions or institutional practices aimed at a material end in a way incompatible with respect for human autonomy and/or the minimal condition required for that autonomy to be respected: the rule of law. Now, putting all this together, it would not be difficult to show, as indicated earlier, how, for a

---

line with his contractarian argument, which he calls a "lexical" ordering principle. However, putting aside for the moment complications introduced by his later Dewey Lectures, I would argue that the interpretation offered here is closer to the requirements of Rawls's theory than some of his own formulations. As stated in *A Theory of Justice* (sec. 40, "The Kantian Interpretation of Justice as Fairness") and in "A Kantian Conception of Equality," *Cambridge Review* (1975), I do not think Rawls can justify the priorities of his original contractors on *Kantian* grounds. The situation is rather as if Hobbesian egoists were forced into a situation with Kantian restraints. See here the criticism of Andrew Levine, "Rawls' Kantianism," *Social Theory and Practice* 3 (1974–75), pp. 47–63. Put another way, I think that the interpretation defended here better explains a "Kantian" interest in the material conditions of freedom stressed in Rawls's second principle (and also helps correct the standard view of Kant used against Rawls by such commentators as Levine).

modern, or even eighteenth-century, European society, this view would condemn slavery or endorse some standard list of basic liberal rights. Moreover, one could also easily show that certain rights, like free speech or vigorous expression of disagreement, are essential to respect for autonomy and that they thus may not be abridged for the sake of any general moral duty we have to aid others in their quest for happiness and so refrain from public vulgarity or sarcastic criticism. But the point at issue now is: do these considerations not only legitimate the "rule of law" *überhaupt,* but also help specify the kind of laws that may be adopted? For example, what should be the permissible extent of ownership and use of property?

Not surprisingly, at least not surprisingly given the above interpretation, Kant deals with such an issue only in a highly abstract way, leaving a very good deal, too much I shall argue, open to contingent legislative decision. For he argues not that property rights are directly derivable from the duty of justice, and certainly not that any particular institution of property is. All he thinks he can claim is that ownership of some property is a "postulate" of justice. Generally, he means by this (i) that ownership of property in some form is not inconsistent with the duty of justice and that it is thus permissible (a *lex permissiva* or *Erlaubnisgesetz*); (ii) that the idea of rendering *any* object a *res nullius,* the property of no one, would be inconsistent with the exercise of freedom, for, "in that case, freedom would be robbing itself of the use of its will in relation to an object of the same will inasmuch as it would be placing usable objects outside all possibility of being used,"[57] and (iii) that therefore, it would be *unjust* to prohibit this permissible exercise of freedom.

In the body of his discussion, however, he is mostly concerned with two more general issues: to show how and why *de jure* possession, or what he calls "*possessio noumenon,*" is possible, and through the use of this concept, to show that *if* there is such noumenal possession, interfering with it would be a violation of justice; and secondly to show how this *de jure* possession is possible only in civil society, not in the state of nature.[58] He thus only claims, as a conclusion, "It is a duty of

[57] *MEJ,* p. 52; *PrAk,* p. 246.

[58] There is thus no "natural right" to property in Kant, nor any "natural" entitlement to property improved through our labor, etc. This is so because without an institutional framework, there would be no way to distinguish empirical possession, which is not, according to Kant, even having property, from noumenal possession. The latter depends on the possibility of possession being recognized, to use the Hegelian notion, *as* property by citizens. That possibility is what makes possession property. However, this just requires some *public* rule specifying what property is so that I can be assured that, if I am subject to these rules in the acquisition of property, others are too, equally. It does

justice to act towards others so that external objects (usable objects) *can* also become someone's [property]"[59] (my emphasis).

This argument, on the one hand, confirms much of what has been said here about Kant's political philosophy, but, on the other hand, stops curiously short of extending that reasoning into more detail. That is, Kant discusses the general issue of property rights in a way we would, by now, expect: as a *condition* for the exercise of autonomy. I cannot value freedom so highly without insuring that there be some means for my exercising my freedom, and the use of objects without threat of theft is just such a means. Even at this level, though, Kant's claims are empirically unstable, since he nowhere argues that private ownership *alone* is an indispensable means for the exercise of such autonomy (as, for example, Hegel does).[60] He does not consider (although he admits the possibility of) collective, legally defined ownership of land.

But more to the point here, Kant has very little to say about the extent to which the general duty of justice might impose *limits* on the possible legislative acquisition of further, more specific property rights. He can show that if there is *de jure* possession in civil society, violation of this possession is an injury to human autonomy, but he has little to say about whether justice requires any specific social institution of private property. Given the case presented above, we might expect him to be able to argue that property rights are rights at all only if they can be shown to be morally permissible and empirically necessary to the exercise of autonomy. But that case defends the value of private property only because of a prior commitment to the moral ideal of autonomy itself. Thus we would also argue that the institution of private property is limitable; no use of private property may be inconsistent with the very ideal which legitimates it. More concretely, we might then argue that no claim about "rights" of ownership in, say, a restaurant, given *why* that right is a right, can be consistent with the exercise of that right to deny persons use of that restaurant on the basis of some claim that denies universal autonomy, such as race. We might even argue that the use of property for profit is, especially in an economic system where there is little or no option about employment

---

not presuppose that all do agree (or implicitly agree), as a general will, on what these rules are. This point is badly confused by Howard Williams in "Kant's Concept of Property," *Philosophical Quarterly* 27 (1977), p. 39. See *MEJ*, pp. 64–65; *PrAk*, p. 256.

[59] *MEJ*, p. 60; *PrAk*, p. 252.

[60] G. W. F. Hegel, *Philosophy of Right*, trans. T. M. Knox (Oxford: Oxford University Press, 1967), pp. 40–57; *Grundlinien der Philosophie des Rechts* (Hamburg: Felix Meiner, 1955), pp. 55–79.

for wage earners, inconsistent with dehumanizing, mechanical labor. Of course, even in such an argument, we would need to be mindful of Kant's concern with securing the minimal empirical conditions for the pursuit of any material end, but, for all his formalistic rigor, Kant is almost excessively concerned with this latter issue.

Thus, for example, when discussing in the 1793 theory-practice essay the moral ("a priori") requirements of equality in civil society, Kant admits:

> This uniform equality of human beings as subjects of a state is, however, perfectly consistent with the utmost inequality of the mass in the degree of its possessions . . .[61]

and he goes on to state the classical liberal formulation of equality as equality before the law alone. However, he also insists in this passage that no one may "stand in the way" of another's equal opportunity for advancement by means of hereditary privilege. Such inheritance of *authority* would be inconsistent with the freedom of all. But Kant simply allows that a subject "may hand down everything else"[62] and thereby "create considerable inequalities in wealth among members of a commonwealth."[63] He just does not consider the issue raised so often in the nineteenth century, whether this inequality alone just as effectively "prevents" equal opportunity of advancement as inherited authority. That is, he does not consider whether his own argument about hereditary privilege should lead him to deny an *unrestricted* right to bequeath property. Given that property rights, as interpreted above, are not directly included within the duty of justice, but are only argued for as "a condition" of autonomy, various empirical and historical factors might convince one that some particular institution of property impeded rather than promoted such universal autonomy, and so violated our duty to promote the highest good.[64]

This hesitation to deal with the details of the empirical conditions of autonomy is visible in several other passages, particularly in those in "Perpetual Peace" where Kant insists on perpetual peace as a moral

[61] *TP,* p. 75; *PrAk,* p. 292.

[62] *TP,* p. 76; *PrAk,* p. 293.

[63] Ibid.

[64] Of course, those who because of unrestricted economic competition are too poor to make use of their "equal opportunity" would, while still free to do so, find this freedom valueless. And Hart is right to point out in "Are There Any Natural Rights?" p. 75, that these are still two *different* evils, not to be confused. Nevertheless, given the argument presented above, once we know why economic freedom *is* a right, that reasoning might just as well convince us that this other worry *is* a politically relevant wrong and hence an object of legislative concern.

ideal for statesmen, but condemns any "precipitate" means toward that ideal, endorsing a notion of prudence so vague as to be almost meaningless (or, at best, Burkean).[65] If the interpretation presented here is at all correct, then his own case for the general duty of justice provides him with the theoretical resources to extend his reasoning about the "conditions" of right in ways far more detailed than he attempted.

That is, in sum, he *need* not have restricted himself, in either of these cases, to his famous legalism. Since, as we have interpreted the argument, our obligation to the laws of civil society is based on general obligation to promote and secure the conditions under which the pursuit of material ends is consistent with respect for autonomy, a theoretical consideration of the social institutions within which this quest for material happiness takes place could certainly be far more detailed, and less open to simple contingencies, than Kant allows. If what we might loosely call the "highest good" form of reasoning is inherently involved in why duties of justice are duties at all, then the famous post-Kantian extension of a concern for justice into social as well as political institutions could be seen as wholly consistent with *Kantian* premises.

Of course, a good deal more methodological and historically relevant detail would have to be provided before this extension could be fully defended, but the structure of such an argument seems to me to be inherent in Kant's own case, or at least in the most successful general reconstruction of it. Providing this detail, that is, would just be to take seriously Kant's own words quoted earlier: "What is to result from this right conduct of ours . . . cannot possibly be matters of indifference to reason."[66]

University of California, San Diego

[65] I. Kant, "Perpetual Peace," trans. H. B. Nisbet, in *Kant's Political Writings,* p. 122; *PrAk,* vol. VIII, pp. 377–78.

[66] See note 47 above. I want to add here my thanks to Gerald Doppelt, Richard Arneson, and Charles Griswold. Their comments on and criticisms of earlier drafts of this article were invaluable, and I am grateful for their help.

8 What Kant and Fichte Can Teach Us about Human Rights

SUSAN SHELL

One of the things that strike a person who has lived both in America and Canada is the extent to which (we) Americans, as distinguished from Canadians, tend to frame political questions in terms of individual rights. Where we Americans speak in terms of such rights—for example, the right to free speech or to privacy or even to welfare—Canadians tend to speak (passing over the interesting exception of language rights) in terms of the general desirability of policies—not do people have a right, say, to free medical care? but is it advisable that they get it?[1] Now there are good historical and legal explanations for this difference, the United States Constitution being perhaps the most important.[2] In any event, what I mean to suggest in drawing attention to this difference in national rhetoric is the extent to which Americans take for granted the importance and coherence of the concept of individual rights. One has only to think of influential recent American works in political theory by John Rawls, Robert Nozick, and Ronald Dworkin, each of whom claims to take rights most seriously. And yet despite, or perhaps because of, the importance of rights in American political discourse, there have been relatively few recent attempts to provide the concept of rights with a firm theoretical foundation. Here Rawls, Nozick, and Dworkin, who seem to take the legitimacy of rights on faith, are no exception.

At first glance, Immanuel Kant and Johann Gottlieb Fichte seem like unpromising thinkers to turn to for a clarification and deepening of our understanding of the problem of rights, as classically conceived

[1] Stories are told in Canada of criminal suspects who expect to receive the "Miranda rights" (without equivalent in Canada) that they see dramatized on American television.

[2] Not all students of the American legal tradition have applauded this emphasis on rights. See for example Alexander Bickel, *The Morality of Consent* (New Haven: Yale University Press, 1975).

by the liberal tradition and as conceived in America today. For one thing, Kant's eighteenth-century Prussia and Fichte's late eighteenth-century Saxony were in many ways illiberal societies, politically and economically closer to feudalism than to the liberal freedoms of contemporary England and revolutionary France. Peasants in many German states were still technically bound to the soil, requiring permission of their lord to choose an occupation or to marry. For their part, many landowners were still required to protect their peasants, for example by feeding them if the crops failed. At the same time, Kant and Fichte were themselves much moved and enthused by the revolutionary political developments in America and France, and by the notion of rights there espoused.[3] Thus their treatment of rights has a certain abstractness; their sense of the politically possible tends toward the hypothetical, rather than growing out of and responding to what they have seen practiced around them.

And yet this very abstractness can also be seen as a kind of advantage. For, combined with a ruthless—even procrustean—theoretical rigor and consistency, it leads them to push certain premises to their logical conclusions, however disagreeable such conclusions may be from the point of view of ordinary common sense. When Fichte deduces a "police state" from what he calls the right to life, or, as he later amends it, the right to live as agreeably as possible from one's labor; or when Kant declares that rights to property must be respected whatever their effect on human well-being, we can perhaps learn something useful about such rights and their possible limits.

Kant and Fichte are radical thinkers, in the sense that they do not take the plausibility of concrete, historical rights for granted in the manner of Burke or Hume, and in the sense that they demand what the great founders of modern natural rights theory, Hobbes and Locke, arguably do not provide—a metaphysically and morally certain foundation for human rights. Kant's and Fichte's demands may have been excessive, even fundamentally misguided. (To this issue we shall later return.) Nevertheless, the extremity of those demands gives them, as I hope to show, a certain critical edge over earlier theories of right.

Both Kant and Fichte are moral extremists. For Kant especially, and unlike Rawls and other latter-day heirs of Kantian thought, individual rights rest on a prior notion of individual moral freedom and dignity.

[3] Kant, who found little to criticize in the American Revolution, was more guarded in his response to that of France. The youthful Fichte was widely regarded as a Jacobin; his early *Beitrag zur Berichtigung der Urtheile des Publicums über die französische Revolution* was written to answer Burke's *Reflections on the Revolution in France.*

Both Kant and Fichte take very seriously—perhaps more seriously than any previous philosopher—the notion of moral freedom; and they take great pains to resolve the conflict they perceive between this freedom and the apparent determinacy of the world. There is, to be sure, an important difference between the two philosophers. For Kant the determinacy in question is from the beginning natural. He is concerned with the mechanical determinacy of nature (attested to by modern science) and the apparent threat it poses to our moral freedom.[4] For Fichte, on the other hand, the determinacy in question is, at least in the beginning, religious. For Kant, the fundamental problem is to resolve the apparent conflict between morality and science. For Fichte, the problem is to resolve the apparent conflict between morality (which requires moral freedom) and the religious notion of an all-knowing, all-powerful God. It is worth noting that Kant starts out as a student of natural science, Fichte, like Schelling and Hegel after him, as a student of theology.

What are the implications of this difference for their respective theories of rights and politics? Kant, the ex-scientist, has a down-to-earth belief in the power of nature to cancel any and all human plans. With an unflinching eye for cosmic disaster, he admits that an errant asteroid could destroy our world tomorrow.[5] And this appreciation of the power of nature leads him to reject the idea of a rigorous philosophy of history, and with it Fichte's brand of political utopianism. Kant is pessimistic about man's ability to conquer nature completely, to make it fully serve human ends. For Kant, our conquest of nature progresses sporadically and always imperfectly. Our technical skill may improve in one direction—we build better ships that enable us to cross new oceans—but new problems develop elsewhere—we have new diseases to contend with. The problem of happiness is ultimately insoluble for man.[6]

For Fichte, on the contrary, the conquest of nature is no sporadic affair but a process of continuous, asymptotic advance. What is the basis of Fichte's optimism? There are some obvious psychological explanations to call upon. Fichte saw progress all around him. A sort of academic Horatio Alger, his own life history might well lead him to suppose that the greatest obstacles to human progress could be con-

[4]In an unpublished note, Kant suggests that the problem of moral imputability lies at the source of his critical philosophy. See *Gesammelte Schriften,* edited by the Prussian Academy of Sciences (Berlin: Reimer, 1902–), vol. XX, p. 335 (hereafter cited as *G.S.*).

[5]*Anthropology from a Pragmatic Point of View,* trans. Mary J. Gregor (The Hague: Martinus Nijhoff, 1974), p. 190; *G.S.*, vol. VII, p. 329.

[6]See, for example, the *Critique of Practical Reason,* trans. Lewis White Beck (Indianapolis and New York: Bobbs-Merrill, 1956), p. 24; *G.S.*, vol. V, p. 25.

quered. And he was physically singularly robust. One contrasts the sickly Kant and his pessimistic insistence that a preponderance of pain over pleasure is a necessary condition of all organic life.[7] But the philosophic basis of Fichte's political optimism was his understanding of morality and religion. For theoretical reasons that cannot here be discussed he argued that the conquest of nature, so that nature should be to us what our bodies already are, is not merely a matter of convenience but an outright moral duty.[8] To be sure, there is a not altogether dissimilar imperative behind Kant's insistence on our duty to perfect our skills and talents.[9] But only Fichte goes so far as morally to enjoin the thorough domestication of nature—its transformation into a place where we can be *zu Hause.* Now what duty commands must, of course, be possible. Ought implies can. The conquest of nature is thus part of our moral destiny or *Bestimmung.* This broad difference of outlook between Kant and Fichte leads to a difference in their respective understanding of human rights, a difference similar in some ways to that dividing liberals and socialists today.

What are rights? Let us call them justifiable claims. But claims to what? Classical liberals (and here Kant is with them) generally speak of formal or procedural rights, rights to hold and exchange property, rights to enter into contract, rights to free expression in matters that do not impinge on the rights of others, rights to formal representation and procedural due process—in a phrase, the right to the *pursuit* of happiness. Leftward-leaning liberals and socialists, on the other hand (and here Fichte is with them) tend to relate rights directly to substantive material goods; they tend to speak of rights to a job and an adequate wage, rights to health care and old age security, rights to representation that protects one's real interests, rights to substantive and not merely formal due process—in a phrase, the right to *happiness,* or to as much happiness as society is able to provide.

Let us then examine Kant's and Fichte's theories of right with greater care. Kant's theory of right and politics begins with a paradox: On the one hand, the ultimate basis of human rights is said to be the absolute worth and dignity of the individual, as free subject of the moral law. On the other hand, the problem of rights and justice is said

[7] *Anthropology,* pp. 99–100; *G.S.,* vol. VII, pp. 230–32.

[8] For Fichte's fullest treatment of this theme see *Das System der Sittenlehre* (Science of ethics), *Fichtes Werke,* ed. I. H. Fichte (Bonn: Adolph-Marcus, 1834–46), vol. IV, pp. 1–365. (*Fichtes Werke* hereafter cited as *F.W.*)

[9] See the *Doctrine of Virtue,* trans. Mary J. Gregor (New York, Evanston, and London: Harper and Row, 1964), pp. 110–14; *G.S.,* vol. VI, pp. 443–47.

to be soluble for "a nation of devils," as Kant puts it in a famous phrase, "if only they are intelligent."[10] Kant's theory of right, it seems, captures in a particularly forceful way a certain liberal ambivalence about human nature: on the one hand, men are bad, or at least aren't to be trusted to be good; on the other, they deserve our honor and respect. Kant's system of justice is designed to work the same for good men and bad, angel and devil alike. For purposes of justice, only our outer actions are taken into account. The inner motives that constitute the moral worth of our actions are, for purposes of justice, irrelevant.[11] According to Kant, virtuous men are just as much in need of coercive laws and penalties as evil men. For, as he puts it, be men ever so righteous and well-intentioned, they will disagree about what is good and so come into conflict.[12] Kant rejects the classical suggestion that a community of the virtuous, united by their knowledge and love of the good, could dispense with justice in managing their mutual affairs and instead rely on friendship. He rejects this suggestion because he believes, with Hobbes, that there is no rationally determinable good for human beings and that therefore each person must determine the good subjectively for him- or herself. Kant, it is true, does acknowledge a "highest good" that all men are enjoined by morality to further. This "highest good" he defines as "happiness commensurate with virtue." But insofar as one component—"happiness"—of this heterogenous good is at best an ideal of the imagination, not of reason, the idea of a "highest good" cannot furnish justice with a strict, rationally determinable foundation. In modern parlance, Kant's theory of justice is "deontological," taking its ultimate bearings from a notion of what is obligatory or right without reference to any prior conception of the (human) good.[13]

How then does Kant's system of justice work in practice? In many respects it resembles the Lockean state (and certain "night-watchman" models of the state advanced today), formed to preserve property—a

[10] "Perpetual Peace," in *On History*, trans. Lewis White Beck (Indianapolis and New York: Bobbs-Merrill, 1963), p. 112; *G.S.*, vol. VIII, p. 336.

[11] By "motive" Kant means that for the ultimate sake of which an action is undertaken. Motive establishes the moral value of an action, which, according to Kant, is morally creditable only if undertaken for the sake of duty (rather than, say, to avoid pain). Proximate intentions do matter juridically in the obvious sense that intentional homicide differs from (and is treated differently by the law than) accidental killing.

[12] *The Metaphysical Elements of Justice* (The Doctrine of Right), trans. John Ladd (Indianapolis: Bobbs-Merrill, 1968), p. 76; *G.S.*, vol. VI, p. 312.

[13] For a thorough and incisive discussion of this distinction see William A. Galston, *Justice and the Human Good* (Chicago and London: University of Chicago Press, 1980).

state in which individuals contract to exchange goods and services and expect the government to see that such contracts are honored. It resembles the Lockean state, but with this difference. Locke's justification of private property and consequent material inequality rests at least in part on an argument that most people are thereby made better off. As he puts it in chapter five of the *Second Treatise of Government,* "a king of a large fruitful territory [where there is no private property] . . . feeds, lodges, and is clad worse than a day laborer in England." What is strikingly different about Kant's justification of private property is his refusal to make any *direct* appeal whatsoever to human welfare or happiness, to what is good for men. Justice, he says, has nothing to do with the end men have by nature, the end of achieving happiness.[14] Rights and justice must be deduced from a priori, rational and objective principles. And notions of welfare and happiness are a posteriori, empirical, and in the last analysis subjective. What will make me and you happy, even what will make me happy from one moment to the next, is subject to any number of empirical contingencies and cannot be rationally (pre)ascertained. Anticipating and going beyond modern welfare economists and other critics of utilitarianism, Kant questions not only interpersonal comparison of satisfaction but intrapersonal comparison as well. If rights and justice are to rest on reason, they cannot take their bearings from human happiness. The aim of Kant's system of justice is not to provide for our happiness, or even the minimal conditions for happiness, but rather to secure formal non-interference among wills. Neither competition among wills nor mutual thwarting of purposes is thereby eliminated. Individuals are, however, assured that nothing is done to them by others to which they have not directly or indirectly consented. The most obvious illustration of such formal non-interference, or what Kant himself calls "external freedom," is the (ideal) marketplace, whose participants are deemed free (without regard for their material circumstances or substantive gains and losses) so long as they are able to enter into voluntary, binding exchanges. Kant's demand for a rational and a priori grounding of rights, combined with his modern conviction as to the contingency and subjectivity of happiness, leads to a theory of rights that lacks all direct concern with the actual satisfaction of human wants and needs. As Kant puts it, "let justice prevail though the world perish."[15] Or, as a similar

[14] *G.S.*, vol. VIII, p. 289.

[15] "Perpetual Peace," in *On History*, p. 126; *G.S.*, vol. VIII, p. 378. In translating the Latin phrase, Kant softens it to read: "let justice prevail though all the rogues in the world perish."

sentiment was put one hundred years later in the United States Supreme Court case of Lochner vs. New York: let freedom of contract prevail, even if that freedom results in people going hungry.

Which brings us to Fichte, Kant's student and critic. For Kant, formal equality and material inequality, equal dignity and unequal happiness, are entirely compatible. "The uniform equality of human beings as subjects of the state is . . . perfectly consistent with the utmost inequality of the mass in the degree of its possessions, physical and mental."[16] Unlike Rawls, Kant draws from the "moral irrelevance" of gifts of fortune the lesson that the lucky may enjoy their boon without guilt, while the unlucky must bear their burden without complaint. Kant does acknowledge that a certain kind of physical and economic dependency may impinge on one's ability to function as a free and equal citizen. He is thinking less of poverty per se than of specific modes of earning a living, for example as a servant, or wage laborer, or wife. Such individuals do not own their own means of earning a living and so, according to Kant, are not fully their own masters. For Kant as for Marx after him, the worker's dependency is constituted not so much by his need as by the fact that he does not own what he produces or produce what he immediately intends. His tasks, in short, are set by others rather than by himself. This leads Kant to distinguish between passive and active citizens, only the latter of whom may participate in public life (e.g., by holding office or by voting).

Kant is at pains to render this qualification of civic equality a question of general type (is this person the owner of his livelihood?) rather than specific amount (how much does he own?). In so doing he strives, perhaps, to play down the extent to which his system of justice, though based on the a priori moral equality of all human beings, must concede to what Kant regards as brute empirical facts—to wit, the inability of certain kinds of human beings (for example, wage earners and women) to participate responsibly in public life.

Fichte, on the contrary, argues (one is reminded of such contemporary socialists as C. B. Macpherson and Michael Harrington) that if material inequality can so impinge on civil equality, then it is the duty of the state to remove that material inequality. Specifically, he contends that citizens have a right not only to formal equality but also to be able to "live by their labor." All must work, but each who is willing to work must be able to live.

[16] *G.S.*, vol. VIII, pp. 291–92.

As it happens, the right to participate in public life proves to be far less germane in the managerial state envisioned by Fichte than in the open republic proposed by Kant. While voters, in Fichte's state, determine the very broadest direction of the laws, experts shape the exacting regulations that assure to all a livelihood and, as Fichte has it in later years, as agreeable a life as possible. Now Kant (unlike Nozick) does grant the state a certain welfare function—for example, poor relief—though not for the sake of the poor but in the interest of public safety: as Kant puts it, "if the supreme power makes laws which are primarily directed toward happiness (the affluence of citizens, increased population, etc.) this cannot be regarded as the end for which a civil constitution was established, but only as a means of securing the right state, especially against external enemies of the people."[17] Fichte on the other hand makes provision of all with a livelihood the first duty of the state, and for reasons (superficially at least) not altogether different from those invoked by Kant in his defense of *formal* freedom.

Conceptually, Fichte claims to derive rights from the (logical) presuppositions of individual self-consciousness. The lines of his argument run roughly as follows: As conscious, the self is subject. As content of consciousness, the self is object: To be self-conscious is thus to be at once subject and object, active and passive, determining and determined. These conflicting properties are only thinkable in conciliation through the experience of interaction with another person. Specifically, I must be called upon or "invited" to manifest my freedom by recognizing the rights of another, by acknowledging the free subjectivity of a human object outside me. I must, if the conditions of self-consciousness are to be fully met, find myself invited by another to manifest my freedom by acknowledging his.[18] As for Rousseau, and in contrast with the early liberals, the development of intellect and sociality go hand in hand. There is, to be sure, nothing intrinsic to guarantee that once awakened mutual recognition of rights will continue to prevail. Thus follows, again conceptually, a mutual demand for an overarching power as each party seeks relief from the other, whose freedom, whose power to do or forbear, each recognizes but whose respect neither can secure. On such quasi-Rousseauian foundations Fichte erects his Leviathan, its coercive apparatus yoked increasingly, as Fichte's thought develops, to a moral change.

[17] *G.S.*, vol. VIII, p. 296.

[18] *Grundlage des Naturrechts nach Prinzipien der Wissenschaftslehre* (Science of right), *F.W.*, vol. III, p. 36.

Justice for (the early) Fichte, as for Kant, is not concerned with our ultimate ends, be they good or evil, but rather with the reciprocal impact of our external activity in pursuit of these ends. But whereas Kant was concerned only with the formal aspect of this impact, the formal relation between wills, Fichte is concerned with supplying the actual material conditions required for us to carry out our plans and achieve our ends. He is concerned with the minimization of frustration and risk.[19] If Kantian politics reflects a free-market conception of liberty, Fichte's anticipates the modern welfare economist's concern with risk aversion and full security.

Consider the following example: I buy your farm. It is a free, uncoerced exchange. Each of us thinks he stands to benefit. But then there is a drought. You have all my money while I go hungry. Now according to Kant there is nothing unjust about any of this; my misfortune is just that, an act of nature or chance for which no one can rightfully be praised or blamed. Fichte, however, sees matters differently. According to Fichte, at least by 1800 when he writes the *Closed Commercial State,* any event that human action could mitigate or prevent is within the pale of justice—is, in other words, a social and not merely a natural occurrence. If I am visited by drought, or fall sick, or find myself unable to earn a living wage, I have a right to help and (he is adding by 1800) as much help as society is able to provide, up to a level comparable to that of my fellows.

> Everyone wants to live as agreeably as possible, and since everyone demands this as a human being, and no one is either more or less a human being than anyone else, in this demand everyone has an equal right.[20]

According to this early and radical version of entitlement theory, people's right "to live as agreeably as possible" derives from their humanity, or more specifically, from the demands each makes upon the others in the name of humanity. What is it, then, that we share, what aspect of our common humanity entitles us to (the aid of others in securing) an agreeable life?

In an early section of his *Science of Right* Fichte derives the fundamental rights of human beings from their mutual experience of one

[19] This concern is more pronounced in Fichte's *Closed Commercial State* (1800) than in the *Grundlage des Naturrechts* (1796). In the later work he describes the pre-juridical state as follows: "No one is free because all are unlimited; no one can pursue anything purposefully nor reckon for a moment upon its enduring." The emphasis in Fichte's juridical state is not on the securing of life for its own sake but on providing risk-free conditions to facilitate purposive activity in general.

[20] *F.W.*, vol. III, p. 402.

another's freedom, a freedom that manifests itself essentially as a capacity to impose the form of reason on an otherwise irrational and recalcitrant nature.[21] To recognize another as human, or as a fellow being with rights, is to acknowledge the existence of another who, like oneself, is capable of exercising his will upon nature the better to command it. It is to recognize, as Fichte suggests in the *Closed Commercial State,* a fellow laborer, engaged, whatever his immediate wants and goals, in the common project of imposing upon nature a human face. It is labor, then, that gives men equal dignity and a right to equal joy. One is reminded of the traditional German expression, perhaps once innocent: *Arbeit macht frei.*

Fichte's enhanced conception of labor blurs Kant's strict distinctions between right and virtue, dignity and happiness; and it prepares the way for the erasure of yet another Kantian distinction (still embraced by Fichte in 1796)—that between juridical and ethical community. For labor is the mode by which man progressively assumes command over nature, a command that is at once his right, his satisfaction, and his (moral) purpose or destiny. Fichte's concept of labor provides him with a substantive common good something like the universal welfare function that Kant and other liberals before and since have found so elusive. His notion of a community of labor bent on the overcoming of nature holds forth the promise of a people internally united by duty and interest, without recourse to external force.

"It is not merely a pious wish for mankind," says Fichte, "but it is also the indispensable requirement of man's right and destiny that he should live as easily, as freely, as much in command over nature, in as truly *human* a manner, as nature will allow."

> Man should labor, but not as a beast of burden that falls asleep under its burden, and that is awakened again after minimal recovery of its exhausted power to bear that burden once again. He shall work without anxiety, with pleasure and joy, and shall have time left over to lift his mind and eye to the heavens for the contemplation of which he is fashioned. He shall not eat with his beast of burden, but rather his food shall be distinguished from its fodder, his dwelling from its stable, just as his body is distinguished from its body. That is his right, for the very reason that he is a man.[22]

Labor for Fichte, as for Marx after him, is not merely a means to other ends, not merely the unpleasant price we must pay, as with Locke, for certain benefits, but itself a source of both satisfaction and

[21] *F.W.,* vol. III, p. 30.
[22] *F.W.,* vol. III, pp. 422–23.

dignity. And this leads us to yet another reason for Fichte's optimism as to the conquerability of nature and consequent possibilities for human happiness. One reason for Kant's pessimism about the possibility of human happiness in any ultimate sense is his belief, which he shares with Hobbes and Locke, that satisfaction is relative to desire and that desire is infinitely expandable. If we want one car this year, we will want two next year and three the year after. There is thus no way our technical skill and productive capacity can keep up with our demands and hence we shall never be fully satisfied. Life, as Hobbes says, is a restless pursuit of power after power ceasing only in death. Now while agreeing that human desire is potentially infinite, Fichte believes, along with Rousseau, that desire can and should be held in check. Desire, though infinitely expandable, is also almost infinitely malleable. We can learn to make do, and to enjoy making do, with less. But how are desires to be limited? Fichte answers this question in the *Closed Commercial State,* a curious work that makes explicit the risk-aversive premises suggested in his earlier treatments of politics. His answer is indicated by his odd title. Liberals such as Kant and Adam Smith taught that human progress depends on open intellectual and commercial borders—a free market in goods and ideas. Fichte, on the contrary, urges nations to close their borders to commerce and travel in order to encourage the development of a homogeneous and self-disciplined citizenry: "the essential transition point from all actual political systems of commerce and trade . . . to the one which, in our opinion, is the only true system and the one demanded by reason is: that the state should entirely cut itself off from all commerce with foreign countries . . . ."[23] There is, to be sure, one exception to the general restriction. Artists, intellectuals, government officials, and in general all those whose cultural level is high enough to permit them and the state to benefit from contact with others are to be permitted to travel. Fichte seems to assume not only that the cultural level of societies will thereby be raised but also that such individuals will not suffer the debilitating distractions of ordinary citizens. What Fichte fears is that tide of rising expectations that awareness of the habits and luxuries of foreigners can cause. Like today's carefully screened cultural emissaries from the east, Fichte's enlightened few are presumed immune to the desire-expanding charms of other nations.

Rousseau had proposed the small, homogeneous, self-contained republic as a perhaps workable *alternative* to progress; Fichte proposes it as a workable *means* to progress, dedicating his book to the "progres-

[23] *F.W.,* vol. III, p. 476.

sive" finance minister of Prussia. What happens if a nation needs something it cannot produce itself? It learns to do without (as we once gave up bananas and now do without Havana cigars); or it assumes what Fichte sees fit to call its "natural" borders, if necessary by force. Fichte uses the device of the closed border to achieve what Marx later thought could only be achieved internationally—a system that progressively solves the problem of human happiness by concentrating on basic needs rather than desires, and by seeing labor itself as a key component of human satisfaction and dignity. In so resolving the problem, Fichte breaches the sharp line drawn by Kant between right and virtue. The problem of justice is no longer seen as soluble for a nation of devils. For Fichte, by 1800, technical and moral enlightenment, knowledge and virtue go hand in hand. Yet despite its moral dimension, Fichte's solution to the problem of justice is more mechanical, less rooted in human deliberation and choice, than that of Kant. Men are to be led to virtue less by the habit of self-government (as with Kant) than by the mechanisms of the market. Despite Fichte's emphasis on national character and love of fatherland, an emphasis lacking in Marx, he shares with Marx a conviction that the ultimate basis of the state is not political but economic. The true creator of national character, according to Fichte, is the introduction of closed economic borders and a domestic currency.[24]

The year 1800 ushers in another development in Fichte's thought. For Fichte, as for Marx, the ultimate function of the state, once it has done its work, is to bring about its own abolition. For, as Fichte argues in a late work, the very notion of right and the state rests on a paradox and contradiction. On the one hand, we all have a right to follow our own moral conscience, our own insight. On the other hand, we may be compelled and may compel others to follow the insight of society at large. This contradiction is only resolved when all individuals are raised to the same level of moral culture or insight. And thus the essential duty of the state is the education of all to the insight of what is right. Only if the state fulfills this condition does it possess the right to exist, for it prepares the way for its own cancellation (*Aufhebung*).[25]

Kant, as we recall, held that the state, with its powers of compulsion, will always be necessary, no matter how virtuous its citizens. Fichte, on the contrary, comes to argue that the withering away of the state is a real historical possibility as well as a moral necessity. The condition of this possibility is the (temporary) governance of society by those at the

[24] See, for example, *F.W.*, vol. III, p. 509.
[25] *F.W.*, vol. IV, pp. 432–44.

forefront of technical and moral progress, rule by a kind of intellectual vanguard. Paradoxically, the equality of enjoyment demanded by justice requires rule by an intellectual elite. And this paradox is only overcome historically—after the fact, so to speak—as the general population comes to share the level of technical and moral culture enjoyed by its most educated citizens. Fichte's demand for rule by the few in the name of equality of right tells us something about the kind of equality of right he envisions. As he puts it in the *Closed Commercial State:* "Everyone has a right not merely to free activity, but also to the most powerful and most successful activity in society which the most educated person can imagine." I have a right, in other words, not only to equality of opportunity but to equality of results, and at the highest level that society can provide. I have a right, assuming that I buy a farm, not only to be protected from drought, but to achieve the highest yield technically possible as well as the highest income generally supportable for all. The (Fichtean) right to live as agreeably as possible, the right not only to *pursue* happiness, in the liberal sense, but to *achieve* it, culminates in what Hegel sarcastically called the "police state,"[26] in which, as Fichte boasts, "the police know pretty much what everyone is doing at any time of day."[27] It culminates in a state that tells people what occupations they can enter, where they can go, and how much they can earn. Fichte's ideal, pursued to infinity, is a society in which there are no surprises, in which external circumstances have been rendered so predictable that no plan, rationally conceived, can fail. But Fichte's abolition of frustration in the name of freedom entails obvious costs to freedom, costs that can only be overcome, in the last analysis, by a quasi-mystical appeal to God, fatherland and history: "the infinite content of freedom . . . the moral task, is incomprehensible, the image of God, because God is incomprehensible and can be experienced only in the revelations of history."[28] Fichte's theory of right stands at a crossroads between liberalism and socialism and at the threshold of modern nationalism. And his theory reveals, perhaps more fully than that of any other modern philosopher, the tensions that obtain among the desires for freedom, security, and community.

What Kant and Fichte principally object to in the classical liberal account of rights is its lack of evident necessity, both rational and moral. Kant, as we have seen, attempted to ground right in the moral

[26] See for example, G. W. F. Hegel, *The Difference between Fichte's and Schelling's System of Philosophy,* trans. H. S. Harris and Walter Cerf (Albany: State University of New York Press, 1977), p. 147.

[27] *F.W.,* vol. III, pp. 185–86.

[28] *F.W.,* vol. VII, p. 581.

freedom of the individual as subject of the moral law. Yet paradoxically this attempt culminated in a system of justice that has nothing directly to do with the teaching of virtue. The problem of politics is soluble for a nation of devils if only they are intelligent. Kant defines moral freedom as radical independence from external, empirical determination. Thus the state could not teach virtue without undermining the very freedom on which virtue, according to Kant, ultimately rests. Indeed the whole project of moral education, however desirable, remains for Kant essentially problematic. Virtue is a matter not of being molded or formed from without but rather of spontaneously exercising one's freedom. Moral education remains for Kant at best a preparation that cannot replace the leap of will that true morality requires.

Kant's attempt to link political rights and moral freedom faces another difficulty. Kant's conception of moral freedom is so radically transcendental as to pose serious questions as to its relation to political or "external" freedom. How does moral freedom, in principle inviolable, dictate a right to external freedom, which can be violated and, indeed, often is? If a person in chains remains morally free, as Kant insists he must, how in any morally relevant way do those chains impinge on his freedom? Kant's clearest answer to this question lies in his concept of man as an "end in himself," that is, as a being who may not be subjected to treatment to which he has not directly or indirectly given his consent. Yet how this concept is to be logically derived from the categorical imperative in all its formal purity is something that Kant does not make fully clear.[29]

Fichte, too, attempts to link rights and moral freedom. He defines that freedom, however, less in terms of the immediate transcendence of nature than in terms of its gradual and progressive overcoming. Freed from Kantian pedagogical reserve by his own enhanced—or inflated—understanding of labor, his attempt culminates in a state

[29] In the *Groundwork of the Metaphysics of Morals* Kant embeds this concept in one of the "formulas" of the categorical imperative, while at the same time leaving the precise logical status of the "formulas" unspecified. The most promising line of argument may look to the so-called typic of the categorical imperative, presented in the *Critique of Practical Reason.* The typic allows us to see that we cannot consistently will an action and at the same time will a world in which such action would be arbitrarily frustrated by the wills of others. Kant, in other words, appears to furnish political rights with a moral ground by trading on the external focus or object of (human) moral willing, its concern with phenomenal results. Whether, however, this phenomenal concern can be made ultimately consistent with the noumenal status of moral willing remains open to question. It is worth noting that Fichte begins with what Kantian dualism arguably cannot provide—an integral concept of (human) action.

that tries to teach virtue, so to speak, by force, and hence in a conflict between freedom and compulsion to be resolved, Fichte optimistically assures us, by history.

Fichte's understanding of labor does allow him to restore the connection, severed by Kant, between happiness and justice. The price of this union, however, is a set of highly utopian hopes concerning the conquerability of nature and possibilities for (an eventually) noncoercive community. Here, then, is the paradox: the recovery in Fichte's thought of the satisfaction of human need as a component of justice results in a politics that is not less rigid and unrealistic in its expectations of human conduct but more so.

A final problem for Fichte: how is moral freedom to be reconciled with a morally progressive history? Doesn't such progress give later generations an unfair moral advantage? No, says Fichte, not when the goal is infinite and moral credit is measured by effort rather than result. Effort or striving becomes for Fichte a kind of intergenerational measure and absolute. Still, won't later generations be happier? Not really, says Fichte. It is not the appeasing of desire (as with Hobbes), or repose (as with Rousseau), or rest after labor (as with Kant), but labor itself that becomes for Fichte the most enduring human satisfaction.

One can't help feeling a little let down, not to say wearied, by this solution to the age-old problem of the relation between virtue and happiness. In a way, Aristotle said something similar: happiness lies in virtuous activity. Aristotle, however, characterized that activity not as labor but as leisure, not as striving against opposition but as *unimpeded.*[30]

Yet if virtue is effort and striving, vice for Fichte can be nothing but laziness. Fichte lacks Kant's sense of the radically evil in man. Fichtean morality is less concerned with reward and punishment than with the development of human power bent on the overcoming of nature. But in so adapting Kant's concept of moral freedom, the notion of individual dignity—the bedrock of Kantian liberalism—loses something of its grip. Freedom is no longer conceived as the inviolable possession of the individual, but as a collective and infinitely receding goal. Freedom catches the individual, so to speak, at infinity, where the individual understood as finite ego ceases to exist. Put otherwise, were freedom fully to be achieved, the finite individual would disappear. The *Bestimmung,* the determination or destiny, of the individual is, in the last analysis, to overcome his individuality. It took Hegel to draw

[30] Aristotle, *Ethics* 1153b.

the fatal and down-to-earth conclusion: the destiny of the individual lies in his death. It is not by willing the moral law (as with Kant) but by one's acceptance of death that, according to Hegel, one shows oneself to be free. Poised between Kantian pessimism and Hegelian fatalism, the wonder is not that Fichte's optimism failed to thrive but that it thrived so well.

It would be inaccurate and unfair to burden all liberals or all socialists with Kant's and Fichte's programs in their entirety. Not all who believe in the benefits of private property need justify, with Kant, the most extreme degrees of economic inequality. Nor need all who defend public welfare as a matter of entitlement endorse, with Fichte, an all-embracing state apparatus. Yet to those to whose political beliefs the notion of human rights is central, the thought experiments of Kant and Fichte must give pause; for they suggest that human rights as classically conceived by both the liberal and the socialist traditions may have some logical consequences that are morally unacceptable and politically unsupportable.

To take the notion of human rights as central in determining what is desirable and just is to take justice in a particular way. It is to assume that justice begins with the claims that human beings can legitimately make upon one another qua human beings. But what is it about human beings that authorizes or grounds such claims? Rousseau, from whom both Kant and Fichte learned much, tentatively suggested that it is will, or freedom, wrested out of and against nature, that furnishes the ground of rights. Men gain their dignity and respect, their claim to rights, in the mutual recognition of one another's freedom. Whether, however, the distinction between nature and will is ultimately sustainable is a question that Rousseau chose pointedly to raise.[31]

Kant and Fichte sought to solidify what Rousseau left questionable. For them the line between will and nature is sharply drawn, if (especially in Fichte's case) drawn oppositionally. There are, to be sure, differences between the two thinkers. Freedom, which Kant understood principally as the capacity for moral desert or imputable agency, is interpreted by Fichte to mean activity in general, or the striving of the finite self progressively to overcome all opposition, thus (re)uniting with the unlimited or absolute self at infinity. The moral focus of Kant gives way to a quasi-religious concern with the relation between

[31] See, for example, Jean-Jacques Rousseau, *Discourse on the Origin of Inequality*, in *The First and Second Discourses*, ed. Roger D. Masters (New York: St. Martin's Press, 1964), p. 114.

the finite and the infinite, the soul and God. Nevertheless, for each, human rights rest on a metaphysic of freedom, an account of things, that in the face of the dispiriting teachings of modern science makes room for and supports the dignity of man and his superiority over nature.

Rights, to be sure, may have other grounds. Of those seeking a foundation "within the limits of reason" and without recourse to revealed religion, some have attempted to derive human rights from the principle of non-contradiction combined with an analysis of the requirements of human judgment and action. Others have accepted rights as an institution imbedded in the complex practices of our society. Hegel, critical of Kant and Fichte, sought in his account of rights to reconcile, by a labored logic, their abstract formulations with the concrete realizations of history. And Aristotle, for his part, would probably have regarded the modern attention to rights as unbalanced in its focus on what is merely one facet of justice.

Still, the utility—in our time—of a rhetoric of rights, its practical contribution to decency, cannot, I think, be doubted. It is true that what may at first appear a near universal moral language often breaks into something closer to babble. The rights one party has in mind are "political," the rights of another "economic." Group rights, language rights, the right to holidays and a paid vacation—all have been seriously put forward at one time or another as belonging to the universal claims of mankind.

For Americans, to whom rights, the "truths we hold to be self-evident," are a national creed, the teachings of Kant and Fichte, whatever their failings, ought to hold special interest. Here were two great thinkers, impressed by our revolution and its guiding principles, unencumbered by at least some of our peculiar prejudices and traditions, placing our concept of rights (or something like it) at the center of their own all-embracing world systems. Their differences continue to find an echo in our ongoing political debates. And their attempted rigor—or rigidity—points up logical difficulties that may be hidden by more pragmatic and easygoing formulations of political doctrine. What can Kant and Fichte teach us about rights? At the very least, they draw attention to a sort of impoverishment to which the liberal understanding of rights and freedom is particularly susceptible. The spirit of liberalism, Abraham Lincoln once suggested, lies not in the mere pursuit of happiness but in the *laudable* pursuit of happiness.[32]

[32] Abraham Lincoln, "Message to Congress in Special Session," July 4, 1861, in *Works,* ed. Roy P. Basler (New Brunswick, N.J.: Rutgers University Press, 1953), vol. IV, p. 438. I am indebted to Robert Faulkner for calling my attention to this speech.

How do we understand that laudableness? How do we take it seriously? On the importance of that question, at least, Kant and Fichte would agree.

Boston College

9 The Place of the Sublime in Kant's Aesthetic Theory

DONALD W. CRAWFORD

I

In the *Critique of Judgment* Kant divides aesthetic judgments into judgments of the beautiful in nature and art (which he calls "judgments of taste") and judgments of the sublime. It is a theoretical division he inherits from many earlier eighteenth-century writers. Much has been written about Kant's theory of beauty. For reasons perhaps having more to do with the concept of the sublime itself than with Kant's treatment of it, much less has been said about his theory of the sublime. The sublime, like the arabesque and the picturesque, now seems a brief episode in the history of taste with few if any living descendants. As one commentator on Kant's aesthetics recently put it:

> A twentieth-century reader might ask, with a certain smile, whether the sublime really needs an analysis. . . . as an aesthetic category with its roots in our culture, the sublime seems largely irrelevant.[1]

And another chimes in:

> Even if there is historical interest in Kant's discussion of the sublime, I think it is safe to assume that his analysis of this particular aesthetic merit will not be of much interest to modern sensibilities.[2]

All citations of passages in Kant's *Critique of Judgment* are given parenthetically in the body of the paper, by listing the section number, as provided by Kant, followed by the page number of the citation as it occurs in volume V of the Akademie edition of Kant's works: *Kants gesammelte Schriften,* herausgegeben von der Königlich Preussischen Akademie der Wissenschaften (Berlin: Walter de Gruyter and Co., 1902–).

[1] Francis X. J. Coleman, *The Harmony of Reason: A Study of Kant's Aesthetics* (Pittsburgh: University of Pittsburgh Press, 1974), p. 85.

[2] Paul Guyer, *Kant and the Claims of Taste* (Cambridge, Mass.: Harvard University Press, 1979), p. 400.

Is the concept of the sublime in nature a quaint romantic relic that should be kept in the "rare idea room"? According to views widely held in the eighteenth and nineteenth centuries, the natural sublime is to be found in grand objects or phenomena that inspire feelings of pleasing astonishment, amazement, awe, and respect: stormy seas, vast deserts, majestic peaks, precipitous cliffs, violent thunderstorms, great waterfalls, and the like. The natural objects thought to produce these effects are those which under normal circumstances often cause us to feel fear, horror, dread, or frustration—in short, a personal concern due to an awareness of the inadequacy of our physical or mental powers. In the case of the storm, its destructive power threatens one's safety; the vastness of the desert or sea presents a barrier to travel and the distance can literally boggle the mind. Reflect for a moment on the positive experiences you may have had in viewing the Grand Canyon, Niagara Falls, or Death Valley; witnessing the eruption of Old Faithful geyser; watching a turbulent surf crash against a rocky shore; experiencing an intense thunderstorm, a torrential downpour, or even an earthquake. Theories of the sublime begin with such experiential data—a positive affective response in the face of nature's power or magnitude. The theoretical question has been how best to account for the overall positive response when the perceptual object is an aspect of nature that appears to be dysfunctional with respect to the interests of the perceiver.

One might wonder why a theory of the sublime, which seems to be largely a psychological phenomenon, falls within the domain of philosophical aesthetics. The easiest answer is the historical one, having to do with the concept of the aesthetic itself. The concept of the aesthetic, as it evolved in the eighteenth century, was consistently identified with perceptually based experiences valued for reasons other than the satisfaction of desires for practical gain, scientific knowledge, or sensuous gratification, or for the realization of religious precepts or moral imperatives. The sublime fits comfortably within this concept, and philosophers have taken it as their task to analyze it. So if your positive response to the Grand Canyon is due to the realization that an underground culvert would suffice to carry the water in the Colorado River while the canyon itself would serve as a landfill site for Los Angeles refuse, your response is not aesthetic and hence not sublime. Similarly, your pleasure in viewing Yosemite's El Capitan is not aesthetic if your interest is solely that of a cliff scaler thinking of the grand challenge you believe will result in personal glory and perhaps monetary reward for doing soft drink commercials from the summit. The sublime in nature, then, has been conceived as an aesthetic category; it has been linked to the experience of natural objects of extensive power or magnitude and characterized by a positive feeling not explained by the satisfaction of these other interests.

Personally, I do not share the view that the aesthetic category of the sublime in nature is irrelevant to current aesthetic sensibilities. I find it alive and well in the writings of recent naturalists and environmentalists; and it has been incorporated into contemporary empirical assessments of the aesthetic quality of landscape. The sublime thus forms a significant philosophical underpinning to contemporary environmental aesthetics, whose shallow roots may lie in Ralph Waldo Emerson, Henry David Thoreau, John Muir, and Aldo Leopold, but whose tap roots are firmly planted in eighteenth-century aesthetic theory.

In this essay, however, I am concerned only with Kant's theory of the sublime and its place in his aesthetics. Each of these topics is not without its difficulties. As in most of Kant's writings, there is the problem of precisely what Kant's view *is:* the dense Kantian text, infused with his own architectonic and terminology, cries out for interpretation and appears to some readers to be riddled with difficulties. Francis Coleman, for example, concludes that "Kant's theory of the sublime is not only logically untenable but seriously distorted in its details."[3] Secondly, there is the problem of the position of Kant's treatment of the sublime within the text of the *Critique of Judgment* itself and its relationship to the rest of Kant's aesthetic theory. Several recent commentators, finding Kant's view on the sublime an obstacle to a unified interpretation of his "Critique of Aesthetic Judgment," tend to ignore it or to cast it aside. The present author's book on Kant's aesthetics provides an instance of the former,[4] while Paul Guyer's recent book exemplifies the latter. Guyer even suggests that Kant's inclusion of an explanation of our response to the sublime in the third *Critique* "seems something of an after thought, or a concession to the standard topics of eighteenth-century aesthetics (or taste!)."[5]

I want to resist these pessimistic conclusions and argue that Kant's theory of the sublime, though not without its difficulties, is significant with respect to the more general aims of the third *Critique.* My proce-

[3] Coleman, *The Harmony of Reason,* p. 120.

[4] Donald W. Crawford, *Kant's Aesthetic Theory* (Madison: University of Wisconsin Press, 1974).

[5] Guyer, *Kant and the Claims of Taste,* p. 399. More recently, however, Guyer has attended to Kant's theory of the sublime: "Kant's Distinction between the Beautiful and the Sublime," *Review of Metaphysics* 35 (1982), pp. 753–83.

dure involves attending closely to the historical influences on Kant and to the compositional history of the text itself, as we can best reconstruct it. In this regard I am indebted to the late Giorgio Tonelli, whose detailed textual analyses of Kantian concepts have helped reveal the evolution of Kant's thought. I shall suggest that in the course of writing the *Critique of Judgment* new considerations emerged that significantly changed Kant's line of inquiry, and that consequently the straightforward, unified theory of Kantian aesthetics sought by recent interpreters is probably not forthcoming. The result may not be a philosophically more acceptable Kantian aesthetics, but I believe it better reveals the programmatic significance of the third *Critique* for the critical philosophy in general. In particular, it helps explain Kant's obscure claim that his critique of the faculty of judgment bridges the gulf between the conclusions of the first and second *Critique*s, making possible the transition from the realm of natural concepts to the concept of freedom.

II

Interest in the sublime as a modern aesthetic category began with the appearance in 1674 of Nicolas Boileau's French translation of the Greek essay "On the Sublime" (*Peri Hupsous*), attributed to Longinus. English as well as other translations quickly followed, as Longinus's piece joined the core of writings on literary art. Although concerned almost entirely with the innate abilities and literary tools required to produce "lofty" or "elegant" writing, Longinus implies that this quality of sublimity in literature can also be known by its effects on the reader:

> For the effect of genius is not to persuade the audience but rather to transport them out of themselves [*ekstasis*]. Invariably what inspires wonder casts a spell upon us and is always superior to what is merely convincing and pleasing.[6]

An analogous point can be made, Longinus claims, concerning natural grandeur and our response to it, and the following brief poetic passage sets the stage for theories of the sublime in nature:

> Thus within the scope of human enterprises there lie such powers of contemplation and thought that even the whole universe cannot satisfy them, but our ideas often pass beyond the limits that enring us. Look at life from all sides

[6] *Dionysius or Longinus on the Sublime,* trans. W. Hamilton Fyfe (Cambridge, Mass.: Harvard University Press, 1939), p. 125.

and see how in all things the extraordinary, the great, the beautiful stand supreme, and you will soon realize the object of our creation. So it is by some natural instinct that we admire, surely not the small streams, clear and useful as they are, but the Nile, the Danube, the Rhine, and far above all, the sea. The little fire we kindle for ourselves keeps clear and steady, yet we do not therefore . . . think it more wonderful than the craters of Etna in eruption. . . . what is useful and indeed necessary is cheap enough; it is always the unusual which wins our wonder.[7]

Three aspects of Longinus's brief discussion of the sublime in nature are important for the development of theories leading to Kant's treatment of the sublime. First, there is the hint of two aesthetic categories in addition to the beautiful: namely, the extraordinary and the great. This seems to have been the source of Addison's influential threefold division of the "pleasures of the imagination" into the beautiful, the uncommon, and the great[8]—a trinity that reigns in British aesthetic theory until Edmund Burke in 1757 dismisses novelty as a unique source of pleasure, leaving only the beautiful and the sublime.[9]

The second fertile idea nestled within the passage is the view that in the experience of the sublime our own powers of contemplation and our ideas are greater than can be satisfied by the sensible world. Joseph Addison takes up this point and suggests (in 1712) that one source of the pleasure in viewing things is their *greatness,* by which he says he means "not only the bulk of a single object, but also the largeness of a whole view, considered as one entire piece"; he gives as examples prospects of an open countryside, vast uncultivated deserts, huge mountains, high rocks and precipices, and wide expanses of water.[10] Addison attempts a double explanation of our pleasure in viewing such sights. On the one hand, he writes, "our imagination loves to be filled with an object, or to grasp at anything that is too big for its capacity"; and, on the other hand, it is pleasing to allow the eye to roam without confinement over a spacious horizon, since this, he says, is an image of liberty.[11] And Addison provides a description of the concomitant affective response: "We are flung into a pleasing astonishment at such unbounded views, and feel a delightful stillness and an amazement in the soul at the apprehension of them."[12] Addi-

[7] Ibid., pp. 225–26.

[8] Joseph Addison, *Spectator,* no. 411 (June 21, 1712).

[9] Edmund Burke, *A Philosophical Enquiry into the Origins of Our Ideas of the Sublime and Beautiful* (1757), Pt. One, sec. I ("On Novelty").

[10] Joseph Addison, *Spectator,* no. 412 (June 23, 1712).

[11] Ibid.

[12] Ibid.

son does not pretend to understand the cause of the experience, but he speculates that the ultimate purpose or final cause of this naturally occurring delight in what is great or unlimited is the contemplation of God.

Addison's remarks on greatness raise a question that becomes increasingly important as theories of the sublime develop in the eighteenth century. Is the sublime properly attributed to physical objects and phenomena (mountains, a storm at sea) or rather to a state of mind (a pleasing astonishment, a delightful horror)? In saying that "wide and undetermined prospects are as pleasing to the fancy as the speculations of eternity or infinitude are to the understanding,"[13] Addison indicates that he does not simply equate the pleasure in the sublime with the pleasure in speculating on ideas. Still, he does claim that the unbounded prospect gives pleasure because it is the image of liberty, and he admits that in viewing the ocean "the imagination prompts the understanding, and, by the greatness of the sensible object, produces in it [i.e., in the understanding] the idea of a Being who is neither circumscribed by time or by space."[14] Thus it would seem that for Addison the unbounded object provides satisfaction not (or not so much) because it is interesting to view *in itself,* but rather because it leads one to do something *else* that is satisfying, such as reflect on the idea of God. As we shall see, if one substitutes for God our own powers of reason, Kant's theory of the sublime pops right out of this early eighteenth-century woodwork.

The third important element in the passage from Longinus is the emphasis on strong feeling or emotion in the experience of the sublime in nature. The affective state is characterized as one of awe, wonder, amazement, or respect in the face of something that in many cases would be a source of fear. The modern historical sources for these descriptions are the emotionally charged autobiographical accounts of some writers who crossed the Alps in the late seventeenth century. Steeped in a tradition identifying beauty with order, harmony, and proportion, but nonetheless finding themselves moved by nature's vastness, power, and apparently infinite variety, numerous writers provided the phenomenological basis for the new aesthetic category of the natural sublime. Thomas Burnet writes in 1684:

> The greatest of objects of Nature are, methinks, the most pleasing to behold; and next to the great Concave of the Heavens, and those boundless Regions where the Stars inhabit, there is nothing that I look upon with more pleasure

[13] Ibid.
[14] Joseph Addison, *Spectator,* no. 489 (September 20, 1712).

> than the wide Sea and the Mountains of the Earth. There is something august and stately in the Air of these things that inspires the mind with great thoughts and passions; We do naturally upon such occasions think of God, and his greatness; and whatsoever hath but the shadow and appearance of Infinite, as all things have that are too big for our contemplation, they fill and over-bear the mind with their Excess, and cast it into a pleasing kind of stupor and admiration.[15]

This positive, emotional response to nature's vastness, power, and variety is clearly expressed in the journals and letters of many late seventeenth-century writers who took similar journeys: Lord Shaftesbury in 1686, John Dennis in 1688, and Joseph Addison in 1699 among them. The emotional spirit and the language of these writings are retained in subsequent British theories as well as in Kant's treatment of the sublime.

What British writers on the sublime prior to Burke might Kant have been familiar with? The only one we can be fairly certain of is William Hogarth, whose *Analysis of Beauty* of 1753 appeared in a German translation (by Mylius) in 1754. Kant repeats Hogarth's example of St. Peter's in Rome almost verbatim in the *Observations on the Feeling of the Beautiful and Sublime* (1763)[16] and refers to it in the *Critique of Judgment* (§26, p. 252). There were also translations into German of Joseph Addison's essay from the *Spectator* (1712) and Francis Hutcheson's *Enquiry* (1725) published in 1745 and 1762 respectively, but I know of no direct evidence that Kant was familiar with these works. The first hint of any opposition between the beautiful and the sublime is found in an anonymous 1739 work, *An Essay on Design and Beauty,* by Isaak Hawkins Browne, an opposition which is then followed by other minor writers of the period.[17] One of them was Robert Lowth, whose lectures on the sublimity of the Hebrew poets were given an extensive exposition in German in 1757.[18] Lowth finds in the sublime an exertion of the imagination in terms either of magnitude or of force. This is a possible source for Kant's distinction between the mathematically and the dynamically sublime.

The most famous eighteenth-century writer on the sublime was

[15] Thomas Burnet, *The Theory of the Earth* (London, 1684); quoted in Basil Willey, *The Eighteenth Century Background* (New York: Columbia University Press, 1941), p. 30.

[16] Immanuel Kant, *Observations on the Feeling of the Beautiful and Sublime,* (1763), sec. one; *Kants gesammelte Schriften,* Akademie edition, vol. II, p. 210.

[17] Samuel H. Monk, *The Sublime* (New York: Modern Language Association, 1935), p. 69.

[18] Lowth's lectures were first published in Latin as *Praelectiones de Sacra Poesi Hebraeorum* in 1753. An English edition did not appear until 1787. The lengthy German account appeared in the *Bibliothek der schönen Wissenschaften,* vol. I (1757), pp. 122–55, 269–97.

causal maxim. Today, independently both of Kant's praise and of his critique, the physiological and psychological aspects of Burke's theory have lost their empirical plausibility. At the same time, Kant's explanation of the experience of the sublime is tied so closely to his transcendental philosophy that one wonders whether it has any relevance to contemporary aesthetic experiences.

Kant sets the problem within the same framework as Burke: How can a mode of pain or displeasure give rise to a satisfaction? Although agreeing with Burke that pleasure and pain (*Lust* and *Unlust*) are psychic ultimates incapable of further definition (cf. Locke's "simple ideas"), Kant's starting point differs from Burke's in two important respects—respects, indeed, that would appear to place Kant's attempt at a theory of the sublime at a decided disadvantage. First, Kant retains the more traditional two-valued model of pleasure and displeasure and does not adopt Burke's third category of *delight* as a satisfaction distinct from pleasure that occurs when pain is diminished or removed. Thus Kant's analysis of the sublime is required to be more direct than Burke's: the displeasure *itself* must be responsible for sublime satisfaction. Second, unlike most of his predecessors, Kant insists that we speak incorrectly when we say that a natural object is sublime. Sublimity, according to Kant, resides not in anything in nature but only in the human mind. "Thus the wide ocean, disturbed by the storm, cannot be called sublime. Its aspect is horrible" (§23, p. 245). All we can truly say is that the ocean is suitable for the presentation of the sublimity that can be found in the human mind. What is this sublime state of mind? Kant says that it is the consciousness that we are superior to nature within us and therefore also superior to nature without us (insofar as it influences us) (§28, p. 264). What is it "within us" which he believes is "superior to nature"? If he means to be referring to our empirical selves, Kant is guilty of being patently inconsistent with what he has said in the first two *Critiques*. For in both of those works he insisted that the empirical self is strictly subordinate to natural causes. Thus it is more plausible to interpret him to be invoking the noumenal self and its freedom in this explanation of the sublime. That this might seem mysterious to the ordinary reader might have occurred to Kant, for he does make the curious remark that the principle he finds underlying the sublime "no doubt seems to be too farfetched and subtly reasoned [*vernunftelt*]." But he then goes on to argue that "it may lie at the root of the most ordinary judgments, although one is not always conscious of it" (§28, p. 262).

Kant's analysis of aesthetic judgments on the sublime begins with a twofold distinction between the mathematically sublime and the dynamically sublime. On the interpretation being presented in this essay, these become two rather distinct ways in which our supersensible freedom reveals itself and thus provides a pleasure in the realization of our nature and destiny. They provide a key to the metaphysical implications of Kant's theory of the sublime for his aesthetic theory.

The experience of the *mathematically* sublime occurs when we encounter and reflect upon a natural object whose size or magnitude is exceedingly great, such as the sea, huge mountains, vast deserts, the night sky. If we proceed logically and mathematically (Kant's own terminology), we can estimate and apprehend their magnitude. All we need to do is to select some unit of measure as a base and proceed according to rule. In this way, regardless of whether the unit chosen is one we can take in at a glance (such as a foot or a mile) or whether it is conceptually arrived at (such as the diameter of the earth), the estimation of vast magnitudes can continue indefinitely. So far, there is nothing surprising in this, nor anything obviously sublime. The sublime occurs, Kant says, when in this process of logical estimation of magnitude "the mind listens to the voice of reason" (§26, p. 254). Reason requires a totality in each and every case, a comprehension in *one* intuition, a *presentation* for all the members of a progressively increasing series. Kant maintains that our reason does not even exempt *the infinite* from this requirement. But the requirement cannot be met. No standard of sense apprehension is adequate to the idea of the infinite. We can *conceive* the infinite, have an idea *of* it, although it surpasses every standard of sense awareness and thus every attempt to sensibly apprehend it.

Let us try to express in less Kantian terms the process of thought he suggests forms the basis of the mathematically sublime. Imagine standing in the middle of a grove of giant sequoias in California and being amazed at the height of one of the trees. You think to yourself: What an incredibly tall tree! It must be as tall as . . . what? What standard can I use to estimate its height?

It must be as tall as eighty men standing head to toe. That's tall! But now that I think of it, how many such trees, placed end to end, would it take to be as high as Mont Blanc? And how many of these measures are there in the distance to the sun, to say nothing of the farthest stars? And what if space extends indefinitely? There is no contradiction in thinking of infinite space. But what standard of measurement could there be for the sensible apprehension of the infinite, of that which is great in magnitude beyond all comparison?

All sensible standards are relative, hence none is adequate. How frustrating it is to realize the inherent limitations of our mental powers! (This is the displeasure part of the experience of the sublime.) And yet we are able to *think* of that which is great beyond all comparison. This must mean that we have a supersensible ability, "a faculty of the mind that surpasses every standard of sense" (§26, p. 254). In other words, this sense of inadequacy of our powers of intuition can make us aware that we have a supersensible faculty which is superior to nature (or to our minds and bodies as subject to nature) in this important respect: it exercises dominion over our own sensible powers (i.e., "nature in us"), directing them to press on toward an adequate sensible representation of our ideas, to make the totality comprehensible.

The experience of the mathematically sublime, on Kant's analysis, is thus functional or purposive (*zweckmässig*) for our understanding. It leads us to strive for a greater and greater totality of systematic knowledge. The initial displeasure or frustration felt in trying to apprehend that which is too great for the imagination (the infinite, for example) arises from an apparent conflict between our faculties. The conflict is between our faculty of intuition (sense awareness) on the one hand and our power of comprehension by reason or understanding on the other hand. But this conflict gives way to a pleasure if, through this very conflict, we apprehend and appreciate our powers of reason, our own power to move us to continue to try to apprehend everything in one totality. True, our feeling of awe and respect in fact is directed to natural objects that appear incomparably great. We call *them* sublime. But, on Kant's view, this feeling is a kind of "subreption," a "conversion of respect for the idea of humanity in our own subject into respect for the object" that occasions this idea (§27, p. 257). We feel awe in the presence of the vast ocean because it gets us to realize that our reason has dominion over our sensibility (over "nature in us").

The experience of the *dynamically sublime* occurs upon encountering and reflecting upon extremely powerful natural objects and phenomena that are capable of exciting fear. Kant gives as examples:

> Bold, overhanging, and as it were threatening rocks; clouds piled up in the sky, moving with lightning flashes and thunder peals; volcanoes in all their violence of destructions; hurricanes with their track of devastation; the boundless ocean in a state of tumult; the lofty waterfall of a mighty river, and such like. . . . (§28, p. 261)

Once again, according to Kant, the sublime experience of these things occasions a *displeasure,* this time caused by the realization of the inadequacy of our physical powers of resistance in comparison with nature's might. Although we are literally helpless in the face of the forces of nature, and our awareness of this helplessness is discomforting, Kant suggests that we can regard an object as *fearful without being afraid of it.* And he believes this can happen in the above cases provided we believe we are properly secure from actual danger. Nature's might causes us to recognize our own physical impotence as beings of nature; but in so doing it discloses to us the unique power we have of a different kind of resistance. The idea thus occasioned in us by these exceedingly powerful aspects of nature is the idea of nature having no dominion over a part of us. In a sense, nature cannot even dominate our physical and sensory natures, for we have the ability through the use of our reason to *direct* our sensible faculties not to feel fear in fearful circumstances. And it is the awareness of this power that produces the pleasure marking the dynamically sublime. The experience of the dynamically sublime is thus purposive for the power of reason. In making us aware of the power of our reason over sensibility it "prepares us to esteem something highly even in opposition to our own (sensible) interest" (§29, p. 267). It too serves reason to direct our lives.

This is a difficult, metaphysically laden claim. Kant's complex thesis begins with the view that the experience of the sublime indicates that we have an ability to think a supersensible idea (which ability requires reason and cannot itself be reduced to a power of sensibility), i.e., a power in us that "is not nature." Kant's thesis allegedly (*a*) explains the psychological or experiential components of the experience of the sublime (a species of pleasure), (*b*) shows how "the aesthetical judgment itself [i.e., of the sublime in nature] is subjectively purposive for the reason as a source of ideas" (§27, p. 260), and (*c*) justifies the ascription of necessity to judgments on the sublime (§§29, 30; pp. 264–80).

There are numerous difficulties with Kant's analysis of the sublime. One problem is in the requirement that we must be safe or at least believe we are not vulnerable in order to experience the dynamically sublime.

> He who fears can form no judgment about the sublime in nature, just as he who is seduced by inclination and appetite can form no judgment about the beautiful. The former flies from the sight of an object which inspires him with awe, and it is impossible to find satisfaction in a terror that is seriously felt. (§28, p. 261)

Kant retains this condition from previous theories of the sublime, but its place in his own theory is puzzling. The ability of an extraordinarily powerful storm to make us fear for our safety is canceled if we are protected from it, say by a secure enclosure. Kant is right in noting that an object can appear fearful to us (i.e., be the kind of object that might or usually will cause fear) without our actually being afraid. But how *this* calls up a special faculty of resistance in us if in fact we do not believe we are in any danger remains unexplained. Furthermore, why couldn't a situation involving *real* danger make us aware of our faculty of resistance? Kant himself wavers on this point, as evidenced by a curious remark on war:

> War itself, if it is carried on with order and with a sacred respect for the rights of citizens, has something sublime in it, and makes the disposition of the people who carry it on thus only the more sublime, the more numerous are the dangers to which they are exposed and in respect of which they behave with courage. (§28, p. 263)

Another problem is Kant's view that we legitimately ascribe necessity and universality to aesthetic judgments on the sublime. Kant says that if someone remains unmoved in the presence of that which we find sublime, we judge the person lacking in a basic human respect. We do not say that the person is lacking in *taste*, as we do if one fails to find beautiful what we sincerely judge to be beautiful, but, Kant claims, we do say that the person "has no *feeling*" (§29, p. 265). Kant admits that a certain amount of culture is required to experience the sublime, but he denies that the experience is *merely* a product of culture or convention. Rather, he finds the experience of the sublime rooted in human nature. Our belief that everyone ought to feel awe or astonishment in viewing the Grand Canyon is based on a subjective presupposition, Kant claims, that we believe we are warranted in making, namely, the universal capacity for *moral* feeling. But Kant does little more than assert that there is this common basis for the sublime in human nature.

Third, Kant's analysis of the sublime reduces the natural objects we call sublime (mistakenly, according to Kant) to mere triggers for the experience of the sublime. Consequently, there is no reason to deny sublimity to *anything* that can arouse an awareness of our supersensible faculty. Kant has no good reason to restrict the sublime to nature; non-natural objects might serve equally well to arouse an awareness that we can think the infinite but never attain an adequate representation of it in intuition. A marathon race, a movie by Andy Warhol, a speech by Fidel Castro, even a passage from the *Critique of Pure Reason*, might do the trick. Thus Kant is not left with a very convincing explanation of the data with which his theory of the sublime began—the awe-inspiring pleasure in experiencing certain aspects of *nature.* In brief, Kant's dismissal of the relevance of specific qualities of natural objects that occasion the feeling of the sublime seems unjustified. We can understand, perhaps, why he thought it necessary to exclude them; like Burke, he wanted a strict dichotomy between the beautiful and the sublime. And if beauty is based on an object's spatial form or temporal composition, that leaves little else about the *object* that could form the basis of a universal judgment on the sublime. Thus Kant resorts to the apparent *formlessness* of certain objects to explain the sublime, and thereby the object's specific properties cease to be efficacious for the experience of the sublime. But such a view is inconsistent with Kant's own examples of the natural sublime. However great, the waterfall is not infinite in magnitude or power and need not even appear so to occasion the experience of the sublime. It seems plausible to suggest that relative greatness is sufficient, but that is definitely not Kant's view; for him, the sublime is that which is *absolutely great,* that which is *great beyond all comparison* (§25, p. 248). Kant's point of view, fortified by Burke's empirical analysis, does take hold, however. The literature of the natural sublime in the nineteenth century abounds with references to what appears to be infinite and to lack definite boundaries. A typical example is to be found in Horatio Parson's *Book of Niagara Falls,* a popular nineteenth-century American tourist guide that clearly shows the influence of Burke as well as Kant:

> The mind, filled with amazement, recoils at the spectacle, and loses for a moment its equilibrium. The trembling of the earth, the mighty rush and conflict and deafening roar of the water, the clouds of mist sparkling with rainbows, produce an effect upon the beholder, often quite overpowering, and it is only after the scene has become somewhat familiar to the eye, the ear, and the imagination, that its real grandeur and sublimity is properly realized and felt. . . . from the end of the bridge, the effect of the Falls upon the beholder is most awfully sublime and utterly indescribable. The sublime, arising from obscurity, is here experienced in its greatest force. The eye, unable to discover the bottom of the Falls, or even to penetrate the mist that seems to hang as a veil over the amazing and terrific scene, gives place to the imagination, and the mind is instinctively elevated and filled with majestic dread.[22]

Other examples are easily found. The sublime was an important element in the nineteenth-century experience of nature. It would be worthwhile to inquire into the extent this kind of experience is still a component of our appreciation of nature. The present point, how-

[22] John Conron, ed., *The American Landscape* (New York: Oxford University Press, 1974), pp. 174–75.

ever, is that, whatever its limitations, Kant's reading of the natural sublime was not an aberration from the mainstream bent to fit his own purposes in the development of the critical philosophy. Kant was on target, both in his identification of the sublime as an important component of the aesthetics of the time and in his analysis of it as making reference to ideas of the supersensible.

IV

How did the Analytic of the Sublime get into the *Critique of Judgment*? Was it part of Kant's original conception of the problem to be addressed in that work? The answer is simple: Not at all! On the contrary, the late incorporation of the treatment of the sublime into the text of the third *Critique* indicates an important shift in Kant's own thinking as to what the *Critique of Judgment* accomplishes.

What is known about the *composition* of the section of the third *Critique* titled the Analytic of the Sublime? We have good reason to believe that Kant had not begun to write the third *Critique* in any substantial way before the end of September 1787, for he says in a letter to L. H. Jakob on September 11 (?), 1787:

> My *Critique of Practical Reason* is at [the printer's] now. . . . I shall now turn at once to the "Critique of Taste," with which I shall have finished my critical work, so that I can proceed to the dogmatic part. I think it will appear before Easter.[23]

Clearly Kant did not envisage the third *Critique* to be anything like the 482-page work it turned out to be. In his famous letter to K. L. Reinhold on December 28 and 31 of that year (1787), he says he is "now at work on the critique of taste" and hopes "to have a manuscript on this completed though not in print by Easter [of 1788]; it will be entitled 'Critique of Taste.'" In this letter Kant also indicates that he believes he has "discovered a kind of a priori principle . . . [for] the faculty of feeling pleasure and displeasure," but that this part of philosophy, which he now refers to as "teleology," is, in his own words, "to be sure, the least rich in a priori principles."[24] On January 6, 1788, Kant's publisher, J. F. Hartknoch, wrote asking about a "Critique of Beautiful Taste" (*Kritik des schönen Geschmacks*); there is no record of

[23] *Kants gesammelte Schriften,* Akademie edition, vol. X, p. 471; translation from A. Zweig, *Kant: Philosophical Correspondence, 1759–99* (Chicago: University of Chicago Press, 1967), p. 125.

[24] Ibid., p. 488; Zweig, pp. 127–28.

Kant's reply.[25] Then on March 7, 1788, Kant writes to Reinhold that he hopes to have his "Critique of Taste" ready for the St. Michael's book exhibition, which would have been on September 29, 1788.[26] But a little over a year later (May 12, 1789) Kant writes again to Reinhold and mentions that his *Critique of Judgment,* "(a part of which is the 'Critique of Taste')" should appear at the *next* Michaelmas (= September 29, 1789).[27] Then on May 26, 1789, Kant writes to Marcus Herz:

> I am still burdened with the extensive work of completing my plan (partly producing the last part of the critique, namely, that of judgment [*Urteilskraft*], which should appear soon . . .).[28]

In summary, the evidence from the correspondence indicates that the Critique of Teleological Judgment and the Analytic of the Sublime were not begun, and perhaps not even conceived, before March of 1788 and that the original project, the "Critique of Taste," was almost certainly complete at this time. This "Critique of Taste" presumably consisted of the Analytic of the Beautiful, the Deduction (of judgments of taste) at least through §40, and the Dialectic. It seems reasonable to speculate that the a priori principle Kant reported having discovered (in December of 1787) for the "faculty of feeling pleasure and displeasure" only later became, in his mind, the a priori principle for the faculty of judgment *in general* and that *this* shift, marked by the change in the title of the work to the *Critique of Judgment* (*Kritik der Urteilskraft*), necessitated the extensive additional time required for its completion.

A detailed analysis of the text itself is essential in questions of this nature. Does the text support the above speculations? Tonelli convincingly documents the fact that the Analytic of the Sublime was relatively late in order of composition, clearly after the Analytic of the Beautiful, the Deduction (excluding §30), and the Dialectic.[29] He also argues that the Analytic of the Sublime must have been written even after the first Introduction, since the scheme given there for the critique of aesthetic judgments on the sublime was not in fact followed. This scheme promised not only a separate Deduction of the Sublime,

[25] *Kants gesammelte Schriften,* Akademie edition, vol. X, p. 491; see G. Tonelli, "La formazione del testo della *Kritik der Urteilskraft,*" *Revue Internationale de Philosophie* 8 (1954), p. 428.

[26] Ibid., p. 505; see Tonelli, ibid.

[27] *Kants gesammelte Schriften,* Akademie edition, vol. XI, p. 39; Zweig, p. 151.

[28] Ibid., p. 49; Zweig, p. 151.

[29] Tonelli, "La formazione del testo della *Kritik der Urteilskraft,*" p. 443.

but also a Dialectic of the Sublime. Neither materialized. In fact, if the scheme of the first Introduction had been followed, the Analytic of the Sublime would appear *after* the Dialectic (concerning judgments of beauty or taste). Although it is impossible to determine conclusively what happened to change Kant's plans, speculations are not altogether fruitless. Tonelli makes two intriguing suggestions. Perhaps Kant's belief in the lack of purposive structure in the *object* we call sublime cast doubt on the structural parallelism between the beautiful and the sublime and on the possibility of a deduction for the latter. The last paragraph of the introductory section to the Analytic of the Sublime (§23) seems to support this suggestion: Kant declares that the concept of the sublime is not nearly so important or rich in consequences as the concept of the beautiful, since it requires no external ground; and he then remarks that the theory of the sublime is a mere appendix or appendage (*Anhang*) to that of the beautiful. Second, Kant may have encountered difficulties in actually working out a separate deduction for the sublime. This is rendered plausible by the fact that even in the Analytic of the Sublime itself, *as published,* Kant promises a separate deduction for the sublime (§25, p. 250), but he never supplies it. He later argues that it is unnecessary (§30).

Further evidence for the lateness of the composition of the Analytic of the Sublime is uncovered by studying those parts of the final text believed to be earliest in composition: the Analytic of the Beautiful, the Deduction, and the Dialectic. In these sections Kant consistently describes his project only in terms of a "Critique of Taste," never as a "Critique of Judgment" or a "Critique of Aesthetic Judgment." And he never claims that judgments of taste include judgments on the sublime; in fact he contrasts these two types of judgments.

Other considerations also raise doubts as to whether Kant originally intended to include the sublime at all in the third *Critique.* In the Analytic of the Beautiful, which is universally accepted as the earliest segment of the text, there is not so much as a single allusion to the sublime. In the Deduction, discounting the transitional §30 which is most likely a later addition, there are only four references to the sublime. The first occurs in §39 (p. 292), where pleasure in the sublime is characterized, in contrast with the pleasure in the beautiful, as a pleasure of "rationalizing contemplation" (*vernunftelnden Kontemplation*). Tonelli rightly observes, following Michel Souriau, that this view of the sublime is not the same as that found in the Analytic of the Sublime, in which the feeling of the sublime is described as one of *movement* as opposed to the *restful* contemplation of the mind in the case of the beautiful (§§24, 27; pp. 247, 258). The second, third, and fourth occurrences of "sublime" in the Deduction are also out of keeping with the analysis of the sublime in the Analytic. In §49 (pp. 197, 197n.) Kant gives two examples—one a poetic description and the other the inscription of the Temple of Isis—both of which he says are sublime or occasion sublime thoughts. And in §52 (p. 325) Kant allows for the combination of the presentation of the sublime with beauty in a tragedy in verse, in a didactic poem, or in an oratorio, and states that in this combination fine art is more *artistic,* even if not more beautiful. But in the Analytic of the Sublime Kant suggests that the sublime is not properly presented in products of art at all (§26, p. 252).

In the Dialectic, as in the Analytic of the Beautiful, no reference can be found to the sublime, either direct or indirect. This is quite surprising, since a discussion of it would have tied directly into two major topics treated therein: the concept of the supersensible and, even more clearly, the question of the idealism versus realism of the aesthetic purposiveness of nature (§58). But in these sections Kant never mentions the purposiveness in aspects of nature occasioning the feeling of the sublime, even though his analysis of the sublime depends on this relationship. So Tonelli may be right in suggesting that the decision to include a discussion of the sublime probably occurred to Kant very late.

V

However late the actual writing of the Analytic of the Sublime, it would be misleading to conclude, as some critics have suggested, that Kant's treatment of the sublime in the *Critique of Judgment* is simply an afterthought. It more likely represents a shift in focus within the third *Critique* itself, first noticeable in those sections of the Dialectic which express a concern with possible purposive relationships between nature and our faculties. That this constitutes a modification of Kant's original project, the so-called Critique of Taste, is supported not only by the changes in terminology,[30] but more importantly by the fact that these considerations do not obviously relate to the major question of the old Critique of Taste: that is, the question of whether our judgments of taste can have a foundation that legitimizes their claim to universality and necessity, which Kant interprets as equivalent to the question of whether the pleasure in the beautiful is based on that which can be presupposed in everyone *as required for possible cognition*

[30] Extensively documented by Tonelli, ibid.

in general.[31] The question in the Critique of Taste is whether there is a common operation of the faculties—necessary for cognition in general—on which a particular subclass of pleasure could be based such that a common basis for aesthetic response is possible. Kant believed this to be sufficient to justify the *claim* to universality on the part of judgments of taste. The judgment of taste, upon analysis, comes to this: If the pleasure I experience in viewing this object is a pleasure in its *beauty,* it must be based on a harmonious accord of my faculties, which accord I can reasonably assume you also would have if you were to view this object in the way I view it (without any interest, etc.); on this assumption I legitimately claim the related pleasure to be a universal pleasure and my judgment of taste to be universally valid.

Issues about the claims of taste are no longer the major issue in the parts of the third *Critique* of later composition, in which the inquiry shifts to *teleology.* In the Analytic of the Sublime, in both introductions, and in parts of the Dialectic, Kant's concern becomes one of explaining what purposes aesthetic responses serve, or, to put it differently, what human interests are served in responding to nature through *feeling,* or judging it merely on the basis of feeling. Trying to explain why we demand of others an interest in the beautiful and the sublime in nature and find them wanting if they *fail* to respond to natural beauty or sublimity involves Kant in various attempts to link aesthetics and morality. In addition, it raises questions concerning the nature of the subjective purposiveness in the experience of the beautiful and the sublime. Both of these concerns nominally appear in the old Critique of Taste, but the emphasis changes significantly. Although the notion of subjective purposiveness is the topic of the Third Moment of the Analytic of the Beautiful and is later claimed to be a common feature of judgments on the sublime and judgments of taste (§24, p. 247), a close analysis reveals that Kant is talking about different things in these two sections of the text. In the Analytic of the Beautiful, the formal subjective purposiveness is nothing more than the ability (or disposition) of an object through its formal properties to produce a certain pleasurable experience in us (without its serving practical or scientific interests, or swaying us by its sensuous charm or emotional appeal). More precisely, the object produces a harmony of the cognitive faculties that causes the pleasure we identify with the experience of beauty. This purposiveness in the object is nonetheless *wholly subjective,* Kant claims, in the sense that it relates to a pleasurable feeling—a state of the judging subject—and cannot be used for any

[31] Cf. §§9, 21, 35, 38, 39; pp. 219, 238, 287, 290, 292–93.

knowledge whatsoever. In the Analytic of the Beautiful (and throughout the Deduction until the last paragraph of §40), there is *no further end* suggested for this pleasurable experience, no further purposiveness beyond the maintenance and the sharing of that pleasurable state. Kant's aesthetic theory in these parts of the text is blatantly hedonistic, albeit a universal rather than an egoistic or relativistic hedonism. Pleasure and the sharing of a pleasure are the only ends hypothesized for our judgments of beauty. Kant believes he has shown that the pleasure involved is intersubjective, that in principle it can be shared by all disinterested subjects, but nothing other than this sharing is suggested as the end of aesthetic activity.

The subjective purposiveness in the case of the sublime, however, from the very outset, is significantly different. The experiential component is still feeling, namely, a displeasure due to the conflict between imagination and reason, but this produces a pleasure (and hence, for Kant, is purposive). More significantly, this pleasure or even the sharing of the pleasure is not the end point. It is not the pleasure per se but pleasure that is quasi-cognitive or propositional in character; it is a pleasure due to "a feeling that we possess pure self-subsistent or self-sufficient reason" (§27, p. 258), a pleasure that is "subjectively purposive for the reason as a source of ideas" (§28, p. 261). In short, the sublime is purposive in relation to *further* mental activity: reasoning about ideas. (Kant should also claim, though for complex and, in my view, mistaken reasons he fails to do so, that great and powerful natural objects that occasion the feeling of the sublime are themselves purposive for us in this way.)

Once this shift is made in the application of purposiveness, it is a simple move to apply the concept of purposiveness at this level to the case of the beautiful. And that, I suggest, is what Kant does in the Dialectic (§§55–59), in his lengthy discussion of genius and the arts (§§40, 44–54), and clearly in both introductions. Here, in sections which are all relatively late in composition, artists and the arts are analyzed and evaluated not in terms of the pleasure they provide or even in terms of the beautiful, but rather in terms of how they can further culture and the mental powers (particularly reason in its attention to ideas).

In addition, in these later sections the pleasure in the beautiful *itself* becomes purposive by supporting the a priori *principle of judgment*—the principle that nature always manifests itself to us in ways conducive to our judging it and to organizing our judgments into a coherent and unified system of knowledge. The pleasure in the beautiful comes to be analyzed as based on *feeling* that nature conforms to our powers of cognition, and this purposiveness of nature becomes for Kant a regulative principle "indispensable for the needs of our understanding"; Kant claims that "it is only insofar as that holds that we can make any progress with the use of our understanding in experience or gain knowledge" (Intro. IV, p. 186). The pleasure we take in natural beauty thus becomes purposive for our cognitive faculties because it instantiates the principle of judgment in non-question-begging contexts. Nature exhibits the beauty of natural forms, independently of our will, and these forms are suitable to our powers of cognition *in general,* i.e., independently of any interest on our part or attempt to gain knowledge. The use of this regulative principle of judgment for the greater goals of a coherent and systematic unity of knowledge is thus furthered. This application of purposiveness in the case of natural beauty brings with it an interest in the *existence* of beautiful forms in nature, as manifestations of the principle of judgment. Kant claims, wrongly I think, that no such concern is present in the case of the sublime, since the sublime is only a state of mind. But Kant cannot have it both ways. Either sublime natural objects only fortuitously trigger the experience of the sublime, in which case almost anything might do equally as well (e.g., a long, drawn-out philosophical essay). But if so, Kant has not provided a very convincing explanation of the special feeling we have towards these aspects of *nature.* Or else the properties of natural objects which occasion the experience of the sublime actually make a difference, or it makes a difference that they are *natural* objects, in which case the issue is the same as it is for the beautiful in nature.

But leaving aside these and other internal criticisms, we find Kant's aesthetic theory shifting during the period of its composition from a concern with the intersubjective *validity* of aesthetic judgments to a concern with whether the response to the beautiful and sublime in nature and in art is a significant human activity and, if so, what this significance consists in. Part of the continued fascination with Kant's aesthetic theory lies in unraveling and assessing his contributions to these enduring questions. If I am correct in my hypothesis as to the change in direction in Kant's aesthetics, we are brought back to Kant's commitment to the Aristotelian doctrine that nothing natural is in vain. Thus, if the experience of the sublime is a natural occurrence, as Kant and the eighteenth century in general believed, what better Kantian explanation is in the offing than that it serves to further our own destiny—our ability to invoke reason and legislate for our wills so as to realize a kingdom of ends, a system of rational legislating beings? Kant's treatment of the sublime thus becomes an integral part of his avowed discovery of a bridge between nature and freedom, and it reaffirms Kant's basic commitment to our having a faculty which we can direct toward "beauty considered as a realm of ends to be made actual by our actions in it."[32]

Kant clearly was aware of these metaphysical themes implicit in his theories of natural and artistic beauty and the natural sublime. In §83 of the "Critique of Teleological Judgment" he discusses what he refers to as the "ultimate purpose" of nature, and of the arts and sciences, that of making us "feel an aptitude for higher purposes which lies hidden [*verborgen*] in us" (§83, p. 434). Let me conclude by quoting a telling footnote to this passage, in which the then sixty-five-year-old Kant reveals some of his deepest philosophical convictions:

> The value of life for us, if it is measured by *what we enjoy* (by the natural purpose of the sum of all our inclinations, i.e., by happiness) is easy to decide. It sinks below zero, for who would be willing to enter upon life anew under the same conditions? Who would do so even according to a new, self-chosen plan (yet in conformity with the course of nature), if it were merely directed to enjoyment? We have shown above [that] what value life has . . . consists in *what we do* (not merely what we enjoy), in which however we are always but means toward an undetermined final purpose. There remains then nothing but the value which we ourselves give our life, through what we not only do but do purposively so independently of nature that the existence of nature itself can only be a purpose under this condition.

University of Wisconsin, Madison

[32] Lewis White Beck, *A Commentary on Kant's Critique of Practical Reason* (Chicago: University of Chicago Press, 1960), p. 162.

10 Aesthetic Form and Sensory Content in the *Critique of Judgment:* Can Kant's "Critique of Aesthetic Judgment" Provide a Philosophical Basis for Modern Formalism?

MARY J. GREGOR

One does not go far in contemporary aesthetics without encountering the theorizing formalist critics of the nineteenth and twentieth centuries: Eduard Hanslick in music and Clive Bell and Roger Fry in the visual arts. Among those who are doing constructive work in aesthetics, the formalist principle is generally taken to be a necessary, though perhaps not the sufficient, condition of aesthetic value. Even those who regard traditional aesthetics as a mistake may recommend that fruitless talk about "beauty" be replaced by investigations into the principles of the various art forms, citing Bell's *Art* and Hanslick's *The Beautiful in Music* as examples.

However, a careful reading of Hanslick and Bell shows that, in trying to secure the foundations for their critical principles, they come to grief on the central problem of traditional aesthetics. So Hanslick insists that beauty is objective, a property that music has quite independently of the subject's response: it consists in musical "logic" or "rationality," which is based on laws of nature, essentially the law of harmonic progression which is determined by the physical conditions governing the production of a musical tone. Yet he admits that this rationality yields only "negative" beauty, without which music is "arbitrary," "capricious," and "ugly." Since his work is largely a polemic against Wagner, whom he charges with having violated the logic of music, he does not seem fully aware that he has not accounted for the "positive" beauty that distinguishes a Mozart symphony from a student's exercise in harmony. Musical beauty itself, he admits, has no "definite ideal," and any discussion of it becomes an account of "aesthetic feeling"—a curious procedure if beauty is independent of the subject's response.

Bell, on the other hand, declares that any system of aesthetics that pretends to be based on some objective truth is so palpably absurd as not to be worth discussing. Beauty, or "significant form," comes into being only when certain combinations of lines and colors stir the viewer's "aesthetic emotion," and aesthetic judgments are reports that the viewer has experienced this peculiar feeling. Where Bell founders is in his attempt to secure some "general validity" for aesthetic judgments. He does not want to say that they are merely autobiographical reports, and unlike Fry he seems unwilling to let empirical psychologists determine whether "sensitive people" get this peculiar emotion from combinations of lines and colors. But he is at a loss for any alternative.

The widespread appeal of the formalist principle lies in its capacity to provide some public basis for aesthetic value judgments. Whatever the individual's private associations may be, we can apparently come together in our apprehension of the object's form. But however useful the formalist principle may be, the relation between form and aesthetic value requires the sort of philosophical investigation it too seldom receives. Hanslick, Bell, and Fry were not philosophers but critics trying to enunciate and justify the principle underlying their criticism. In so doing, they encountered problems they were not equipped to deal with. In the ongoing debate they started, the participants are too often content to appeal, directly or indirectly, to introspective data. In reply, those who are unwilling to have aesthetics turned into a branch of psychology insist on the objectivity of beauty, despite our inability to specify the property that would differentiate the beautiful from the merely correct. Unless we are willing to accept the formalist principle on purely pragmatic grounds, we are apparently left with the traditional dilemma: If "this is beautiful" is a cognitive judgment, why cannot we specify the characteristics contained in the concept "beauty" and settle aesthetic disputes as we do scientific disputes? If it is not a cognitive judgment—if the term "beautiful" does not express a concept but rather the subject's feeling of pleasure—how can we reasonably expect others to agree with our judgment?

Since the aesthetic formalism of Kant's *Critique of Judgment*[1] grew

[1]More precisely, of "The Analytic of the Beautiful," which deals with judgments which do not subsume the manifold under an empirical concept. These are to be distinguished from judgments of dependent beauty, in which we do apply empirical concepts. From one point of view, judgments of free beauty are of primary importance. As containing no predicate, they are neither cognitive nor practical; as involving a claim to intersubjective validity, they require a critique. From another point of view, however, they may turn out to be less important than judgments of dependent beauty. In arguing that Kant's epistemology could provide a basis for modern formalism, I do not mean to suggest that, in aesthetics, Kant is a formalist in the sense of Hanslick or Bell.

out of the eighteenth-century dialogue concerning the objectivity or subjectivity of beauty, it is worth inquiring whether he has something relevant to say in the contemporary debate as to whether beauty is a matter of cognition or of feeling, and—more specifically—whether his account of free judgments of beauty provides a sorely needed philosophical basis for the theories popularized by Hanslick and Bell. The most obvious obstacle to relating Kant's aesthetic theory to contemporary work in the field is the intimate connection of his aesthetics with his theory of knowledge. But any properly philosophical aesthetic theory presupposes epistemological commitments, and it can only be to the advantage of aesthetics to make these explicit.

Precisely because of the relation between the first and the third *Critiques*, it is considered problematic whether Kant can provide a philosophical basis for modern formalism, on the ground that his epistemological commitments require him to limit the aesthetically relevant characteristics of objects to their spatiotemporal relations. The basic contention of the third *Critique,* so the argument runs, is that in judging an object "beautiful" we are making a claim that our pleasure in the object be shared by everyone who appraises it according to the principle of reflective judgment. We must therefore be able to assume that the representation on which we are reflecting can be shared by everyone: the communicability of the pleasure presupposes the communicability of the representation. But on the level of perception it is only spatiotemporal relations that are a priori and therefore communicable: sensations are variable, dependent on the state of the sense organs. Hence the form, reflection on which issues in a pure judgment of taste, is limited to spatial and temporal relations within the object—the organization of shapes in painting and, in music, the temporal pattern of sounds.

This "restrictive formalism" is, of course, quite inconsistent with Hanslick's "musical beauty" and Bell's "significant form." Nor does the view that color is aesthetically irrelevant in painting or melody and harmony in music have anything to recommend it. Before attributing such a view to Kant, however, we should ask whether he does regard sensations as incommunicable in such a way as to lead to a restrictive formalism. My thesis is that there was only a brief period in Kant's philosophical development during which he was logically compelled to exclude sensation from the beautiful—the period from 1769 when he broke with the rationalist tradition regarding sensibility to whenever it was during the "silent decade" that he worked out the transcendental deduction. If Kant had, at the time of his *Inaugural Dissertation,* seen his way clear to a philosophical treatment of beauty, he would have produced a restrictive formalism. But it was not until 1787 that he saw the possibility of an a priori principle—teleology—for an irreducible third faculty of feeling, and by that time his view of sensation had undergone a significant change. By 1790 he was not committed to any restrictions on aesthetic form that the modern formalists would not agree to, and in the *Critique of Judgment* he, in effect, turns the question of form in music and painting over to the "empirical investigations" of Hanslick and Bell.

Although Kant published nothing of lasting importance in aesthetics before 1790, his *Nachlass* show that he reflected a good deal on the problem of beauty.[2] It was not, for him, a mere corollary to metaphysics and theory of knowledge but a subject of interest in its own right. It was, however, a problem that could not be solved in isolation, and each major step toward the third *Critique* followed upon a major development in his theory of knowledge. Thus, in his earliest reflections, Kant repeats the rationalist view that beauty is perfection as known by the lower or sensitive cognitive power, i.e., perfection conceived clearly but indistinctly. Perfection is unity in variety, the ordering of the manifold in a thing to a common purpose. To know perfection by the senses is to represent the thing as a number of clear sensations united into a particular. But a clear image is a confused or indistinct idea, since on this level of thought we cannot enumerate the notes or marks that distinguish this sort of thing from others. Once we begin to consider separately the characteristics of the thing, we have begun the process of logical analysis or definition by which we represent perfection through the higher or rational cognitive power. At this stage of Kant's thought, judgments of taste are cognitive judgments, but the discipline that investigates them cannot be a science properly speaking, since science operates with distinct concepts, and to make concepts distinct is to rise above the level of clear but confused ideas that differentiates aesthetic from rational perfection. As long as Kant remained in the rationalist tradition, he had no problem about including sensations in the beautiful. To know the beautiful is to

[2] In the approximate dating of the *Nachlass,* I rely on Adickes's method, as explained in his introduction to volume XIV of the Akademie edition and defended in volume XVII. Quotations from the *Critique of Pure Reason* and the *Critique of Judgment* are taken, with occasional modifications, from the translations by Norman Kemp Smith and James Meredith, respectively.

In his excellent study *Die Entwicklung des Begriffs des Schoenen bei Kant* (Bonn: H. Bouvier, 1970), Hans-Georg Juchem explores Kant's relations with his German predecessors and contemporaries. He does not, however, deal in a positive way with the development of Kant's view of sensation.

apprehend clear sensations as coordinated into a whole (Ak. XV #403; XVI #1748, #1766, #1784).

But the "great light" of 1769, which revealed the radical difference between sensibility and thought, also revealed that beauty is not perfection thought indistinctly. Beauty lies on the side of the particular, apprehended by sensibility, and the difference between sensibility and intellect is not a logical one, in terms of distinctness of representations, but a difference in origin and content. The representations of sensibility are not thoughts, concepts, cognitions, and beauty is a matter not of knowledge but of feeling (which itself is not a confused representation). It is no longer a question of feeling that follows upon sensitive knowledge of perfection. It is rather that, in judging something beautiful, we are reporting the pleasure we take in a representation that is not itself knowledge. Yet we intend our judgments to have more than "private validity": we regard the pleasure we feel as valid for others (Ak. XV #640; XVI #1780). Hence we must be appraising something that has universal validity. What the rationalists called knowledge by the lower cognitive power has become empirical intuition and, not surprisingly, Kant turns to that aspect of intuition which, though "subjective," is universally valid—its spatiotemporal form. Typical of the reflections from this period is the following:

> . . . beauty is not something that can be known, but is only felt. What pleases us in the object, and what we regard as a property of it, must consist in what is valid for everyone. Now relations of space and time are valid for everyone, whatever sensations he may also have. Hence in all appearances the form is universally valid, and this form is also known according to common rules of coordination. Consequently, what is in accord with the rule of coordination in space and time necessarily pleases everyone and is beautiful. (Ak. XV #672)

And again:

> Beauty has a subjective principle, namely, conformity with the laws of intuitive knowledge; but this does not interfere with the universal validity for men of our judgments about beauty, if the intuitions [*Erkenntnisse*] are one and the same. (Ak. XV #625; cf. also #627)

A number of texts which contrast the universal validity of our pleasure in the form of intuition with the merely private validity of our pleasure in its matter, sensation, base this difference on the assumption that the mind is active in coordinating sensations but merely passive in receiving them. The pleasure we get from sensation has only private validity because in sensation "the mind is regarded as merely passive, in so far as it is affected by the presence of a thing"; taste, pleasure that we regard as valid for everyone, can be had only from form, which "arises from the laws of the activity of the subject (especially of the lower cognitive [power], which coordinates)" (Ak. XVI #1789); "their form is given by the proper activity of the soul" (Ak. XV #619). Again, "In so far as our sense representations have a determinate form, they require an ordering together of sensations, not a mere taking together. This ordering together is a combination through coordination," on the basis of space and time, and gives the form or *Gestalt* (Ak. XV #683).

This view of sensation clearly stems from the *Dissertation,* in which the few texts that deal with sensation stress the causality of the object and the independence of sensations from any activity of the mind. "Sensa" arise from the presence of objects which "strike the senses": they are "impressions from the object affecting the senses" (Handyside translation, p. 45) and "exciting this act of the mind" (i.e., the production of intuitions) (ibid., p. 66). From this it follows that sensation is doubly subjective, so to speak. Space and time are subjective in the sense that they are forms under which objects appear to our senses, but they are universally valid, "a certain law inborn in the mind for co-ordinating" sensa into "some whole of representation." Sensation, on the other hand, "depends for its quality upon the nature of the subject, so far as it is modifiable by that object" (ibid., p. 45).

What is notable here is Kant's assumption that, while intuition is passive (i.e., it receives impressions under the conditions of space and time) (ibid., p. 50), the mind is active "in co-ordinating its sensa according to unchanging laws" (ibid., p. 66). What is connate in our concepts of space and time is only "the law of the mind, according to which it combines in a fixed manner [i.e., according to the principles of space known from geometry] the sensa produced in it by the presence of the object" (ibid., p. 66). In fact, Kant has no way of accounting for the formation of these "wholes of representation." This is a problem that he cannot resolve until he has the categories to relate sensibility and thought and produce these "wholes" of empirical intuition. In the *Dissertation* he has, on the one hand, the real use of intellect, in which concepts and relations are given "through the very nature of the intellect" and through which we know noumena or things in themselves (ibid., p. 47). On the other hand, he has the logical use of intellect in empirical knowledge. Mere intuition is not knowledge: to have experience as distinguished from appearance we must reflect on and compare a number of appearances and subordinate them to common concepts and general laws (ibid., pp. 45–46). This activity, however, presupposes that "wholes of representation" are available for it to work on. And while we know that this combination of sensa will conform to the nature of space and time, we have no account of the mental activity itself. What we have in the *Dissertation* is sensibility and reason: what is lacking is understanding. We have no categories, least of all any mathematical categories.

In fact, Kant does not have at this time the equipment for either a restrictive or a non-restrictive formalism in aesthetics. The reflections quoted above reveal an unresolved tension in his thought. On the one hand, he is looking for the source of a communicable pleasure in something that is not knowledge; on the other hand, he seeks it in the "laws of intuitive knowledge." To validate the sort of claim we make in pure judgments of taste, Kant must connect beauty with a priori principles of cognition, hence with laws of mental activity. As he puts it in the third *Critique:* "only knowledge, or what pertains to it, is communicable" (Ak. V, 217). Until he has settled the relation of sensibility and intellect, of intuition and intuitive knowledge, the fact that space and time are a priori will not solve his problem; and the process of clarifying this relation changes his view of sensation. Even so, he has still to explain the communicability of pleasure in a representation that is not knowledge. In the meantime he continues to worry about the problem, and one of his attempts to solve it, though unsuccessful, is singularly instructive.

The fact that the objects we call beautiful are manifolds of sensa coordinated in space and time is, he recognizes, inadequate to account for our pure judgments of taste, since any empirical object fulfills these conditions. Something more is required to produce the pleasure on which our judgment is based, and in his search for this additional factor Kant brings together two lines of thought he has been pursuing. First, that while a "mere" sensation is not beautiful, "compared sensations"—sensations as differentiated, harmonized and contrasted—belong to the form that is beautiful (Ak. XV #624, #625, #653, #639);[3] the play of sensations or the form or *Gestalt* that pleases universally includes "not merely the form of the object according to relations of space and time in the appearance, but also the matter, i.e., sensation (color)" (Ak. XV #638). Second, that form in this extended sense produces universally valid pleasure by indirectly facilitating the

[3]Caution must be used in these texts. Kant is not yet sure whether there is a distinction between sensation and feeling, and, if so, precisely what this distinction is. Hence *Empfindung* tends to be used rather indiscriminately. Cf. Ak. XV ##207, 605, 606, 619, 630, 631. In XVI #1831, "Beauty is the harmony of sensations," he may well be talking about "feeling." Moreover, it is not always clear whether "the play of sensations" is to be distinguished from or identified with the "form" or *Gestalt*. Cf. XV ## 638, 655.

activity of the intellect. The contrast and consonance of sensations, as facilitating the distinction of the manifold, is an element in "everything estimated by taste," along with relations or proportions (Ak. XV #625). The former make it readily intuitable; the latter, readily intelligible (*begreiflich*). "That the form of the object facilitates the activity of understanding pertains to enjoyment and is subjective; but it is objective that this form is universally valid" (Ak. XV #630).

That the feeling expressed in the pure judgment of taste is produced by the free play of imagination in harmony with the lawfulness of understanding looms large in the third *Critique:* it is even said that the pleasure is a feeling of the mutual "quickening" of the cognitive powers (Ak. V, 219, 222, 238, 244). At the time of the *Dissertation,* however, Kant's attempt to solve his problem along these lines would have put him back in the rationalist camp. He could not, like the rationalists, appeal to the activity of discriminating and clarifying sensations: this meant taking notice of them, and the activity of paying attention to them involved thought or apperception, which in turn made sensations confused thoughts or concepts. It would make the beautiful a clear but indistinct concept, pleasing because it is itself sensitive knowledge and the material for rational knowledge.

> The question is, whether the play of sensations or the form and *Gestalt* of intuitions is immediately pleasing or only pleases in so far as it provides understanding with intelligibility [*Begreiflichkeit*] and facility in the taking up together of a great manifold, and also distinctness [*Deutlichkeit*] in the whole representation. (Ak. XV #638)

The attempt failed because it would involve the absurdity of "sense representing its objects by concepts" (Ak. V, 228) and, in the process, make the beautiful instrumentally rather than immediately pleasing.

What Kant needs, ultimately, is the principle of reflective judgment to account for immediate pleasure in what is not itself cognition.[4] More urgently, however, he needs to clarify the relation between empirical intuition and thought, before he can decide what can be admitted into the representation "this" in the judgment "this is beautiful." To space and time as conditions of the beautiful he adds conformity with the "rules of reflection" (Ak. XV #648). But, he concludes, the sources of pleasure are merely empirical. We can de-

[4] As Kant points out in the "Critique of Aesthetic Judgment," "The attainment of every aim is accompanied by pleasure" (Ak. V, 187, 242). But if reflection on the form of the object does not yield knowledge, he cannot account for our pleasure in reflection in terms of knowledge attained.

scribe the phenomenon of taste, but its proof is a posteriori (Ak. XV #622, #623).

Until we reach the Transcendental Analytic, the first *Critique* does not progress much beyond the *Dissertation,* as far as sensation is concerned. The Introduction asks, rhetorically, how our cognitive power could be awakened to act unless objects affecting our senses not only aroused it but also "of themselves produced representations" (B 1), "the raw material of sensible impressions" (A 1). In the Transcendental Aesthetic we hear a good deal about space and time as pure intuitions and as the forms of empirical intuition, but little about the matter of empirical intuition, "that in the appearance which corresponds to sensation."[5] What is conspicuous by its absence is reference to "the activity of the mind" in coordinating the manifold. The form of appearance is that which so determines the manifold that it allows of being ordered in certain relations (B 34), but nothing is said about the activity of ordering. Sensibility, receptivity, has been methodologically isolated from thought, and combination is the work of thought, activity, or spontaneity. The manifold, both pure and empirical, belongs to sensibility, but the synthesis of the manifold belongs to thought and takes place according to its principles.

What Kant does have to say about sensation, in the context of distinguishing the well-known subjectivity of sensations from the subjectivity of space and time, is not altogether consistent. On the one hand, sensations "do not of themselves yield knowledge of any object, least of all any *a priori* knowledge": they are not properties of things but only "changes in the subject, changes which may indeed be different for different men" (B 45). On the other hand, when he wants to distinguish appearance from illusion, we find sensations on a par with space and time to the extent that they are predicates which can be ascribed to the object itself in relation to our senses, though not to things in themselves (B 70n.). Strictly speaking, Kant should not be talking here about the reference of sensations to objects, since this is the function of thought. But after his revision of the Transcendental Deduction, he should have revised these passages, making it clear that in becoming aware of sense data which we cannot predicate of external objects, we get knowledge of ourselves, as objects of inner sense:[6] even illusions give us information, if not of external objects, then at

[5] A 20 = B 34. "The effect of an object upon the faculty of representation, so far as we are affected by it, is sensation."

[6] Cf. Lewis White Beck, "Did the Sage of Koenigsberg Have No Dreams?" in *Essays on Kant and Hume* (New Haven and London: Yale University Press, 1978), pp. 38–60.

least of our own mental state. The *Prolegomena*'s theory about judgments of perception which do not subsume sense data under the categories, together with Kant's insistence that the pure judgment of taste does not subsume under a concept, might suggest that the representation "this," in "this is beautiful," escapes the categories.[7] If this were so, Kant would be no better off after the first *Critique* than in the *Nachlass* from the period of the *Dissertation.*

Like the *Dissertation,* the provisional treatment of sensibility in the Transcendental Aesthetic no more warrants a restrictive than a non-restrictive aesthetic formalism. Since the question is that of the communicability of the representation "this" in judgments of taste, let us formulate the problem in terms of communicability—a legitimate procedure since "objects of experience" are by definition public. Kant holds that propositions are communicable to the extent that they contain an a priori and hence universally valid element. So far, we know only that space and time are a priori, not that there are a priori principles for combining the spatiotemporal manifold. Even were we to grant, however, that propositions of pure mathematics are communicable, it does not follow that empirical spatial relations are communicable. These are dependent in part on what is given to sensibility, and we need assurance that the procedure in constructing pure intuitions is the same as that in forming empirical intuitions. This assurance we get through the category of extensive magnitude, and only through it could we get even a restrictive type of formalism. As for a non-restrictive formalism, the category of intensive magnitude does not of itself provide for this, but it is the wedge that opens the possibility.

The difficulty arises that Kant says repeatedly that the pure judgment of taste is independent of concepts. That it does not subsume the manifold under an empirical concept is clear: the representation is only subjectively final, the purposiveness is without a purpose. The manifold which we unify in the "this" "permits of being understood and reduced to concepts, but in the aesthetic judgment it is not so

[7] Kant's failure to discuss in any detail the relation of his theory of knowledge to the representation on which we are reflecting has led at least one commentator to complain that Kant sometimes writes, in the third *Critique,* as if he had not read the *Critique of Pure Reason.* We must remember, however, that Kant's primary concern is with the communicability of pleasure: his discovery of an a priori principle for feeling was the breakthrough that released him from the impasse where he had been stuck from 1769 till 1787, and made a "Critique of Aesthetic Judgment" possible. But he does indicate that, were it not for the account he has given of the relation of our cognitive powers, men would be "unable to communicate their representations or even their knowledge." Ak. V, 290n. The basic condition of communicability is the same in both cases.

reduced" (Ak. V, 266). The "this" is, therefore, not a full-fledged "object of experience" in the sense of the first *Critique.* But if the gist of the Transcendental Deduction (at least in B) is that becoming aware of any representation as a manifold involves bringing it to the objective unity of apperception, and that the categories are ways in which we bring the manifold to this unity, then the reflective activity which produces the "this" must involve the categories. In reflecting on the form of the object we are relating elements—lines, tones—to each other and ultimately to the unity of the representation "this," which is clearly a product of human consciousness and involves the categories.

It is with the categories of quantity that we are primarily concerned. These categories do not ensure that our perceptions of empirical spatial relations and intensities of sensations will be the same: both are dependent to some extent on the state of our sense organs. What these categories do ensure is that statements about these relations will be communicable because there is a principle of a priori synthesis operative in perception. Because objects in space and degrees of sensations are measurable, I can distinguish how the object appears to me from how it is. Although in discussing mistakes in judgments of taste Kant is more concerned with confusion between contemplative pleasure on the one hand and "charm and emotion" on the other, the confusion of objective with subjective is not limited to feeling. Unless we can talk about perceiving the object correctly, we cannot make a claim on others' feelings about the object. The categories ensure not that our perceptions will be veridical, but rather that it is meaningful to distinguish between veridical and non-veridical perception.

The function of the category of extensive magnitude is, in part, to guarantee the communicability of our judgments about empirical spatial relations. Kant's argument here is that the conditions of perception guarantee that objects will be measurable or, to put it differently, that unless we could measure an object we could not intuit it. From the Transcendental Aesthetic we know that we cannot have empirical intuition except under conditions of space and time, and that any portion of the space and time occupied by the object is itself made up of spaces and times. Hence it is always possible to take some portion of space or time as a unit and apply it successively to the space and time occupied by the object. By reproducing in consciousness the portions already traversed as we add each new unit, we arrive at the mathematically determinant judgment that the object is, e.g., six feet long.

Given the orientation of the first *Critique,* Kant's concern is primarily with mathematically determinant judgments. But he is not saying that we cannot perceive an object without going through the measuring process. As long as the object is enclosed within points or limits we can apprehend it "aesthetically" or "by the eye" as an indeterminate quantum (B 456n.): indeed, in the case of empirical objects our apprehension of the unit of measurement is always "aesthetic"—otherwise we would be measuring *it* rather than taking it as the unit of measurement. Moreover, we can make "aesthetic estimates" of the relative size of objects.[8] This, I suggest, is what we are doing when we reflect on the form of an object with a view to the judgment of taste: we are, in part, estimating "by the eye" the relative magnitude of portions of the object. The object conducive to reflection on its form must be fairly complex in its internal structure. Simple geometrical figures are not objects of taste (Ak. V, 241–42), partly because there is not sufficient complexity in them to induce reflection on the form. If so, our apprehension of the beautiful is, in part, apprehension of the total object by discriminating and relating the parts of varying magnitude, on which its coherence depends. Since these internal relations are measur*able,* this aspect of the beautiful is communicable; and this is all that Kant should mean when he talks about "claiming the assent of every man."[9]

The category of intensive magnitude, which ensures the communicability of our statements about the intensity of sensations, seems more meager in its aesthetic implications: the relative loudness of tones in music and brightness of colors in a painting are aspects of aesthetic form, but certainly not the whole story. What is important here, however, is the principle established. In the Introduction Kant referred to sense impressions as the "raw material" of experience, which arouse the mind to the activity of synthesizing them into experience. One implication of the Transcendental Deduction is that the existence of this "raw material" is the result of an inference from what we are aware of: the sensations we are aware of are already a product of the mind's synthetic activity. What Kant is arguing in the Anticipations of Perception is that the intensity of sensation is communicable because it is measurable. In so far as we are aware of the content that

[8]Apart from the Axioms of Intuition in the first *Critique,* Kant's most important discussion of extensive magnitude occurs in the context of the mathematically sublime, Ak. V, 248ff. When he talks, there, about "aesthetic appraisals" of relative size, he has in mind comparing an object with others of the same kind; but an extension of the principle seems warranted. If shape or figure is a quality, it is one that is dependent on the relative magnitude of component parts.

[9]As Kant indicates in Ak. V, 191, the cognitive equivalent of a pure judgment of taste is a singular empirical judgment. For a discussion of the sense in which pure judgments of taste are "necessary," cf. Lewis White Beck, "On the Putative Apriority of Judgments of Taste," in op. cit.

fills a portion of space and time, this content has some internal complexity which is brought to unity by the activity of thought. Sensations have magnitude, though their magnitude is not determined by the successive addition of parts. It is rather one of degree or intensity, and hence can be represented as containing within itself all degrees between it and zero, which would be represented by empty space and time.

There are a great many difficulties here. An important one for our purposes is: what, precisely, is it that has intensive magnitude? We are told that it is "sensation, and the real that corresponds to it in the object" (A 167), and again that it is "the real that is an object of sensation" (B 207). What distinction is Kant drawing between "sensation" and "the real"? The distinction is, I think, that between sensation as a mental event and sensation as referred to external objects, between "green" as a modification of inner sense and as a property of grass (Ak. V, 189, 206).[10] Both, he indicates—"every sensation . . . and likewise every reality in appearance"—have degree (B 211); in the third *Critique* he seems to include feeling as well.[11] As in the case of extensive magnitudes, we can always estimate the degree "aesthetically," by comparing it with others. When it comes to the question of measuring, as distinguished from measurability, however, complications arise. To measure the intensity of a light or sound we apparently have to translate it into terms of extensive quantity,[12] and this seems to limit mathematically determinant judgments of intensive magnitude to sensations as properties of external objects. Moreover, in the case of feelings and of sensations as objects of inner sense, we cannot draw a distinction between how it appears to me and how it is. These complications, however, need not concern us here, since the "this" which we are reflecting on in taste is an object open to public inspection. The relevance of Kant's discussion of intensive magnitude to aesthetic form consists in four points. (1) There is in every sensation a "specific

[10] Although it is sometimes said that by *realitas phaenomenon* Kant means force, he clearly indicates that this is an application of the principle, which has no place in the *Critique* itself. A 171 = B 213.

[11] ". . .appraisal of things as great or small extends to everything, even to all their qualities. Thus we call even their beauty great or small," since anything presented in intuition is "in its entirety a phenomenon, and hence a quantum" (Ak. V, 249–50). However, Kant's position that we have some justification for attributing beauty (though not sublimity) to the object, as if it were a quality of the thing—although "apart from any reference to the subject's feeling" it is nothing—makes this text somewhat indecisive. Cf. Ak. V, 218, 245.

[12] This is pointed out by H. J. Paton in *Kant's Metaphysic of Experience* (London: Allen and Unwin, 1936), vol. II, p. 147 n. 3.

quality" which is strictly empirical, dependent on the state of the sense organ affected, and therefore incommunicable. (2) But sensations contain, besides, a manifold, an internal complexity, that permits of being ordered. (3) The manifold is such that it permits of measurement. Hence (4) to this extent, something about sensation is communicable. This, apparently, is all that can be said about sensation on the level of "conditions of possible experience." To the extent that sensation is measurable, it is communicable.

If we consider Kant's discussions of the aesthetic relevance of tone and color in the third *Critique*,[13] we find, I think, that their inconclusiveness stems largely from his hesitations as to whether anything about sensations, other than their intensity, is measurable. Every sensation has an incommunicable "specific quality" and a communicable degree of intensity. But should we draw a distinction between *Sinnesempfindungen,* such as those of smell (and presumably taste), in which the only complexity is that which yields degree, and sensations of vision and hearing, which contain a further mathematically determinable structure? A *Sinnesempfindung* is not merely a sensation, but the real in sensation as referred to cognition (Ak. V, 291), and in the context of the third *Critique* this takes on the added meaning of reference to an object *as existing,* hence producing the interested pleasure of sensuous gratification (ibid., 209). "It is not merely the object, but also its real existence that pleases." The contemplative pleasure of taste presupposes formal determinations to reflect upon (ibid., 324–25). Whether some sensations contain such formal determinations is a question for the physicist, the physiologist, and the psychologist.[14]

[13] The two extended discussions are to be found in Ak. V, 223ff. and 324–25.

[14] Kant's discussion, in the *Anthropologie,* of the distinction between the "more objective senses," which (as long as the sensation is moderate) inform us about the object, and the "more subjective senses" of taste and smell, by which we are aware primarily of the sense being affected, is of interest in this regard. In the case of the more subjective senses "the idea they give us is more an idea of our *enjoyment* of the object than knowledge of the external object. So men can easily come to an understanding about the more objective senses, whereas one man can feel affected quite differently from another in the more subjective senses. . ." (Ak. VII, 160). Perhaps the intimate connection between feeling and sensation in the "more subjective senses" contributed to Kant's long-standing difficulty in distinguishing sensation from feeling. In the first *Critique* he discusses together color and taste, then notes that they are grounded in sensation "and, indeed, in the case of taste, even upon feeling (pleasure and pain), as an effect of sensation" (A 29). Even after his clear distinction between sensation and feeling in the third *Critique,* he sometimes uses *Empfindung* where we would expect *Gefuehl.* It is possible that the untranslatable term *Sinnesempfindung* incorporates this notion of a sensation that cannot be clearly distinguished from its agreeableness or disagreeableness.

It will be noted that Kant's references to *Sinnesempfindungen* (Ak. V, 281, 291, 303,

Kant's position seems to be that *if* empirical investigation reveals perceptible, mathematically determinable structures within some sensations, *then* these sensations and the relations among them can be beautiful. Melody and harmony, in that case, do not merely draw attention to the temporal form, the rhythm, in music: they are elements in the communicable form. And so too, "by analogy," relations among colors.

It is a recurrent theme in Kant that the "pure" part of philosophy should be kept distinct from its applied part. Philosophy, he says, benefits from this division of labor, not only because it obviates confusion of the empirical with the a priori, but also because the talent required for the two parts may not be found in the same person. The "Critique of Aesthetic Judgment" is essentially the pure part of aesthetics. Kant's incursions into the aesthetics of music and the visual arts may be considered unfortunate addenda. Having set forth his transcendental principles, he should have handed the question over to David Prall's analysis of "the intelligible structures in the aesthetic surface"[15] and to the development of musical aesthetics by Hanslick and, less successfully, the aesthetics of the visual arts by Bell and Fry. But it is perhaps more important, in our time, to recognize the need for a properly philosophical foundation for aesthetic theory.

San Diego State University

306; compare 223, 238, 324, 330–31) usually occur either in the context of distinguishing the subject's passivity regarding them from his reflective activity, or in that of the overlapping distinction between the agreeable and the beautiful. The lower animals and man share "the agreeable," but only in man does it give rise to an interest, since an interest involves thought. It would seem that the senses of taste and smell are primarily, though not exclusively, those which would provide material for an interest: they are, as Kant points out, important primarily from a biological point of view. Ak. VII, 158–59.

[15] It is worth noting that Prall doubts whether the so-called lower senses yield material for aesthetic analysis: at least we have not been able to discover any intelligible structures in the area of odors and flavors. Moreover, the color cone is a poor approximation to the musical scale as a systematization of these structures.

11 Kant's Evaluation of His Relationship to Leibniz

CHARLES M. SHEROVER

The year 1790 saw publication of Kant's third *Critique.* In that same year, Kant had published an explicitly polemical essay in which he defended the first *Critique,* originally published only nine years earlier, against vehement—and, he thought, virulent—attack. The conjunction of publication is telling. While Kant was seeing the capstone of the Critical philosophy into print, he had an essay published which seeks to instruct us as to how he wished his first *Critique* to be interpreted and understood.

This polemical essay was directed against the charge by one Professor Johann Eberhard—that the first *Critique* had made no philosophic advance beyond Leibniz. Kant's defense of his own accomplishment concludes with this statement: "Thus the *Critique of Pure Reason* may well be the real apologia for Leibniz, even against his partisans whose eulogies do him no honor."[1]

Against subsequent textbook expositions, Kant thus situated himself within the Leibnizian tradition. Claiming to be Leibniz's true successor, he did not seek mere reiteration of Leibnizian doctrines but rather sought to carry forward Leibnizian themes—by 'seeking out Leibniz's intentions' and looking beyond the particular words used in order to comprehend and fulfill the task that Leibniz had set for himself.[2] In this vein, Kant had, in the first *Critique,* already suggested that we often find that "we understand [a philosopher] better than he has understood himself," for, insofar as he may not have sufficiently clarified his own basic concepts, he may have "spoken, or even

[1] Immanuel Kant, "On a Discovery according to Which Any New Critique of Pure Reason Has Been Made Superfluous by an Earlier One," trans. Henry E. Allison as *The Kant-Eberhard Controversy* (Baltimore: Johns Hopkins University Press, 1973), p. 160 (hereafter cited as *K-EC;* N.B.: I have made minor revisions in some of the translated citations).

[2] Cf. *K-EC,* p. 160.

thought, in opposition to his own intentions" (A 314 = B 370).[3] Kant then suggested that, by clarifying conceptual conflicts and thinking them through, the first *Critique* seeks "the same objective," the development of a "coherent system of metaphysics,"[4] and thus carries forward the work that Leibniz had begun.

Kant seems to be claiming that he understands Leibniz better than either Leibniz or his immediate successors did, that his own *Critique* manifests an essential loyalty to the Leibnizian perspective, that his specific criticisms and divergent doctrines are to be seen as attempts to bring greater coherence to the central thrust of monadological idealism. In order to examine this claim within this brief compass, I first briefly review some specific mentions of Leibniz in the *Inaugural Dissertation* and the first *Critique,* and then turn to concluding passages of this polemical essay as well as some of his letters; finally, I conclude with a few considerations of my own. In the end, I think we should be able to accept Kant's own judgment about his own intent and accomplishment as largely justified, if, perhaps, somewhat overstated; we should see the first *Critique* as presenting a radical modification of some Leibnizian doctrines but nevertheless remaining fundamentally accordant with Leibniz's philosophic perspective. For Kant's *Critique* is neither an external attack nor a repudiation; it is a reformulation of the Leibnizian outlook and remains within the household of the Leibnizian way by seeking to present an internal criticism and consequent redevelopment.

I

The Kant biographies suggest two publication dates that had a profound impact on the development of Kant's thinking. Leibniz's prime sustained work, his critique of John Locke's *Essay,* the *New Essays on the Human Understanding,* although written in the 1690s, was first published in 1765. Three years later, in 1768, the *Leibniz-Clarke Correspondence,* concerned with the metaphysical nature of time and space, was reissued. Apparently Kant read them both with care; for their timing is accordant with Kant's claim that, one year later, in 1769, a "great light"[5] had dawned for him. Turning from the contem-

[3] All citations from the *Critique of Pure Reason* are from the translation by Norman Kemp Smith; when I have modified the translation, this is indicated by an asterisk (*) within the reference.

[4] Quoted in Arnulf Zweig, ed., *Kant, Philosophical Correspondence, 1759–99* (Chicago: University of Chicago Press, 1967), p. 179 n. 1 (hereafter cited as *KPC*).

[5] Lewis White Beck, *Early German Philosophers* (Cambridge: Harvard University Press, 1969), p. 432.

porary dogmatisms back to Leibniz as his point of departure, he promptly gave voice in the *Inaugural Dissertation* of 1770 to what is now called the Critical turn: it was here that he announced his radical thesis of the subjectivity of the forms of time and of space, a thesis which, to the end, he regarded as his fundamental innovation, fundamental just because the entire Critical problematic flows directly from it. Radical as this thesis might at first appear to be, I will suggest that it is but a necessary modification of the monadic outlook.

Already in its formal title—*On the Form and Principles of the Sensible and Intelligible World*—the *Dissertation* presumes the twofold Leibnizian perspective, which Kant held to the end: the world may be considered in two distinct ways: as the object of sense experience and as intelligible by reason alone.

Leibniz is explicitly mentioned three times in the section entitled "On the Principles of the Form of the Sensible World." Kant, arguing against the Cartesian doctrine that the moments of time are ontologically real,[6] voices the Leibnizian rejoinder—that "*time is a continuous quantity*" and that separate 'moments' are not parts of time "but *boundaries* by which we distinguish the parts of time."[7] Expressly defending Leibniz's doctrine of "the metaphysical law of *continuity*," Kant then presents his own twofold criticism of Leibniz, a criticism that presages the central doctrine of the Transcendental Aesthetic and is fundamental to all that follows: first with regard to time and then with regard to space, Kant attacks the Leibnizian thesis that these are *real* relations of things. This Leibnizian thesis regarding time, he says, propounds a "vicious circle" and also neglects the crucial temporality of simultaneity, "the most important consequence of time";[8] insofar as Leibniz had defined space in terms of 'simultaneity', this leads Kant directly to his criticism of Leibniz's theory of space qua the real relations of things, a theory which, Kant argued, is "in headlong conflict with phenomena themselves and [with] . . . geometry";[9] thus, it is as unsatisfactory as the 'English notion' of absolute space which leads to a 'world of fable'.

Announcing the new Critical thesis that time and space are not

[6]See René Descartes, *The Philosophical Works of Descartes,* trans. E. S. Haldane and G. R. T. Ross (Cambridge: Cambridge University Press, 1968): "Arguments Demonstrating the Existence of God (Addendum to Reply to Objection II)," Axiom II, vol. II, p. 56; and "Reply to Objections, V," vol. II, p. 219, sec. 9.

[7]Immanuel Kant, *Inaugural Dissertation,* in *Kant: Selected Pre-Critical Writings,* trans. G. B. Kerferd and D. E. Walford (Manchester: Manchester University Press, 1968), p. 64 (hereafter cited as *Dissertation*).

[8]*Dissertation,* p. 66.

[9]*Dissertation,* pp. 70–71.

general abstractive concepts but "principles of *sensible* cognitions,"[10] Kant promptly proceeded to an immediate consequence, a consequence largely ignored in the literature even as it seems to provide a prime point of the title of the first *Critique,* a consequence that immediately challenges Leibniz's faith in the competence of pure reason alone to attain knowledge either of particular spatiotemporal presentations or of the world as such: Kant subsumes logic *under* the form of time.[11] This grounding of conceptual (or 'general') logic within time itself would itself ground the Critical doctrine and restrict the reach of possible cognition to phenomenal appearances in temporal form. Kant's later reformulation of this particular thesis in the *Critique* did not in any way augment the competence of pure reason—for the restriction of logic to analytic judgments continued the same outcome: logic as such has no empirical cognitive object and thereby "no [cognitive] authority and no field of application" (A 151 = B 191).

In the balance of the *Dissertation,* Kant voices cardinal theses which were prominent in Leibniz's metaphysics: (i) the distinction between the sensible and the intelligible vantage points as the "ground" upon which the world is to be regarded as one whole;[12] (ii) the distinction between form and matter,[13] a distinction that underlies the structure of the *Critique* but whose roles are to be reversed as the heart of Critical doctrine; (iii) the fundamentality of "the concept of time [which] supposes the perdurability of a subject";[14] and (iv) the belief that the finite power of the human mind is sustained by the pervasive force of God.[15] These theses are to be carried forth in the Critical enterprise, albeit in more or less revised form. Additionally, the *Dissertation* already voices the essential thrust of Kant's later "highest principle of synthetic judgments," a principle which I would argue is the fulcrum upon which the Critical doctrine of cognitive objectivity rests and which, I will suggest, embodies Kant's essential cognitive revision of Leibniz's principles of sufficient reason and pre-established harmony.

II

The first *Critique* is as notable for its lack of specific citations as it is for the paucity of its direct references to Leibniz—aside from the

[10] *Dissertation,* p. 72.
[11] Cf. *Dissertation,* p. 73.
[12] *Dissertation,* p. 75.
[13] *Dissertation,* p. 75.
[14] *Dissertation,* p. 79: "supponit perdurabilitatem subjecti."
[15] Cf. *Dissertation,* pp. 78–79.

concluding section of its Analytic which discusses some fundamental Leibnizian concepts. Before turning to it, however, we must first consider the prime thesis of the Transcendental Aesthetic—just because it poses the problem which, in large measure, the balance of the *Critique* aims to address.

If, as Kant insists, it is only by means of sensibility that we may be affected by objects, then the structure of sensibility predetermines the possible scope of empirical knowledge. If sensibility and conceptual understanding are to be distinguished, then conceptual understanding can only be cognitive insofar as it is able to enter into that form in which sensibility reports, the form of time which is the form of inner sense, of consciousness. The consequent need for temporalized concepts (set out in the Schematism)—as the structure of conceptual knowledge (delineated in the Principles)—and the temporal bar to the cognitive force of supra-temporal speculation (summarized in "Phenomena and Noumena")—are but entailed by this initial thesis.

In opening the Transcendental Aesthetic, Kant made it clear that his concern was not with knowledge in general, but with human knowledge, the kind of cognitions attainable by us, the kind of knowledge within the competence of the human perspective—or, in Leibnizian language, the particular ways in which human monads are able to reflect, each in his own consciousness, the universe as it appears to them.

The first *Critique,* then, rests on an ontological thesis concerning the nature of time, of space, and of human (monadic) being insofar as it is affected by—or reflects—the things of the world among which it finds itself. About space and time, the dual forms of the human outlook, Kant asks: "What, then, are space and time?" (A 23 = B 37)—*not* 'how may we know them?' *but* '*what* are they?'. He reiterates the *Dissertation* rejection of the two alternatives: (i) what he had called 'the English view': that they are real existent entities; and (ii) Leibniz's view: that they are "relations of things [but] yet such as would belong to things even if they were not intuited" by us. Kant's foundational ontological thesis is that space and time are "such that they belong to the form of intuition [i.e., the form of the sensory outlook = *Anschauung*] and therefore to the subjective constitution of our mind, apart from which they could not be ascribed to anything whatsoever" (A 23 = B 37–38). Within the structure of the human kind of outlook, time and space are the pervasive forms in which all particular representations are constituted; only as so constituted do these representations become referential objects of our cognitive thinking; only as the constituting forms of all possible apprehended objects do they provide the horizon within which our particular cognitions may be had.

This principle, that space and time are 'empirically real' in our experiences, but 'transcendentally ideal'—as forming the structured horizon of any possible experience—encapsules the ontological principle upon which all else builds. Some years later, Kant but underlined the primordial import of this when he said of "the critical philosophy (. . . I could better call [it] the principle of the ideality of space and time)."[16]

From this ontological foundation, all particular differences from Leibniz flow. But we ought to note just how Leibnizian this principle really is. Kant has effectively accepted Leibniz's relational view of space and time as being, not things-themselves, but the relations of things—with one crucial restrictive qualification: We are not warranted to say that they are real relations of things as such just because we can only rightfully speak of things *as* reflected in our (monadic) consciousness; all we may legitimately say is that time and space are the prime relations of things *as we are able to perceive them,* as we are able to take cognizance of them, as they are able to appear to the peculiar capabilities of the human outlook. Time and space are then still continuous and relational—but as structuring our perspectival outlook; as such, we can account for their universality *in* our experiences, just because we cannot see things in any other way; but, for that same reason, we have no way of knowing whether they might also be something more.

The Aesthetic thus only internalizes the relational doctrine of time and space by thinking through the meaning of Leibniz's principles of the primacy of perspectivity. It also carries forward Leibniz's revolutionary reversal of the traditional priority of space to time: Plato's influential myth had time brought into a preexistent spatial receptacle in order to provide a principle of ordered change. But Leibniz had reversed the ensuing spatial priority in two ways: (i) he defined both time and space by means of temporal predicates—time as the order of succession and space as the order of simultaneity; (ii) his principle of individuation saw the uniqueness of each monad to be the totality of its internalized temporal relational predicates, the temporal biography of each monad. Kant thus but carried forward this priority of the temporal. For time, as the form of all consciousness, includes all spatial predicates within it: although outer perceptions must be in spatial form, they must be brought into the form of time, the form of

[16] Letter to Beck, December 4, 1792, *KPC,* p. 198.

inner sense and consciousness, if we are to be aware of them. If we look forward to Kant's Schematism, this requisite of temporality becomes the bedrock *and* limitation of the Principles of knowledge; for the *essential* predicate of any cognitive use of the categories regarding spatially perceivable objects—and the absolute limit of any cognitive claim concerning them—is representation by us in temporal form. Time, as the form of inner sense, is the form of all consciousness, of any cognitive thinking about our own selves or about representations of external things. One chief focus of Kant's revision of Leibniz is insistence on the import of spatial apprehension (cf. A 46 = B 64); but spatial representation remains for Kant, as it was for Leibniz, a form of temporalization.

Time and space, Kant argues, are the forms in which all external apprehensions must be received; but form without matter is empty and matter is now but the particularity of time-formed sensibility (cf. A 42 = B 60). Form is given, not by the world, but by us; it is this "subjective constitution" that "determines" in advance the form which any entity must be able to meet if it is to appear to human consciousness (cf. A 44 = B 62). It is this reversal of the roles of form and matter that yields the transcendental questioning.

Echoing, then, the subsumption of conceptual ('general') logic to time in the *Dissertation,* Kant, in his only mention of Leibniz in the Aesthetic, criticizes him, along with Wolff, for having reduced the difference "between the sensible and the intelligible" to the "merely logical" (A 44 = B 61) (and, incidentally, Kant uses Leibniz's own example of a rainbow to draw the distinction between the empirical and the transcendental).[17] Rather, Kant's thesis urges, the differentiation of the sensible from the intelligible is essentially reducible to the question of time, to the temporal form of the internal constitution of the perceiving monad and the consequent limitations inherent in the way by which human monads are able to apprehend the objects they represent to themselves in consciousness.

III

Concluding the Analytic—and thereby able to presume the work and doctrine developed—is an essay entitled "The Amphiboly of the Concepts of Reflection," a critical examination of some prominent

[17] Cf. *Critique of Pure Reason,* A 45–46 = B 62–63, and Leibniz, *New Essays on Human Understanding,* trans. P. Remnant and J. Bennett (Cambridge: Cambridge University Press, 1981), pp. 146 and 219.

Leibnizian concepts which, Kant charges, are ambiguous in their legitimate application.[18] These concepts, which are used for comparing conceptual judgments with each other, are: (i) identity-and-difference, or the principle of the identity of indiscernibles; (ii) agreement-and-opposition, or the cognitive force of logical contradiction; (iii) inner-and-outer, or the principle of the community of substances; and (iv) matter-and-form, or the distinction between the form and the content of sensibility.

These reflective concepts, Kant here argues, are not fundamental just because they do not address the transcendental question of the sources of our knowledge; thus they may only be applied cognitively to what has already been taken up into consciousness, i.e., reports of sensibility as synthesized by temporalized categories. Because Leibniz had not clearly recognized the distinction between sensibility and understanding, but had subsumed the former under the latter, Kant argues that he had not been able to take these concepts to the primordial ground of their cognitive possibility, application to objects of spatiotemporal apprehension. For this same reason, Kant charges, Leibniz had not been able to explain the relation of a mind to its objects, and thereby had not seen the crucial import of outer sense, of spatiality, for the apprehension of conceptually identical, but numerically distinct, objects of perception. Leibniz had given the name 'phenomena' to the objects of our perceptions, not because he recognized sensibility as a separate source of knowledge, but because he regarded sensibility as a somewhat confused form of conceptualization. Ignoring the question of how general concepts can directly apply to the particularity of appearances, he believed that knowledge of particulars can arise out of mere conceptual comparison. Thus he could only offer an essentially ambiguous doctrine of how these concepts are to be used in the construction of knowledge.

Let us briefly look at Kant's criticism of each in turn:

(i) The principle of the identity of indiscernibles, Kant argues, can only apply to conceptual comparison of *kinds* of things, not to specified experiential objects which may be spatially distinct while being conceptually identical, e.g., separate drops of rain. The validity of this principle is, then, "only as an analytic rule" for the comparison of concepts of things, not for their appearances as particular objects;

[18] Prior to this is one critical comment on Leibniz—in a final note to the System of Principles added to the B edition where Kant argues that if monads were restricted in their activity to thinking, then any community of monads would require the "mediating intervention" of God to maintain it (B 293).

it is, then, "no law of nature," but only a valid rule for conceptual comparison of the *kinds* of things represented or instantiated as *spatially* pluralized in our experiences of them (A 272 = B 328).

(ii) The force of conceptual logic, embodying the law of contradiction, does apply to comparison of distinct concepts, "but has not the least meaning in regard either to nature or to anything in itself. For real conflict certainly does take place" within the experiential world (A 273 = B 329). Kant notes that although Leibniz had accepted the principle of contradiction for making assertions, it was Wolff who had only later made it a first principle of knowledge. Valid as it may be for conceptual analysis, it is blind to real objects appearing in the forms of space and time and is thus not applicable to the objects of experience, just because it recognizes no conflict but that of logical contradiction.

(iii) The distinction between inner and outer was not really acknowledged by Leibniz; because the only power available to monad-substances was seen as that of representation in thinking, Kant explains, Leibniz was unable to account for the reciprocal physical influences of things on each other and had to fall back on his principle of harmony. But our own experience is of being involved with physical forces that are spatially *related to us.* Phenomenal substance, Kant argues, is spatial and "its inner determinations are nothing but relations, and it itself is entirely made up of mere relations" (A 265 = B 321; cf. A 274 = B 330). These relations are empirically real and are forces that attract or repel other entities.

(iv) The juxtaposition of 'matter' and 'form' underlies the argument of the *Critique.* "These two concepts," Kant tells us, "underlie all other reflection." Kant's radical reversal of their traditional roles is at the heart of his Copernican Revolution. "Logicians," he instructs us, "gave the name 'matter' to the universal, and the name 'form' to the specific difference" (A 266 = B 322). True to this tradition, Leibniz had invested his simple monadic substances with the power of representation of time and space as the forms of the relations of substance-things to each other. If this were indeed the case, Kant points out, then pure understanding might well apply directly to things-themselves insofar as space and time would be their determinations; but this is foreclosed by the principle of his Copernican Revolution.

This traditional priority, Kant points out, is explicitly reversed from the outset of the *Critique;* it teaches that "the form of intuition (as a subjective property of sensibility) is prior to all matter (sensations)" (A 267 = B 323)—for space and time, as forms of sensibility, are prior to our representations of things and, indeed, make such representations possible. Matter, then, is phenomenal substance: it is merely thought by us as in the things we think about; its ground "is a mere something of which we should not understand what it is, even if someone were in a position to tell us" (A 277 = B 333).

"The conclusion," Kant then draws, "is that we must either abstract from any and every object (as in logic), or, if we admit an object, must think it under the conditions of [the two forms of] sensible intuition." To think "in a merely logical fashion" (A 279 = B 335) is to compare concepts without reference to the particular things they claim to describe. Limited as we are to human modes of apprehension, outer sense is the form of our only contact with what is external to us. By the ambiguous use of these reflective concepts in the reach of the intellect directly to things-themselves, Leibniz, "one of the most acute of all philosophers" (A 280 = B 336), unfortunately sidestepped the necessary mediation of the senses.

Leibniz's prime error, then, was to ignore the fact that the mere concept of a thing is a selective abstraction from the requisite conditions for knowing it. Only formed intuitions, i.e., representations, present that which is not to be met with in a mere concept, namely, "a space which, with all that it contains, consists solely of relations; whether these are purely formal or also real, I cannot say" (A 284 = B 340*). Therefore, nothing can be known through pure categories alone, just because any particular appearance "consists in the mere relation of Something as such to the senses" (A 285 = B 341*). Concepts can legitimately be used for speculation only by recognizing that speculation is not cognition (cf. A 288 = B 344). In order for categories to function in cognitions of things, they must be schematized, temporalized, brought into the form of time, and used with reference only to particular appearances apprehended as spatial.

We are here engaged in looking at Leibniz through Kant's eyes, just because it is Kant's perception that must count in evaluating his claim of justification. Were we rather to be looking at Kant through Leibniz's eyes, I would explicate my reasons for believing that some of Kant's criticisms may be construed as unfair or even away from the mark. But what is pertinent to this discussion is not the fairness of Kant's particular criticisms of Leibnizian concepts but rather his uses of them; these uses, to which we soon turn, can only arise from his own evaluative assessments.

One additional divergence between them, however, must be noted. Leibniz not only claimed that each particular monad—and not just its species—represents a complete (temporally constituted) concept; he also insisted that such complete concepts can only be known by God, who is able to discern them by analytic reason alone. In speaking of men as 'little gods', Leibniz had urged that we should, to the extent of our finite created capabilities, seek to emulate the mind of God and, in any event, that we must have some insight into divine purposes in the creation if we are to comprehend the created world. In principle, then, the gulf between human minds and that of the divine, and thereby the essentially finite reach of possible human knowledge, was acknowledged at the outset—but as a differentiation in degree and not in kind.

With this theodicy Kant emphatically disagreed. Arguing on the essentially Leibnizian ground that species are differentiated by their modes of representation, Kant insisted that God's mode of knowledge is wholly different from ours—at least in that it possesses that intellectual intuition we lack. Unlike God's, our cognitions are "*not original*" (B 72) just because they are based on our subjective forms, which cannot provide the existence of the objects of our intuition; instead, our intuitions are dependent upon being affected by something we do not originate. And just because Kant could not concede that our cognitive insights can extend to reading the purposes in the mind of God leading to the creation, Kant, agreeing that a concept of purpose is requisite for the understanding of nature, had insisted (at the end of the Dialectic and in the third *Critique*) that attributions of purpose in nature could not be cognitive but could only be regulative. On this theodicean point, then, Kant joined the Cartesian principle that the mind of God is inscrutable by us; but then there is not only a difference in degree but also, in accord with the Leibnizian mode of defining the differentiation of species, a difference in kind. This theological divergence from Leibniz but buttresses Kant's insistence on the limitations of purely conceptual or logical reason.

Kant was thus seeking to deal only with human, not with divine, understanding. On this ground, Kant's disavowal of the cognitive force of Leibnizian concepts, taken as fundamental, is not a repudiation of them, but an exposure of fundamental ambiguity, i.e., "amphiboly," in Leibniz's presentation of them. Kant, in this essay, has conceivably distanced himself further from Leibniz than he really was. For he has repeatedly claimed that were the world of things-themselves directly knowable by our intellectual understanding alone, it would almost certainly be very much like its Leibnizian portrait.

Kant's claims in this discussion, when translated into Leibnizian terms, are that our proper concern is solely with the capabilities and inherent limitations of the representational power of the human kind of monad; that spatial predicates are intrinsic to our perceptions of things and are thereby internalized in our consciousness of them; that externally perceived relations, internalized in consciousness, depend upon the conditions of sensibility to be effected; that as constituted in the human kind of outlook, our concepts of those things we take as external to us contain the predicates of spatial relation as intrinsic to any individual particularity with which we may have a cognitive relationship.

If we accept Kant's claim that an apprehended appearance is only a complex of relations with our senses (cf. A 285 = B 341), then Kant is effectively voicing the Leibnizian primacy of monadic perspective and the internality of all perceived relations in inner sense, in consciousness. If we accept Leibniz's thesis that each monad perceives the world in its own way from its own peculiar point of view, it would seem that Kant, insisting that the forms of time and space are fundamentally ingredient to that perception, has taken Leibniz with fullest seriousness; for he is insisting that the forms of time and space are intrinsic to the way in which human monads are able to 'reflect' in consciousness the objects constituting their perceptual field. If this is the case, then no human monad can rightfully claim to *know* that time and space are in things-themselves as they might be outside of his perspectival mode of seeing them; thereby, the sole legitimate use of human cognitive reason is necessarily confined within the time-form of what is given by inner sense, by consciousness.

Aside from Kant's insistence on the coordinated status of sensibility for knowledge and of spatiality as its form that provides contact with 'external' objects, his most serious divergence from Leibniz has been the denial of conceptual logic as an empirically cognitive instrument; he has carried this forward in the present essay. The possible relevance of merely logical thinking to noumenal reality has been left open; but Kant has initiated what Hermann Lotze was later to call the "delogicization" of (at least) experiential reality. Concurring with Leibniz that the sensible has non-sensible grounds, Kant has left the non-sensible ground of sensibility as a "secret" (A 278 = B 334) beyond our possible grasp.

Kant's own announced restriction of inquiry to the nature of the human kind of outlook picks up the announced task of Leibniz's *New Essays.* It is fully consonant with the central thrust of Leibniz's general monadological outlook—just because of the Leibnizian thesis that each species of monad has its own mode of representation which differentiates it from all others and defines its place in the chain of being.

IV

When we turn to the Dialectic and the Doctrine of Method, we find Leibniz mentioned some six times. Five of these can be quickly noted: In the First Antinomy, Kant gives a qualified approval to Leibniz's claim that we cannot conceive the world as bound by a non-time and a non-space. In the Second Antinomy, he comments on Leibniz's use of the word *'monas'*. On concluding his refutation of the ontological argument, he refuses Leibniz's claim that it can be grounded on the concept of logical possibility—a point of special interest in view of Kant's acceptance of Leibniz's priority of the possible to the actual, a point to which we must return. And, in the final historical retrospect, Leibniz is portrayed as a non-mystical Platonist.

But the sixth mention demands attention. In the Canon of Pure Reason, Kant accepts, without reservation, Leibniz's distinction between the 'kingdom of grace' and the 'kingdom of nature'. The first is described as that of rational beings functioning under the moral law, the second as that in which rational beings, while standing under moral law, yet expect the consequences of their necessarily free actions to accord with the laws of nature. This Leibnizian duality is indeed crucial to the entire unity of the Critical edifice: it provides the Kantian divide between practical and cognitive reason, between noumena and phenomena, between the necessary freedom of moral obligation and the determinist necessity of nature (cf. A 812 = B 840). It is one form of Kant's basic acceptance of the Leibnizian distinction, already set forth in the *Dissertation,* between the world qua sensible and the world qua intelligible. Although Kant does not here introduce the principle of pre-established harmony, it would seem apparent that the unity of these two 'realms' depends upon it. Leibniz had not only argued for the harmonic unity of the two 'realms' but insisted that that of nature ultimately depends upon that of grace. Kant's first *Critique* continually reaffirms this (cf., e.g., B xxviiff.; B 72, A 696 = B 724ff.; A 797 = B 825ff.), and it is voiced again in the second *Critique*'s forthright subordination of cognitive to practical reason.[19]

[19] Cf. *Kritik der praktischen Vernunft,* ed. J. Kopper (Stuttgart: Philip Reclam, 1966), p. 193. Also, cf. *Logic,* trans. R. Hartmann and W. Schwarz (Indianapolis: Bobbs-Merrill Co., 1974), p. 94. N.B.: In this regard we might note that Kant's moral doctrine can be seen as perhaps having taken inspiration from what Leibniz had already claimed in 1686: that morality requires "the right intentions" and not success; cf. *Discourse on Metaphysics,* #11, in Wiener, ed., *Leibniz Selections* (New York: Charles Scribner's Sons, 1951), p. 295.

V

Insofar as the few references to Leibniz in the second *Critique* are sparse and casual and I have found none in the third *Critique*, we can proceed to the polemical essay with which I began. The body of this essay is largely concerned to refute charges which Eberhard, in two reviews, had directed against the first *Critique*. Kant, deliberately leaving Leibniz out of the discussion,[20] devotes himself to refuting the specific charges and to claiming that it is Kant rather than Eberhard who represents the forward march of Leibnizian philosophy. In passing, Kant makes some remarks with an import beyond this polemic: they address themselves to widely held misunderstandings of the Critical philosophy and throw light on both the similarities and the differences Kant saw between his own work and that of Leibniz. Let me note just three:

(i) Conceptual logic: We have already seen the continuity of Kant's condemnation of its cognitive claims. Having announced it in the *Dissertation* of 1770, he developed it in the first *Critique* of 1781, and still in 1799 he expressly repudiated Fichte's *Wissenschaftslehre* precisely on this ground as he summed up his continuing position by saying:

> . . . the principles of logic cannot lead to any material knowledge. Since . . . *pure logic* abstracts from the content of knowledge, the attempt to cull a real object out of logic is a vain effort.[21]

Logic is selectively abstractive just because it only addresses itself to that aspect of its object that interests it; therefore, we require the particularization of sensibility in order to be able to make direct reference to the world of objects.[22] Most crucially for Kant, conceptual logic cannot yield material knowledge because it has "nothing to do with the possibility of knowledge in regard to its content,"[23] and thus can provide no information "concerning the question: how synthetic propositions are possible a priori."[24] The distinction between analytic and synthetic judgments is effectively already present in Leibniz; Kant insisted that conceptual logic can only deal with analytic judgments and for this reason found it necessary to develop a new transcendental logic as "a logic of truth" (A 62 = B 87) requisite for synthetic judgments, judgments which relate concepts, not to other

[20] Cf. *K-EC*, p. 107.
[21] "Open Letter on Fichte's *Wissenschaftslehre*," August 7, 1799, *KPC*, p. 253.
[22] Cf. *K-EC*, p. 117n.
[23] *K-EC*, p. 154.
[24] *K-EC*, p. 152.

concepts, but to experiential things, and which are thereby cognitive by referring directly to the world as experiential.

(ii) Things-themselves: Kant's belief that appearances are not hallucinatory, not self-sustaining, but merely representations of things-themselves, is crucial to the Critical enterprise. As Paton pointed out, without this presumption, "the whole of the Critical philosophy falls to pieces."[25] The attack on the existent independence of the entities we seek to know as phenomenal appearances, in the name of pure logic, was the beginning of post-Kantian idealism. That move from the Critical philosophy Kant had already branded as illegitimate; and its illegitimacy rests on a Leibnizian ground: our knowledge, though limited by the perspective we bring with us, is yet knowledge of a real world, albeit from the limited vantage point of the human thinking outlook. In the first *Critique,* Kant had noted the absurdity of "appearance without anything that appears" (B xxvi–vii; cf. B 72). In this polemical essay, he explains: "Space and time are merely conceptual entities and beings of imagination. This is not to say that they are invented by the latter, but rather that they underlie all of its combinations and inventions."[26] Further, "their *ultimate* grounds are things-themselves, all of which the *Critique* likewise literally and repeatedly affirms."[27] However far we go, Kant insists, "we nevertheless arrive at *things-themselves*"[28]—whether these be those things that appear to us as external objects, our own selves as irreducible entities, or the primordial being who provides existence.

> Now this [Kant says] is precisely what the *Critique* constantly asserts. The only difference is that it places the ground of the matter of sensible representations not itself again in things as objects of the senses, but in something supersensible, which *grounds* the sensible representations, and of which we have no knowledge. It says: the objects as things-themselves *give* the matter to empirical intuition (they contain the ground of the determination of the faculty of representations in accordance with its sensibility), but they *are not* the matter of these intuitions.[29]

Although Kant criticizes Leibniz's cognitive use of conceptual logic and criticizes Leibniz's apparent belief that sensibility provides merely confused ideas which the intellect must then sort out, clarify, and transcend, he adamantly stands with Leibniz in the insistence that all

[25] H. J. Paton, *Kant's Metaphysic of Experience* (London: George Allen and Unwin, 1936, 1961), vol. II, p. 462.

[26] *K-EC,* p. 120.

[27] *K-EC,* p. 124.

[28] *K-EC,* p. 130.

[29] *K-EC,* p. 130.

of our appearances "have [super-sensible] *objective* grounds"[30]—even though the Kantian limitation of the cognitive reach of the human perspective requires that those ultimate and objective grounds must remain unknown and unknowable to us.

(iii) Innate ideas: In order to explain conceptual thinking, Leibniz had proposed a radical modification of Descartes' theory of innate ideas. As fundamental organizing ideas, Leibniz argued, they cannot be acquired from sensory experience and therefore come from within us—not as concepts readily available, but as concepts *in potentia,* as 'virtual', to be developed as experiential occasions bring them forth. It is, I think, fair to read Kant's a priori forms and temporalized categories as his specification of these *virtual* innate ideas, viz., as specific conceptual capacities which can only be realized as they are developed by use in the particularities of experience. Kant explains this in terms of the form of space:

> Only this first formal ground, e.g., the possibility of a representation in space, is *innate,* not the spatial representation itself. For impressions are always required in order to first enable the faculty of knowledge to represent an object (which is always its own act). Thus, the formal *intuition,* which is called space, emerges as an originally acquired representation (the form of outer objects in general), the ground of which (as mere receptivity) is nevertheless innate. . . . The acquisition of these [determinate concepts of things] is an *acquisitio derivativa,* as it already presupposes universal transcendental concepts of the understanding. These likewise are acquired and not innate, but their *acquisitio,* like that of space, is *originaria* and presupposes nothing innate except the subjective conditions of the spontaneity of thought (in accordance with the unity of apperception).[31]

The subjective constitution of the a priori structure of human thought may thus be taken as Kant's development of the notion, left very ambiguous by Leibniz, of virtual innateness waiting to be born. What Kant suggests is that the ways in which we are able to receive sense experiences, as the categorial ways in which we are able to integrate and interpret them, are inherent in the structure of our human perspectival outlook; like Leibniz's virtual innate ideas, they require utilization in order to be realized; they provide the structure in terms of which human monads reflect the universe, thus define the mode of representation which characterizes the essential nature of the distinctly human kind of experience.

All this is to say that my experiences are conditioned, rendered possible, by the encompassing harmony of two fundamental realities

[30] *K-EC,* p. 133.
[31] *K-EC,* p. 136.

which are always and necessarily presupposed as being far more than can possibly be revealed in the inherently finite reach of these limited modes of my human understanding: the objective structure of my subjectivity, of my representational capacity, which I bring to bear in forming any experience I might have, *and* the objective world of things-themselves that have being independent of my thinking and which appear to my consciousness as my representations of appearances to me, appearances in the limited ways in which I am able to apprehend them; these "objective grounds, namely, the things-themselves, are not to be sought in space and time, but in what the *Critique* calls their extra or super-sensible substrate (noumenon). . . . [That the] *ultimate* grounds [of all appearances] are things-themselves . . . [is what] the *Critique* likewise literally and repeatedly affirms."[32]

With Leibniz, then, Kant insists on the super-sensible, or perhaps better, trans-sensible, ground of all that appears within my sensible experience. Their essential dispute in this regard is merely about the extent to which the human mode of understanding can penetrate into that substrate of experiential reality which grounds it and which remains, to borrow Plato's phrase, 'unseen and invisible' in the human perspective.

Leibniz's faith in the competence of human cognitive reasoning had gone so far as to suggest some rational insight into the mind of God. But, as already noted, Kant, to the end, on this point which is consonant with his whole argument, insisted that the ultimate ground of all existents, the mind of God and its purposes, must remain for us wholly "inscrutable."[33] And this on the Leibnizian ground that, as Kant sees it, God's mode of representation is wholly different from ours.

Thus Kant has unreservedly disavowed Leibniz's faith in what pure reasoning alone can attain. But it would seem that Kant has really taken Leibniz's notions of the supremacy of the 'kingdom of grace' over that of 'nature' and the essence of monadic being qua activity more seriously than Leibniz himself did. For Kant, to the end, had insisted that it is *not* by means of rational understanding, but through the activity of "freedom . . . [that we] can extend reason beyond the bounds to which every natural, or theoretical, conception must remain hopelessly restricted."[34]

As radical a change as this was in Leibnizian rationalism, Kant's

[32] *K-EC,* pp. 123–24.

[33] Immanuel Kant, *The Critique of Judgment,* trans. J. C. Meredith (Oxford: Clarendon Press, 1952), Second Part, p. 160 (hereafter referred to as *CJ*).

[34] *CJ,* p. 149.

move was clearly predicated on his understanding of three central principles of Leibniz's metaphysics: (i) the principle of sufficient reason, (ii) the thesis that monads are simple substances, and (iii) the principle of the pre-established harmony. Claiming that these three principles were misunderstood by friend and foe alike, Kant's polemical essay concludes with his attempt to salvage these three principles, albeit it in modified form:

(i) The principle of sufficient reason: Kant points out that Leibniz recognized the insufficiency of the principle of contradiction and the consequent need for synthetic judgments in knowledge. The principle of contradiction, already limited by Leibniz to necessary truths, is, then, one of mere conceptual comparison. For experiential knowledged to emerge regarding specific objects, Kant notes, something *must be added by us,* viz., the principle of sufficient reason, which is, therefore, requisite to our modes of explanation; it thus shows us the need for a subjective principle *in us* that is requisite for the objectivity of any particular cognitive claims we may justifiably make.

(ii) Monads as simple substances: Kant understands this, insofar as it claims that 'all bodies are composed of simple parts', to apply, not to the physical world—because then space would be not relational but rather a composite thing itself—but to "its substrate, the intelligible world [of things-themselves] which is unknown to us."[35] Nothing can then be properly inferred regarding sensible things because they can only be understood by us, as Leibniz might well have said, only as related to our own capabilities of perceiving and understanding them. Leibniz's principle that sensibility is but confused intellection is, then, a grievous error when taken literally, and it effectively subverts the coherence of his system. When, however, taken in the context of his intent to show that sensibility alone can*not* place us in cognitive contact with the world as it may be in itself in its intelligible ground, we should be ready to accept it.

(iii) The pre-established harmony: Kant points out that Leibniz had advanced this principle, on one count, to explain the relation between body and soul. If we take it literally in this particular regard, Kant asks why we should accept the notion of body at all—for it would then seem that all of body might be explicable in terms of unembodied soul. Rather, body and soul seem to be 'completely different kinds of beings': what we call 'body' and what we call 'soul' are but the appearances to us of a substrate "completely unknown to us."[36]

[35] *K-EC,* p. 158.
[36] *K-EC,* p. 159.

If appearances, Kant argues, are conditioned by our intuitional forms of outlook, they belong to the constitution of our minds as their defining mode of representation. Taken in this light, the principle of harmony provides the cognitional unity of understanding and sensibility—and it is this internal harmony that the *Critique* teaches. It is an internal functioning harmony requisite to the possibility of experience as such—because without it, no object could be taken up into the unity of consciousness, no object could appear within our ken. We cannot explain this harmony, why it functions, why it enables us to have the limited kinds of empirical cognitions we attain—even if we trace it back to a "common, but to us unknown, root" as Kant did in the first *Critique* (cf. A 15 = B 29 and A 835 = B 863); we cannot explain—and he cites the third *Critique*—why we are enabled by this harmony to experience nature in terms of particular laws which are not even given a priori. By this principle of harmony, Kant suggests, Leibniz meant to indicate "that we must conceive a certain purposiveness in the arrangement by the highest cause of ourselves as well as of all things outside of us,"[37] a theme carried forward in Critical terms, at the end of the first *Critique* (cf. A 642 = B 671ff.) and the third, as the regulative use of reason. With regard to the possibility of knowledge, the principle of harmony points up the predetermination of the power of the mind to stand "in a reciprocal relationship" with the objects of its knowledge by permitting an a priori openness to them; "this," Kant says again, "is just what the *Critique* teaches."[38] And, indeed, this principle of harmony receives Critical expression in Kant's "highest principle of synthetic judgments," to which we must return.

Leibniz, concerned to justify our knowledge of objects, did not try to explain this agreement between our minds and the objects we cognize in our limited ways; but he used his principle of harmony in a way Kant fully endorses—not only to indicate a purposiveness in the created order, but to point out the harmonic unity of the two very different orders of 'grace' and 'nature', a harmony requisite to Kant's own explanation of how freedom can be operative in a naturalistically conceived determinist world. Agreeing with Leibniz that freedom is the power of self-determination, that it is yet operative in a world of things to be understood by us as sequentially ordered, Kant effectively grounded their ultimate unity in a principle of harmonic integration. But this says that the determinist necessity by which natural sequential relations are to be understood by us can be neither ultimate

[37] *K-EC*, p. 159.
[38] *K-EC*, p. 159.

nor self-sustaining: that they are grounded together in an inherently ordered world which yet guarantees the possibilities of freedom—which is immediately known by us "as a matter of fact"[39] and yet extends beyond our sense-oriented capabilities of understanding.

VI

Having surveyed Kant's own references to Leibniz, let me add a few general observations.

Kant's own application of the Critical outlook to a theory of nature was worked out, in 1786, in his *Metaphysical Foundations of Natural Science,* which only underlines his continuation of the Leibnizian orientation. He there joined Leibniz in a rejection of the thesis of physical atoms, espoused a field theory of physical interaction, and argued that physical substance is to be understood as a field of forces. With Leibniz, Kant there but developed their fundamental understanding of time and space as relational continuities—even if now internalized.

Kant's fundamental departure from Leibniz, announced in the *Dissertation,* was worked out in the *Critique,* where he said: Leibniz's reduction of the difference "between the sensible and the intelligible" to the "merely logical has given a completely wrong direction to all investigations into the nature and origin of our knowledge" (A 44 = B 61). On this ground, he saw Leibniz as having intellectualized phenomena by assuming that the entirety of an object can be conceptually grasped by us; having ignored the crucial role of spatiality in the particularity of perception, Leibniz had thus completely blurred his own distinction between the intelligible or noumenal and the experiential or phenomenal. Kant's transcendental turn was to separate the sensible (as phenomenal) from the intelligible (as noumenal), limit cognition to the former, and direct attention to the grounds of cognition in its possibility rather than try to describe the world itself without first confessing in advance the limiting perspectival bias of any cognitive human description.

Kant understood the cognitive process to be a synthesis of what temporal sensibility provides as interpreted by the temporalized (schematized) categories of the human understanding. But such synthesis is not a thing; it is an activity. The *'ich denke'* in which all assertions are lodged, Kant clearly said, is "the *actus*" (B 423n.). As Leibniz had already said, "to think and to be thinking are the same."[40] Kant

[39] *CJ,* p. 142.

[40] *New Essays on Human Understanding* (hereafter cited as *NE*), IV, vii, 7; in Wiener, p. 469.

later explained: "The synthesizing itself is not given; on the contrary it must be done by us; we must *synthesize* if we are to represent anything as synthesized";[41] this "*synthesizing* is related to inner sense, in conformity with the representation of time, on the one hand, but also in conformity with the manifold of intuition (the given) on the other hand."[42] The mental activity of synthesizingly thinking is not only directed to what is given as temporal; it is itself a temporal process of the perceiving monad's activity of being.

Kant has thus appropriated Leibniz's insistence that mind is known, not as a thing, but as a temporal activity; for it is not as an obscure mental substance but as the activity of synthesiz*ing*, judg*ing* and decid*ing* that we experience mind. It is the appear*ing* of such activities in consciousness that Kant termed the 'empirical ego' as distinguished from the 'transcendental ego' which is presumed as its enabling unificatory substrate; in forcing this distinction, he seems to have worked from an essentially similar distinction which Leibniz had already made in pre-Critical terms: "As regards the *ego,* it will be well to distinguish it from the *appearance of the ego* and from consciousness."[43]

Most fundamentally, Kant appropriated the Leibnizian dictum that 'there is nothing in the intellect that was not first in the senses—except what the intellect produces out of itself';[44] what the intellect produces out of itself according to Leibniz are the fundamental virtual innate principles by which we think (including the principles of mathematics); their confirmation is to be found in the "exact and decisive proof of these principles [which] consists in showing that their certainty comes only *from what is in us.*"[45] It would seem that Kant but developed this thesis in his doctrine that what the mind produces out of itself are precisely the forms of sensibility and the imaginative (temporalized) categories of understanding, with the consequence that their proper cognitive function is the comprehending integration of what sensibility provides.

The opening passage of the first *Critique* described experience as the result of understanding's "work[ing] up the raw material of sensible impressions" (A 1). In the second edition opening, Kant's famous sentence appears: "But though all our cognition begins with [sensible] experience, it does not follow that it all arises out of experience" (B 1*). These two topic sentences may perhaps be rightfully

[41] Letter to Beck, July 1, 1794, *KPC,* p. 216.
[42] Letter to Tieftrunk, December 11, 1797, *KPC,* p. 245.
[43] *NE,* II, xxvii, 9; in Wiener, p. 444.
[44] Cf. *NE,* I, i, 2; in Wiener, p. 409.
[45] *NE,* I, i, 2–4; in Wiener, p. 399 (italics mine); cf. p. 400.

construed not only as setting forth the themes to be developed but as having taken their inspiration from Leibniz's statement:

> . . . in the present state the external senses are necessary to us for thinking, and that, if we had none, we could not think. But that which is necessary for something does not for all that constitute its essence. . . . The senses furnish us the matter for reasoning, and we never have thoughts so abstract that something from the senses is not mingled therewith; but reasoning requires something else in addition to what is from the senses.[46]

Noteworthy in Kant's appropriation of Leibnizian themes is his continuing use of Leibnizian distinctions and terms upon which to ground his own distinctive terminology. However modified in import or meaning, we have already seen several instances—such as those between analytic and ampliative (synthetic) propositions, the sensible and the intelligible, the phenomenal and the noumenal. Kant's description of time and space as empirically real but transcendentally ideal carries forward the Leibnizian distinction between them as 'well-founded phenomena' and as "ideal possibility."[47] Kant's theory of knowledge seems to pick up Leibniz's delineation of 'perception' as "the inner state of the monad representing external things."[48] Leibniz's coinage of '*aperception*' (from the French *aperçevoir*) was taken up by Kant in the title of an apex concept of the Critical system, the 'transcendental unity of apperception', to designate the integral functioning unity of consciousness.[49]

Perhaps most crucial is Kant's full acceptance and development of one of Leibniz's most radical moves, which must be paired with his assertion of the primacy of time before space, i.e., the companion reversal of the traditional primacy of the actual over the possible. Possibility, Leibniz had argued, must be prior. If all particular existents are to be constituted by means of temporal relations, then a given state must first be possible before it can become actual; even God, Leibniz had argued, was confined in his decision to create this particular world to what things and laws were possible together. Kant's concern is not with actual cognitions but with the enabling ground of their possibility, with what is "possible, to man at least" (A 19 = B 33) in the realm of attainable cognition. This is most clearly seen in "The Postulates of Empirical Thought," where Kant has, in

[46] "On the Supersensible Element in Knowledge, and on the Immaterial in Nature," in Wiener, p. 364.

[47] "On Newton's Mathematical Principles of Philosophy," in Wiener, p. 258.

[48] "The Principles of Nature and of Grace, Based on Reason," in Wiener, p. 525; cf. pp. 523–24.

[49] Cf. Remnant and Bennett translation of *New Essays* (see note 17 *supra*), p. xxvii.

systematizing the relationship of the modal principles of possibility, actuality, and necessity, derived the second and the third from the first, from possibility: "That which agrees with the formal conditions of experience, that is, with the conditions of intuition and of concepts, is possible" (A 218 = B 265). And clearly in application of the "highest principle of synthetic judgments," "The postulate of the *possibility* of things requires that the concept of the things should agree with the formal conditions of an experience as such" (A 220 = B 267*).

Kant's reconstructional development proceeded on the ground that Leibniz had provided. It developed the Leibnizian distinction between his two principles of rational thought: the principle of contradiction and the principle of sufficient reason, a distinction which Kant saw as presaging his own "between analytic and synthetic judgments."[50] Kant had severely limited the principle of contradiction, as the first principle of purely logical thought, to that of mere abstract conceptual comparison—and this fundamental departure from Leibniz has been pointed out to be one prime reason for Kant's radical limitation of the cognitive competence of pure reason alone.

But the principle of sufficient reason, as Kant developed it, is central to the entirety of the Critical doctrine. Leibniz had described this principle as "the apex of rationality in motion"; by it, he said, "every true proposition which is not known *per se* has an a priori proof . . . [i.e.] a reason can be given for every truth"; its application, Leibniz claimed, is to the contingent truths of the possible "existence of things."[51] Kant may be seen as having regarded this Leibnizian principle as "a remarkable foreshadowing of investigations which were yet to be undertaken in metaphysics."[52] The principle of sufficient reason provides the principle of explanation for particular experiential objects; as such, Kant developed it into the principle of synthetic a priori judgment. As thus developed, Kant claimed, it is "unequivocally presented in the whole *Critique* from the chapter on the schematism on . . ."[53]—which is to say that the principle of sufficient reason binds the entire "System of all Principles of Pure Understanding," Kant's principles of empirical cognition, and perhaps the Dialectic and the Doctrine of Method as well. It is explicitly invoked in the discussion of the Second Analogy, where Kant clearly says:

[50] Quoted, *K-EC*, p. 101 n. 84.

[51] "The Principle of Sufficient Reason," in Wiener, pp. 93–95.

[52] Cf. Martin Heidegger, *Vom Wesen des Grundes*, 5th ed. (Frankfurt: Klostermann, 1965), p. 17.

[53] Letter to Reinhold, December 12, 1789, *KPC*, p. 141.

The principle of sufficient reason is thus the ground of possible experience, that is, of objective cognition of appearances in respect of their relation in the order of time (A 201 = B 246*).

Its most pointed use is in the "highest principle of synthetic judgments," which is, I suggest, the development of an early Leibnizian principle that states:

. . . there must be something in me *which not only leads to the thing but also expresses it.*

The means of expression must include conditions corresponding to the conditions of the things to be expressed.[54]

Kant's own summary of his "highest principle of synthetic judgments" reads:

. . . the conditions of the *possibility of experience* are at the same time conditions of the *possibility of the objects* [*Gegenstände*] *of experience,* and [it is] for this reason [that] they have objective validity in a synthetic a priori judgment (A 158 = B 197*).

This "highest principle" undergirds the Critical justification of the possibility of objective cognitions and thus constitutes its first principle of cognition. Presuming the principle of harmony, it explains how objective conditions of external objects are possible. It exemplifies the principle of sufficient reason on two gounds: first, it tells us that our subjective conditions for empirical cognitions must be met—the first condition for warranting an empirical proposition is that it incorporates the categorial integration of spatial and temporal apprehension; second, the cognitive claim must refer to an object apprehended as spatial and temporal, an appearance of an external entity represented by us as an object categorially comprehended as such in consciousness. That which appears, however it might be in itself,must yet be such as to be amenable to our modes of perception (representation) in order to be perceived by us in terms of our temporally structured categorial concepts. We are not only told about *our* subjective conditions enabling our cognitive outreach; we are also told that the things about which we may have cognitions must themselves be such that they can, in some aspects of their being, be representable by us in the peculiar ways in which we humans are able to do so.

Kant's Critically modified principle of sufficient reason thus presumes the principle of pre-established harmony—as obtaining a priori or in advance of any particular apprehension so that it may be

[54] "On Newton's Mathematical Principles of Philosophy," in Wiener, p. 281.

possible—between our cognitive capabilities *and* some aspects of things-themselves insofar as they are able to enter into our peculiar kind of perspective and thus, as perspectively conditioned representations, into our possible experiences of them.

In developing these two principles, Kant remained remarkably loyal to Leibniz's metaphysical priorities and distinctions of temporal order. For Kant's presentation of the three Analogies, as one central example, is faithfully Leibnizian in order of presentation. The First Analogy takes up the prime Leibnizian question: 'what is the nature of substance?'—which Leibniz had described as "the most real thing"[55]—and immediately ties this question of substance to the most fundamental Leibnizian conception of time: continuity. If one properly translates Kant's title of the First Analogy as "Principle of Persistence (or Striving) [*Beharrlichkeit*] of Substance,"[56] it is readily apparent that Kant has also built into it Leibniz's principle of *vis viva,* or 'living force'. Having joined the question of substance to temporal continuity and living force in the First Analogy, Kant then proceeded in the Second Analogy to the question of their sequential relation, the "principle of succession" of substantive states, the sequential order of substantival appearances. Leibniz had defined time as the order of succession, and space as the temporal order of coexistence or simultaneity; thus, it is only as the third of the three analogies that Kant can present his "principle of coexistence," or the reciprocity of coexistent entities in a spatial order. Taken together, the three Analogies—proceeding from substance-as-continutity-of-force to the order of sequentiality to spatial reciprocity—reveal a deep insight into and acceptance of Leibniz's fundamental metaphysical priorities.

In order to avoid the solipsism suggested (but not, I think, intended) by Leibniz's famed phrase 'windowless monads', Kant had insisted on the import of spatial form as requisite for our cognitive contact with external things, as requisite for them to be able to appear to us. This spatial form must be such as can be incorporated into the temporal constitution of our consciousness, so that they may both be represented in our awareness, so that they may be thought by us.

Kant's doctrine, then, claims to tell us about the nature of our own functioning selves, about cognizable aspects of the things we seek to know, and about a requisite principle of harmony between things-themselves and us so that we may develop a cognitive relationship with at least some of the aspects of the things constituting our world;

[55] "On Substance as Active Force Rather than Mere Extension," in Wiener, p. 163.
[56] See my "The Question of Noumenal Time," *Man and World* 10/4 (1977).

at least some of the things in the world are such that, by mediation of our spatial outlook, they can be temporally perceived and temporally comprehended by the temporal form of the activity of our human kind of consciousness. This is no mere epistemology; this is metaphysics.

Loyal to the Leibnizian principle that the nature of human cognition presupposes some notion of the nature of the world in which cognitive activity occurs, Kant seems to have employed the principle of harmony in at least three ways: (i) the harmony between sensibility and understanding as requisite to the possibility of empirical cognitive claims; (ii) the harmony between the subjective constitution of our modes of knowing and the thing-world insofar as aspects of it can enter into our representations; and (iii) the harmony between the cognitive and the practical, the phenomenal we experience and the noumenal that grounds it, the necessary sequentiality of the world of nature as we may understand it and the necessity of freedom for the practice of moral reason; between the kingdoms of grace or wisdom and of nature so that freedom can actually function.

VII

One cannot read Leibniz's *New Essays,* or even its Preface, without a presentiment of Kant's *Critique* as an attempt to retrieve and develop the philosophic possibilities Leibniz had presented. Kant's *Critique* then appears as an attempt to rethink basic Leibnizian themes, follow through their implications, and systematically work out their consequents.

Leibniz's prime maxim declared that every individual reflects the entire universe in its consciousness—but from its own peculiar point of view. In his own philosophic system, he seems to have tried to transcend his own finite individual perspective in order to see the world order as it truly is, as such—but from what vantage point? Taken as given, this attempt is incongruous and self-negating. His principle of the primacy of perspective means that we cannot hope to see the world as such, or to share the point of view of God or that of any other kind of being.

Kant's *Critique* seeks to explicate the defining constituting structure of the *human* point of view; it maintains that only within that structure may the truths attainable by human thought be lodged. Kant's criticisms of Leibniz, as his uses of Leibniz, function within this more limited and feasible task. From beginning to end, he moved within the self-conscious limitations of the human perspectival outlook, within this essentially Leibnizian metaphysical framework of monadic perspective. As Norman Kemp Smith observed, Kant was "profoundly convinced of the essential truth of the Leibnizian position" regarding what might be rationally grounded if only our reason could reach that far;[57] he persistently maintained that there must be "non-sensible objects" which, from our finite point of view, "must be viewed as transcendent" to us;[58] that "our [finite] power of conferring objective reality upon our concepts is not a limitation of the possibility of things"; indeed, by the principle of harmony between nature and grace, by means of "the practical ideas of reason" we might even be able to extend "the use of the categories. . . when considering the supersensible."[59] That there is a real world beyond our limited intellectual horizon Kant never seems to have doubted, as he never called into question Leibniz's 'kingdom of grace' as ontologically prior to that of 'nature'. For, in perhaps his most audacious move beyond Leibniz, Kant continually insisted that it is not intellectual understanding but the activity of freedom which represents our participation in the 'kingdom of grace', our one direct contact with the noumenally real: only by the exercise of free practical reason are we permitted direct access to what is beyond the horizon of phenomenal appearances.

Some fifteen years before his death, Kant had said, in a retrospective moment, that it was "the antinomy of pure reason," the consequence of human reasoning reaching beyond the horizon of the cognitive competence of its own perspective, that "first aroused me from my dogmatic slumber."[60] The Critical enterprise then appears as his attempt to bring Leibnizian reasoning, as human reasoning as such, within the self-Critical confines of the defining human perspective. By thinking through the Leibnizian principle of monadic perspective in strictly human terms, by reconstructing and developing fundamental Leibnizian concepts within this more limited horizon, Kant believed he had indeed provided the philosophic vindication of the work that Leibniz had bequeathed.

It has been suggested that Leibniz's metaphysics had but given a new voice to the philosophic tradition.[61] And Kant, following in Leibniz's wake, has urged, in his own defense, that a Critical self-appraisal

[57] Norman Kemp Smith, *A Commentary to Kant's 'Critique of Pure Reason'* (New York: Humanities Press, 1950), p. 419.

[58] Letter to Tieftrunk, December 11, 1779, *KPC*, p. 247.

[59] Letter to Reinhold, May 12, 1789, *KPC*, p. 142.

[60] Letter to Garve, September 21, 1789, *KPC*, p. 252.

[61] Cf. Beck, op. cit., p. 429.

of reason itself provides the vindication, not only of Leibniz, but of other past philosophers as well.[62] Let me then suggest, from something of a Kantian perspective, that his work may well be the vindication of much of the philosophic tradition all the way back to Heraclitus. For Kant seems to have fully accepted, and brought into rich development, the dynamism of experiential reality that Leibniz shared with Heraclitus. But Kant seems to have taken, with utmost seriousness, the largely neglected Heraclitean thesis: beyond or behind the world of visibly changing things, there is "the hidden harmony [that] is stronger (*or,* 'better') than the visible."[63] It is this primordial harmony that must be presupposed by us and yet remain "hidden" to our understanding.

Hunter College
City University of New York

[62] Cf. *K-EC,* p. 160.

[63] Fragment 54 in K. Freeman, trans., *Ancilla to The Pre-Socratic Philosophers: A Complete Translation of the Fragments in Diels, Fragmente der Vorsokratiker* (Cambridge, Mass.: Harvard University Press, 1927), p. 28.

12 Hegel on Kant: Being-in-Itself and the Thing-in-Itself

KENNETH L. SCHMITZ

In a letter written in 1822 Hegel still urged the study of Kant's philosophy, adding that he had been brought up on it.[1] Indeed, T. M. Knox defended the somewhat surprising view that Hegel remained a Kantian in ethics.[2] Henry Harris has shed detailed light upon the relationship between the two thinkers. He distinguishes Hegel's early and careful study of Kant's critical writings from his somewhat later gradual retreat from Kant's philosophy. He insists, however, that the retreat was from Kant's *Critique of Practical Reason,* especially from his formulation of the postulates of practical reason; and he finds no corresponding retreat from the *Critique of Pure Reason,* but rather an advance beyond it from reflection to life.[3] That advance would even-

[1] Letter to Duboc, 30 July 1822 (and insert b), *Briefe von und an Hegel,* hrsg. v. Joh. Hoffmeister, 2 Aufl., 4 Bde. (Hamburg: F. Meiner, 1962), II, pp. 325–30: "Da Sie, wie ich aus Ihrem Briefe sehe, ein geborner Franzose und dann ein in gesunder Wirksamkeit lebender Mann sind, könnten Sie bei [einer] deutschen, hypochondrischen Ansicht nicht stehen bleiben, welche sich alles Objektive vereitelt hat und dann nur noch dieser Eitelkeit in sich selbst geniesst. [[b] Desgleichen hier aus dem Konzept eingeschoben: "Indem ich dies sage, verkenne ich das Verdienst der Kantischen Philosophie nicht—ich habe mich an ihr erzogen—für den Fortschritt, ja die Bewirkung einer Revolution der philosophischen Denkweise insbesondere."] Aber auch abgesehen von den übrigen Verdiensten der Kantischen Philosophie will ich doch dies anführen, wie es interessant und lehrreich ist, bei Kant nicht nur in seinen sogenannten Postulaten das Bedürfnis der Idee, sondern auch die nähere Bestimmung derselben zu sehen."

[2] See "Hegel's Attitude to Kant's Ethics," *Kant-Studien* 49 (1957–58), p. 70. Cf. the more general thesis of W. H. Werkmeister, "Hegel's Phenomenology of Mind as Development of Kant's Basic Ontology," *Hegel and the Philosophy of Religion: The Wofford Symposium,* ed. D. Christensen (The Hague: Nijhoff, 1970), pp. 93–110.

[3] *Hegel's Development: Toward the Sunlight, 1770–1801* (Oxford: Clarendon, 1972), passim; pp. xx–xxi: "Leutwein tells us that Hegel was not much interested in the current discussions of Kantian philosophy in the *Stift.* This is confirmed by remarks made and attitudes adopted later by Hegel himself in his letters. But he certainly *studied* Kant carefully in these years [1788–93]. During his second year he read the *Critique of Pure Reason* and quite a lot of other philosophical works. If he had not already read the

tually carry off reflective understanding into the service of the Hegelian speculative reason that purported to lie beyond mere reflection. In his foreword to a study of Hegel's critique of Kant, Walter Bröcker remarks upon the well-known fact that Hegel took his understanding of Kant from Fichte, that is, from what amounted to a reinterpretation (*Umdeutung*) of what Kant had meant. Bröcker concludes that the actual Kant remained unknown to Hegel in his basic import and that no genuine confrontation of their philosophies occurred, so that if such is to occur it must be undertaken by us.[4] But, if no actual confrontation with Kant took place by way of a historically exact representation of his philosophy[5]—any more than Heidegger confronted

---

Critique of Practical Reason by then he certainly read it before very long. . . . This gradual retreat from Kant was a retreat from the *Critique of Practical Reason;* and specifically from Kant's formulation of the 'postulates of practical reason'. There was no corresponding retreat from the *Critique of Pure Reason:* on the theoretical side the philosophical expression of the ideal involved rather an advance from a merely pragmatic adoption of Kant's position (for purposes of argument and effective communication) to its justification as the highest expression of reflective thought. But even so the standpoint of reflection was still subordinate to the higher standpoint of life itself."

[4] See Ingtraud Görland, *Die Kantkritik des jungen Hegel* (Frankfurt am Main: Klostermann, 1966), pp. v–vi. Also W. Bröcker, *Auseinandersetzungen mit Hegel* (Frankfurt am Main, 1965), pp. 7–32: "Hegel zwischen Kant und Heidegger." Gillian Rose, *Hegel contra Sociology* (New Jersey: Humanities, 1981), chaps. 6 and 7, makes Kant's distinction between *Grenze* and *Schranke* (placed in the context of Fichte's practical philosophy) the pivot for Hegel's *Umdeutung.* For Fichte's own *Umdeutung* of Kant's philosophy, see Charles Griswold, "Fichte's Modification of Kant's Transcendental Idealism in the *Wissenschaftslehre* of 1794 and the Introductions of 1797," *Auslegung* 4 (1977), pp. 133–51.

[5] Merold Westphal, "In Defense of the Thing in Itself," *Kant-Studien* 59 (1968), pp. 118–41, argues (pp. 134–41) that the Hegelian criticisms (by Stace, Kroner, and Hegel himself) are "variations on the theme that to be aware of a limit is to be beyond it," and that they equivocate on the term "absolute," taking it once as a negative principle of limit and again as an affirmative principle of completeness. Moreover, they fail to recognize that Kant's dualism is rooted, not in his problematic realism, but in his theism (p. 134). Indeed, "Hegel leaves the reader to discover for himself how the ability to think such a mode of knowledge [i.e., the intellectual intuition of noumenal reality] shows that the thinker actually possesses it [i.e., knows it as actual rather than merely represents it to himself in thought]" (p. 140). He concludes that Hegel is "unable to raise any substantial objection to the dualist and finitist conclusions which are so odious to him," so that a refutation of Kant is "a much more complicated affair than Hegel himself sometimes makes it appear" (p. 141). It seems to me significant that, in meeting the Hegelian criticisms, the author is drawn towards an interpretation of Kant that is very close to that *Umdeutung* associated with the post-Kantian transcendental idealists. The author speaks, for example, of "the *centrality* of intellectual intuition in Kant's dualism" (p. 135); and further: "There may well be aspects of reality in some sense beyond the scope of human knowledge, but the idea of reality entirely unavailable to any consciousness whatever is one Kant does not favorably entertain. As a theist *the direction of his thought* is toward the identity of thought and being, but not in man" (p. 122; the italics are mine). What is at issue here is the nature, role, and weight to be assigned to intellectual intuition in determining the philosopher's knowledge of the real. Hegel very early in his public career outgrows the language of "intellectual intui-

the historical Kant in this way—nevertheless, Hegel had to reckon with Kant in the process by which he came to formulate his own philosophy.[6] So that a sort of confrontation occurred in relation to and within Hegel's own thought, which he saw as nothing less than a redefinition of philosophy.[7]

In the *Vorbegriff* to the *Encyclopedia of Philosophical Sciences* in which Hegel sets forth his system, he devotes a section to the consideration

---

tion" in favor of "syllogism" and "system." Indeed, Westphal understands that the conflict is one between "entire philosophical system[s]" (p. 137) rather than "brief polemical forays." The same author considers the relationship of the two philosophers from a Hegelian context in *History and Truth in Hegel's Phenomenology* (Atlantic Highlands, New Jersey: Humanities, 1979), pp. 1–14 and throughout. For a vigorous defense of Hegel's criticism of Kant's practical philosophy, see Jonathan Robinson, "Hegel's Criticism of the Postulates of Practical Reason," in *Le Congrès d'Ottouais de Kant* (Ottawa, 1974), pp. 234–52."Hegel is often accused of distorting Kant's account of the moral consciousness; and given this premise it is not difficult to conclude that while Hegel's arguments may be ingenious, and even have a certain intrinsic interest, they have little to do with Kant himself. Gueroult, for example,. . ." (p. 234). Robinson maintains, on the contrary, that "the difficulties in Hegel's treatment of the postulates find their source in Kant's work, not in Hegel's presentation" (p. 241). The author thinks that Hegel's criticisms are directed, not towards the Analytic of the second *Critique,* but towards the Dialectic (p. 242). That is, the criticism does not bear upon the "emptiness of the categorical imperative," but upon "the difficulties of reconciling Kant's doctrine of the categorical nature of morality with what he says about happiness" (p. 243). On the one hand, "moral purposes and nature are *independent and indifferent* to one another" (p. 244), yet, on the other, if moral purpose is to be realized in the actual world of nature there must be some *ontological* provision for such realization (p. 245). This is the moral significance of the idea of *summum bonum* and happiness. But, maintains Robinson (and Hegel), the moral attitude is inconsistent (p. 251), since it claims pure autonomy (independence) while yet demanding ontological completeness (dependence). What results, according to Robinson, is "a synthesis of elements held together by imagination rather than by reason" (p. 249). Finally, "the conclusion of the whole matter is that once we admit the summum bonum is an integral part of the Critical Philosophy then Kant's moral teaching lies exposed to Hegel's attack" (p. 252). I have italicized the terms "independent and indifferent," because it is just this state and relationship that lies at the root of Hegel's criticism of Kant's practical philosophy and also translates that criticism into a quite general refutation of Kant, touching upon ontology and epistemology as well as upon morality.

[6] Westphal, op. cit., p. 1: "We can therefore expect Hegel's philosophy to take the form of a continuous debate with the critical philosophy; and we should not be too surprised when he defines philosophy as the refutation of Kant."

[7] Jean Hyppolite, "La Critique Hegélienne de la Réflexion Kantienne," *Kant-Studien* 45 (1953), p. 83. (Also in *Figures de la pensée philosophiques: Écrits (1931–1968),* I, pp. 175–95.) The entire article is helpful, especially with regard to the structure of the judgment. John E. Smith, "Hegel's Critique of Kant," *Hegel and the History of Philosophy,* ed. Jos. J. O'Malley et al. (The Hague: Nijhoff, 1974), pp. 109–28 (reprinted from *Review of Metaphysics* 26/3 [March 1973]), considers three basic issues in respect to Hegel's criticism of Kant: (i) Kant's conception of "critique" as prior to and separate from actual knowing (Hegel is not averse to the critical role of reason in philosophy, but thinks that criticism should be "immanent," i.e., operative within the "categories at work" [p. 114]); (ii) Kant's conception of the "thing-in-itself" and his consequent "subjectivism" (here Smith argues that Hegel cannot reduce Kant's transcendental idealism

of the critical philosophy.[8] In a *Zusatz* he is reported to have said that

> the Critical Philosophy has one great negative merit. It has brought home the conviction that the categories of the understanding are finite in their range, and that any cognitive process confined within their pale falls short of the truth.[9]

In another *Zusatz* we read that

> Kant did valuable service when he enforced the finite character of the conditions of the understanding founded merely upon experience, and stamped their contents with the name of appearance.[10]

And even more generally, to insist, as Kant did,

> that the contradiction introduced into the world of Reason by the categories of understanding is inevitable and essential was to make one of the most important steps in the progress of modern philosophy.[11]

It is not surprising, then, that Hegel's redefinition of philosophy was worked out within a problematic heavily influenced by Kant (as well as by Fichte). But he came to see him as a one-sided culmination of the entire history of philosophy: "Kant had only a sight of half the truth."[12] The redefinition, then, takes the form both of an advance from his contributions and of a restoration of what had been suppressed by him. Through such a preservation and restoration Hegel was sure that he would restore to philosophy its ancient claim to full intelligibility, consonant with the modern principle of subjectivity.[13]

---

to "empirical psychology" or "psychological idealism" [pp. 115–18]; and, although the pure categories may be merely subjective, they are not thereby "meaningless" [pp. 119–22]); (iii) the primacy that Kant gives to the finite understanding over transcendental reason (here Smith gives serious weight to Hegel's criticism of "the basis upon which Kant declares the subjectivity of reason," for "if the subjectivity of reason depends in the end on a choice and a postulate, it cannot be as well-founded a thesis as the critical tribunal is supposed to deliver" [p. 128]).

[8] *Encyclopedia: Logic*, ##40–60 (considerably expanded in the second edition [1827]): *Enzyklopädie der philosophischen Wissenschaften* (1830), hrsg. v. F. Nicolin u. O. Pöggeler (Hamburg: F. Meiner, 1959[6]).

[9] From *Hegel's Logic*, trans. W. Wallace (1892[2]), ed. J. N. Findlay (Oxford: Clarendon, 1975), *Zus.* to #60, p. 93.

[10] Ibid., *Zus.* to #45, p. 73.

[11] Ibid., *Zus.* to #48, p. 77.

[12] Ibid., *Zus.* to #60, p. 93.

[13] Cf. S. Avineri, *Hegel's Theory of the Modern State* (Cambridge, 1972), pp. 64–65: "While Kant maintained that ultimate reality is opaque to human knowledge, Hegel returns to the classical Aristotelian position that reality is intelligible. Kant's *Ding-an-sich* ultimately left human knowledge knocking, to no avail, at a closed door. . . . Yet while the classical Greek tradition viewed *logos* as given, Hegel sees it as unfolding in the procession of human manifestations—in history." Cf. *Wissenschaft der Logik*, hrsg. v. G. Lasson (Hamburg: F. Meiner, 1967), Bd. I, pp. 25–32 (*Hegel's Science of Logic*, trans. A. V. Miller [New York: Humanities, 1979], pp. 45–51).

He was sure, too, that within his own philosophical viewpoint, Kant's basic insights would remain permanent contributions to philosophy. Indeed, Hegel often depicts Kant as anticipating the key philosophical principle, for (according to Hegel) Kant recognized the speculative nature of the concept (*Begriff*); that is, Kant recognized an original synthetic unity which expressed itself in opposing extremes, an opposition that created both the need and the means for the restoration of the original unity. That recognition, however, remained implicit in Kant, who raised the finite to absolute primacy and let the original unity he had glimpsed fall apart into unresolved conflict.[14]

The purity of Kant's summons to a moral autonomy founded upon reason undoubtedly attracted the young Hegel and his schoolfellows. He seems at first to have accepted the basic structure of Kant's practical philosophy with its moral postulates, but he was not satisfied with it for two reasons. First, Hegel's initial interest in Kantian philosophy was practical and moral, religious and aesthetic; and it is unlikely that Hegel ever thought that Kant's emphasis upon the individual could adequately reconcile the conflicts inherent in social life. Second, Kant's moral ideal postulated a rule for what life *ought* to be; but it remained in principle unrealized and unrealizable; and so, it failed to meet the test of actual life. Along with the stirring events of the French Revolution and the dawn of Reason, Hegel and his friends found a vivid enthusiasm for all things Greek.[15] Indeed, the young Hegel thought that the Greeks had reconciled their rational moral convictions with the actual demands of their lives. And he set out to recover the spirit of harmony that filled this ancient Greek world, so that the same harmony might be brought to actual realization in his own time through a revitalization of religious and public life.[16]

The thrust of Hegel's basic criticism of Kant is inherent in this early interest in religion as a unifying social force. In his Frankfurt period (1797–1800) he had already begun to work out a process for the

[14] For example, see *Glauben und Wissen,* hrsg. v. G. Lasson (1928) (Hamburg: F. Meiner, 1962), pp. 6, 36, and throughout (*Faith and Knowledge,* trans. W. Cerf and H. S. Harris [Albany: S.U.N.Y., 1977], pp. 60, 92, and throughout). Or again, in the *Lectures on the History of Philosophy,* trans. Haldane and Simpson, 3 vols. (London: Routledge and Kegan Paul, 1928, 1968), vol. III, p. 472 and elsewhere in the section on Kant.

[15] Cf. A. T. B. Peperzak, *Le Jeune Hegel et la Vision Morale du Monde* (The Hague: Nijhoff, 1960), pp. 5ff. Also H. S. Harris, *Hegel's Development,* p. 152 n. 2.

[16] About 1795 (the Berne period). See H. S. Harris, *Hegel's Development,* pp. 194ff., on the *Life of Jesus* ("Die reine aller Schranken," hrsg. v. H. Nohl, *Theologische Jugendschriften* [Tübingen: Mohr, 1907], pp. 75–136).

reconciliation of the ancient and the modern, and of the individual and the social. In place of the Kantian *synthesis,* he speaks of unification (*Vereinigung*); in place of the Kantian product of that synthesis, i.e., in place of *representation* (*Vorstellung*), he speaks of the life of men;[17] and in place of the rational *faith* of the Kantian practical reason which culminates in a moral ideal and its postulates, he speaks of love.[18] Kant had described synthesis as that which "gathers the elements for knowledge and unites [*vereinigt*] them" into a representation, says the young Hegel, but a synthesis in knowledge or faith does not guarantee harmony in actual life. Indeed, within the strictures of the Kantian pure reason, asks Hegel, how is such a union even possible? According to Kantian principles, the synthesis of thought and life cannot be theoretical, for that would produce a wholly objective and determined result, and we would then lose the possibility of freedom in the actual life of society. But neither can the synthesis be practical, for in giving laws practical reason annihilates the object and remains subjective. Presumably, practical activity annihilates the object because, as the sole source of active power, it wholly determines the object and appropriates it.[19] It is on some such basis that Hegel links the Kantian philosophy with traditional Christianity as opposite forms of the master-slave relationship. Thus, as lawgiver, Kantian reason asserts its ideal autonomy and proclaims its mastery over the contingent actualities of life. In opposite fashion, the traditional Lutheran religion demands that reason submit to its positive authority and take up the position of captive in relation to the grace received from outside it as a given revelation. The young Hegel thinks that neither Kantian autonomy nor Lutheran heteronomy is capable of doing justice to the conflicting demands of self and other, of freedom and necessity, of thought and life, of individual and society. The young Hegel finds that the principle of healing lies neither in rational autonomy nor in religious belief, but in love as the overriding principle of union:

> Only in love are we at one with the object, it does not assert mastery [as does autonomous reason], and it is not mastered [in religious faith].[20]

[17] Letter to Schelling, 2 Nov. 1800, *Briefe,* I, pp. 59–60: "I ask myself now, while I am still occupied with this [i.e., with reflection], how I am to find a way back to intervention in the life of men." (Quoted by Harris, *Hegel's Development,* p. 406.)

[18] See H. S. Harris, op. cit., pp. 316–17; for the next quotation, p. 312.

[19] Harris, op. cit., p. 316 n. 2.

[20] In H. S. Harris, *Hegel's Development,* pp. 293–94. Cf. ibid., p. 316: "Love is the 'only possible union' and the 'only possible being' in which the two 'modes' sundered by reflection are properly reintegrated."

Love, says the young Hegel, is far removed from the demands of duty, from the mastery of Kantian moral reason and the slavery of traditional positive faith. It is, therefore, also removed from the fetters of inequality, and the parties or sides in the conflict can achieve the harmony of equilibrium:

[A truly rational] religion is one with love. The beloved is not opposed to us, he is one with our own essential being; we see only ourselves in him—and yet also on the other hand he is not we—a miracle that we cannot grasp [by mere Kantian reflection or by mere traditional positive faith alone].[21]

About this time, under the inspiration of Schelling, and against the background of something like a turn towards intellectual intuition in terms of Fichte's philosophy, Hegel breaks free from the non-cognitive restrictions of Kant's practical reason and of traditional religious belief as he has come to understand it. He sets about to work out a union (*Vereinigung*) in terms that far outstrip the modest claims of Kant's theoretical reason. Neither traditional positive belief nor Kantian *theoria* or *praxis* will suffice. Rational religious love points towards a solution; but this indicator places before philosophy the task of making clear the nature of reason and its career as the reconciliation of opposites. In his consideration of the family in the *Phenomenology of Spirit* (chap. 6), and many years later in his *Philosophy of Right,* he was to show how he was to move beyond the Kantian morality with its categorical imperative to the more concrete ethical sphere of the family. In those works he distinguished the familial relationship from moral relationships by the effective presence of love in the family, a love that incorporates sexual desire but much more besides. Such a love is the effective source of a union that results not merely in an abstract mandate which ought to be followed by the individual, but in an actual ethical community.[22] Nevertheless, although Hegel never retreats from the importance of ethical love, he will soon abandon it as the central and overriding conception for the reconciliation of opposites. It stresses the immediate union of the parties and so tends

[21] Nohl, op. cit., p. 377; cited by Harris, *Hegel's Development,* pp. 316–17 and n. 2 (beginning on p. 316).

[22] *Grundlinien der Philosophie des Rechts,* #158. Cf. Avineri, op. cit., p. 137. Also, H. A. Reyburn, *The Ethical Theory of Hegel* (Oxford, 1921, 1967), pp. 197, 205, 210: "Morality is an abstraction. . . . Emotions broaden out into love. Love is not mere impulse, for it is a self-conscious and relatively permanent disposition. It is the feeling side of a persistent social organization, and it has the durability and continuity of that outward union. Love is not mere liking or inclination. . . . It is the feature of a stable form of life, and renders in terms of feeling the self-conscious unity of the family. From this point of view we have to put aside much that delights the romanticist. . . . Ethical love is a higher principle than consanguinity."

to slight the element of conflict and struggle that sharpens the differentiation needed for the prelude to a more radical and systematic reintegration. It is to Kant's credit that, by means of the antitheses rampant in his philosophy, he voiced the antinomies endemic in modern European culture.[23] The problem is to resolve them. It is clear, then, that even for the young Hegel of the Berne (1793–96) and Frankfurt (1797–1800) periods, the problematic is not the same as Kant's. For the young Hegel sought more than a moral canon by which the reasonable individual could live; he sought nothing less than the ancient harmony of thought and life under the new demands made by modernity. *Ens et verum convertuntur:* this convertibility of being and thought was in need of the most radical grounding. Ultimately, Hegel would ground it in the *Science of Logic* as the convertibility of being and nothing, and then trace that convertibility through the logical and natural categories into the domain of social life.

The general lines of Hegel's mature Kant-interpretation are already evident in two Jena essays of 1801 to 1803.[24] They focus upon the concept of *reflection* in the critical philosophy of Kant and Fichte. Indeed, Hyppolite considers *Glauben und Wissen* to be Hegel's most profound treatment of the Kantian system as a philosophy of reflection. The essays are written under the influence of Schelling more than Hegel's later criticisms of Kant, but the assessment of Kant has reached maturity in Hegel's mind. In the two Jena essays the perspective and language have shifted from that of rational religious union in love to philosophical speculative synthesis of subject and object, of thought and being. A genuinely speculative philosophy, according to Hegel, is one that recognizes reason as the all-inclusive and original unity that both differentiates itself and reconciles those differences in a higher truth and a more concrete reality. As already mentioned, Hegel credits Kant with an inchoate insight into just such a speculative idea of reason. It is, however, an insight that belongs rather to the spirit of the Kantian philosophy than to its letter, to its promise rather

[23] *Vorlesungen über die Ästhetik,* 3 Bde. (Frankfurt/M: Suhrkamp Theorie Werkausgabe, 1970), I, pp. 80–81. Cf. K. L. Schmitz, "Hegel's Attempt to Forge a Logic for Spirit," *Dialogue* 10/4 (1971), pp. 661–66.

[24] *Differenz des Fichte'schen und Schelling'schen Systems der Philosophie* (1801), hrsg. v. G. Lasson (1928) (Hamburg: G. Meiner, 1962) (Hegel, *The Difference between Fichte's and Schelling's System of Philosophy,* trans. H. S. Harris and W. Cerf [Albany: S.U.N.Y., 1977]). And *Glauben und Wissen* (1802–3), hrsg. v. G. Lasson (1928) (Hamburg: F. Meiner, 1962) (Hegel, *Faith and Knowledge,* trans. W. Cerf and H. S. Harris [Albany: S.U.N.Y., 1977]). The critical text is in *G. W. F. Hegel, Gesammelte Werke,* Bd. 4 (1968).

than to its fulfillment. Moreover, the transcendental or productive imagination is also a genuinely speculative idea, but Kant's articulation of it falls away from speculation into reflection.[25] The "primary and original" bilateral identity of the imagination presents itself in active and passive form: as active, in the categories of the understanding, but as passive, in the dispersed forms of intuition. It is the primordial synthetic unity that is the hidden ground or "root" of the judgment. That is why Kant's principal question is so promising: viz., How are synthetic judgments a priori possible? For the judgment expresses and reflects a more original division (*Ur-teil*). In this way, it expresses the nature and possibility of reason itself; that is to say, that elements which are in themselves not identical—the subject and the object, the one particular, the other universal, the one in the form of being, the other in the form of thought—that these non-identical elements are in truth identical. For the identification of non-identities is the very nature of reason itself.[26]

Kant did not take thinking to be a merely subjective form, but made it into an object of reflection, something in itself.[27] Kant's attention to the synthetic a priori held speculative possibilities, but, in putting thought over against itself as the object of its own reflection, Kant lost that speculative opportunity and introduced a plurality of heterogeneous elements torn loose from their original unity.[28] Kantian reflection closed off the possibility of working out a genuine synthesis of thought and being; the convertibility was lost. In the closure of thought into itself, Kant let being go, so that it escaped from knowledge, lying beyond knowledge as the unknowable thing-in-itself. This radical self-division of thought from itself produced the dualism of thing-in-itself and objects of appearance; and that dualism underlies all the other famous Kantian antinomies: of spontaneity and receptivity, of understanding and sensibility, of thought and intuition, of necessity and freedom, of duty and inclination. Indeed, years later, Hegel was to say that these very antitheses had not been invented by Kant, but had shaped and troubled modern culture and modern

[25] *Differenzschrift*, pp. 3–4 (*Difference*, pp. 79–81); *Glauben*, p. 17 (*Faith*, pp. 71–72). Cf. Heidegger's criticism of Kant's supposed withdrawal, in edition B, from the implications of the doctrine of the transcendental imagination (the "common root" of sensibility and understanding) as Kant had initially proposed it in edition A: *Kant and the Problem of Metaphysics*, trans. J. Churchill (Bloomington, Indiana, 1962), esp. pp. 166–76. On the power of (transcendental) imagination in Kant's philosophy, see *Glauben*, pp. 18–19 (*Faith*, p. 73).

[26] *Glauben*, pp. 15–16 (*Faith*, pp. 69–70).

[27] *Glauben*, p. 25 (*Faith*, p. 79): "nicht subjectiv, sondern an sich genommen."

[28] Hyppolite, art. cit., p. 89.

consciousness, and that Kant best illustrated them by forcing them to the point of most unbending contradiction.[29] In *Glauben und Wissen,* he calls the philosophies of Kant, Fichte, and Jacobi "nothing but the culture of reflection raised to a system."[30]

The unresolved contradictions of the Kantian philosophy, however, led to a double devaluation. On the one hand, critical idealism, in the name of practical reason, postulated as its highest word an empty and unrealizable moral ideal, while, on the other hand, it condemned knowledge to mere appearances. That it did postulate even an ideal is for Hegel the sign that the speculative idea of reason remains in the Kantian philosophy as the unifying foundation of the life of reason. As an ideal, however, the moral postulate remains inactual, forever what *ought* to be, but never what actually *is.* In the face of the demands of ethics, it collapses into an empty formalism that preaches duty for duty's sake.[31] Its highest maxim, "Do your duty," becomes "You ought to do it."[32] In addition to the failure of practical reason, the rational faith of Kantian philosophy tolerates the failure of theoretical knowledge which, in moving towards reality, meets only the empty and

[29] See n. 23.

[30] *Glauben,* p. 10 (*Faith,* pp. 64–65): "die Erhebung der Reflexionskultur zu einem System." This reflective spirit of "modernity" is most clearly defended, against any Hegelian attempt to reconcile the antinomies, by Oswald Weidenbach, "Die Welt—Ohne Absolutes Gedacht," *Kant-Studien* 50 (1958–59), pp. 188–90 (italics mine): "*Kant beurteilt* in der *Kritik der reinen Vernunft richtig,* wenn er mit allem Nachdruck die Behauptung aufstellt, dass die Vollendung in einer Ganzheit der Gegensätze *immer nur eine regulative Idee bleibt,* der niemals eine Wirklichkeit entspricht. Wir würden sagen: Die Idee der Vollendbarkeit ist nur eine Arbeitshypothese, unter der die der Logos eine Tätigkeit stellt, um dadurch den faustischen Antrieb zu erhalten, unermüdlich weither zu forschen. . . . Die Welt ist Kampf und Geschichte—nicht Sein-an-sich; sie ist Ethos nicht Logos. . . . Tertium non datur. *Entweder* ist die Welt ein vollendetes An-sich-sein; dann ist Ethos und Ethik Illusion—*oder* Ethos ist ihr Sinn; dann muss sie unvollendbar sein und bleiben." Hegel recognizes that, insofar as the conception of reflection is accepted, "Kant is quite correct in making this empty unity a merely regulative and not a constitutive principle—for how could something that is utterly without content constitute anything?" (*Faith,* p. 80; *Glauben,* p. 26). Cf. also *Glauben,* pp. 24–25; *Faith,* pp. 78–79.

[31] In discussing Fichte's development of Kantian reflection, Hegel remarks that "in a true ethic [as distinct from a merely formal morality] subjectivity is suspended" (*Faith,* p. 184; *Glauben,* pp. 118–19). Cf. *Philosophy of Right,* #135 and Zusatz: "Identity without content."

[32] The empty ethical formalism is rooted more deeply in the logical, i.e., ontological, structure of the ought, *das Sollen;* see *Wiss. der Logik,* Bd. I, pp. 121–24; *Science of Logic* (Miller), pp. 133–36. It is testament to the constancy of his criticism that the references to the Kantian and Fichtean philosophies, while they are absent from the first edition of the *Logic* (Pt. I, Bk. I) (Göttingen: Vandenhoeck und Ruprecht, 1966), are present in the revised edition of 1831. Critical edition is in Bd. 11 of the *Gesammelte Werke,* hrsg. v. G. Hogemann, W. Jaeschke (Hamburg: F. Meiner, 1978).

unknowable beyond reason.[33] Knowledge is limited in favor of faith. In the realm of theoretical knowledge itself Kant carves out a field for the meeting of thought and reality, but that field is a space and time that is transcendentally ideal, while yet both the I and the thing lie beyond it. The object known in that field is devalued by having the merely ideal form of appearance.[34] Objectivity is a value that holds only for the subjective conditions of consciousness. The critical idealism of Kant comes to rest in syntheses that have subjective force only.[35] In sum, then, consciousness has been devalued by being offered unreality in the form of a moral ideal and unreality in the form of phenomenal knowledge. We can see how this is so by looking more closely at the structure of the Kantian synthetic a priori judgment in order to see the divisive nature of the reflective consciousness that expresses itself in and through such a judgment.

It would not be an exaggeration to say that, for Hegel—if the Kantian account of the synthetic a priori judgment is true—the faculty of the understanding is an instrument that brings about by violence a sort of "shotgun wedding" between two parties that retain their indifference to one another, just because each is something in itself (*an sich*). Moreover, in a *Zusatz* to the *Encyclopedia*,[36] Hegel is reported to have said that "the world of sense is a scene of mutual exclusion." Now, it is upon just this dispersed manifold that the Kantian forms of judgment rest as upon their material base. For, according to Kant, the understanding receives its content from the world of sense as from an alien source, and so it builds itself up with what lies outside of it. But the relationship itself, between the understanding and its content, is intrinsic to neither, and remains unaccounted for. Hegel knows, of course, that, in the Transcendental Deduction of the categories in the first *Critique*, Kant claimed to have shown that the pure categories can be legitimately *employed* only in combining the manifold of sense. But the unification remains a merely external connection. What, it seems, Hegel expects of a speculative proof is that it will show that the categories cannot *be* without the original unity of form and content, of

[33] "Als ein Leeres für die Erkenntnis" (*Glauben*, p. 27; *Faith*, p. 81).

[34] Cf. Hyppolite, art. cit., pp. 92–93.

[35] *Glauben*, p. 23 (*Faith*, p. 77): "Auf diese Weise wird also die Objektivität der Kategorien in der Erfahrung und die Notwendigkeit dieser Verhältnisse selbst wieder etwas Zufälliges und ein Subjektives. . . . Die Dinge, wie sie durch den Verstand erkannt werden, sind nur Erscheinungen. . . ." See also *Glauben*, p. 20 (*Faith*, pp. 74–75). Cf. Hyppolite, art. cit., p. 91.

[36] *Zusatz* to #42 (*Hegel's Logic*, p. 69).

understanding and sense, of thought and being. He looks for a tighter, intrinsic and concrete unity of differences. The most that the categories of the understanding can achieve on Kantian grounds, however, is to relate the entire formal structure of the judgment and of the understanding itself to an external content. The coalescence is thus brought about in an ultimately unintelligible way.[37] The most that can be achieved within these presuppositions, then, is a conditioned finite result. Hegel calls it a relative, rather than an absolute, identity; that is, an identification brought about by external relations only.[38] Instead of the truth that is we get only the relativism that appears. And he distinguishes such half measures from the absolute integration that philosophical reason must bring about. Philosophical reason is meant to bring about the absolute resolution of differences; it is meant to resolve conflict and opposition by working with what is intrinsic to the opposites. Such absolute knowing is not to be caricatured as omniscience, but is rather knowing inasmuch as it has recovered and justified its own presuppositions. In this way, nothing will remain simply given, data alien to thought. Such is the measure to which philosophy must aspire; for if a philosophy cannot resolve the conflict and opposition of thought and its other (being), then it cannot hope to resolve the conflicts endemic in the actual life of society.

Hegel agrees that Kant's idealism is fundamentally sound in its instinct, for it placed the principle of unity in thought. But Kant so conceived the subject of thought that it neither contained nor could develop the determinate content it needed for knowledge. Again, he was correct when he asserted the original synthetic unity of consciousness as the ground for all knowledge; but he went on to separate out the principle of unity into the "I think" which contains nothing manifold and which stands over against the manifold of sensibility whose unity in turn lies entirely outside of itself in the "I think." In other words, Kant closed off thought from its content and set the content over against thought; in that way the content came to have *its* unity outside of itself. The Kantian "violence," however, was directed ultimately by thought against its own possibilities and nature.

The Kantian account of the synthetic a priori judgment simply reflects the duality of the heterogenous elements of sense and understanding. The understanding is supposed to unify form and content in the representation of the object; but what makes its appearance in

[37] A merely formal unity is left to assemble with its opposite in a non-conceptual way: "auf eine unbegreifliche Weise koaleszieren muss" (*Glauben*, p. 22; *Faith*, p. 76).

[38] *Glauben*, pp. 14–17 (*Faith*, pp. 67–70).

as follows: (1) Kant correctly placed unity in thought, but in such a way that the two sides of thought—form and content, unity and plurality—fell outside of and over against each other. (2) In grasping itself after the manner of a conditioned, ideal (i.e., conscious) thing, something in itself, thought condemned itself to finitude. (3) This self-imprisonment left it empty of its own content, and so unable to reach the truth. (4) In striving to know the object, the Kantian judgment is a violent act of combination, in which a finite understanding imposes its forms upon an alien content that is external and indifferent to it. Under these conditions, to say "is" is to claim mastery, but the mastery is merely ideal, for the "it is" is reduced to "it seems."

Where are we to put our finger, if we are to touch the deepest grounds of Hegel's discontent with Kant? Harris argues convincingly that even in 1793 Hegel already considered the philosophies of both Kant and Fichte to be philosophies of abstract reasoning, i.e., of the understanding (*Verstand*). As such they were unable to resolve the conflict posed by actual existence and life. This evaluation matured into a conception of *reflection*, so that by 1800 Hegel had characterized these philosophies as philosophies of reflection.[48] His mature consideration of reflection which launches the treatment of essence in the *Science of Logic*[49] may, therefore, be viewed as a continuing inner confrontation with Kant. For Hegel, it is the most radical philosophical confrontation, because through it he produces the redefinition of philosophy contained in the mature works. The brief but difficult section on reflection establishes a sort of paradigm for the treatment of other themes in the middle part of the *Logic*. A glance at the table of contents in the book on essence is enough to illustrate the Kantian flavor of the themes: the thing-in-itself, appearance, the modalities of actuality and possibility, of contingency and necessity, and the analogies of substance, causality, and reciprocity. The book on essence in Hegel's *Logic* is at once a commentary upon Kant and a confrontation with him. For, in the context of the *Science of Logic*, all considerations of a strictly historical interpretation fall away. Hegel has made his decision about what Kant holds in principle, even in part against his intention, and it is to the question of principle that Hegel addresses himself.

[48] See W. Cerf's introduction to *Faith*, pp. xvi–xxiv. Also the introductions by H. S. Harris, in *Faith*, pp. 1–50, and in *Difference*, pp. 1–75. Harris's essay in *Faith* is the best succinct treatment of the period in English.

[49] *Wiss. der Logik*, Bd. II, pp. 13–23 (*Science of Logic*, pp. 399–408).

What Hegel takes to be Kant's fundamental inadequacy is that Kantian thought reaches out towards being only to fall back upon itself as upon a hard central core. That core is not, of course, the famous thing-in-itself (*Ding an sich*); it is rather, in Hegelian terms, being-in-itself (*Ansichsein*). We have already seen Hegel characterize the Kantian conception of consciousness as "something in itself" (*an sich*). Now, being-in-itself is a definite ontological structure in Hegelian philosophy. It can be found in many forms—finite and infinite, qualitative and quantitative—but its paradigm is that of qualitatively determinate being, "something" (*Etwas* or *Dasein*).[50] Moreover, that paradigm "infects"[51] whatever form that engrafts itself onto that definite ontological structure. It is incurably finite, even when it assumes the form of the genuine infinite. More precisely, it remains finite in one respect at least: opposition or differentiation takes the form of an external relation between two apparently self-sufficient and indifferent units. The paradigm, once again, is the relation of one determinate being to another, the connection between something and other.

Of course, the paradigm belongs to the Hegelian logic of being, not to that of essence or thought, and at first glance, the paradigm doesn't seem to fit Kant's critical idealism very well. However, Hegel remarks editorially, in the introduction to the logic of essence,[52] that, while essence is the domain of being that is not only related to itself in and through another (*Ansichsein*) but also self-related (*Fürsichsein*), it is the domain of self-relation in-and-for-itself in the form of being-in-itself. In the German jargon: *An-und-für-sich-sein als Ansichsein.* Rendered into Kantian terms: Reflection is the activity of consciousness by which it grasps itself as an ideal (conscious, subjective) something-in-itself. Now, if the paradigm holds, then it is not surprising that such a consciousness should be the source of distinctions whose elements exclude each other, and whose primary relations with others are external connections.

The core of Kantian self-relatedness (*Ansichsein*), then, is not simply a humble or prudent confession of limits, as though knowledge neither can nor should go farther in order to make room for faith. The restrictive self-relatedness that constitutes the radical subjectivism of Kantian consciousness is such that it renders inert and dead the

[50] Ibid., Bd. I, pp. 95–110 (Ibid., pp. 109–22).

[51] "Negation mit einem Anderssein behaftet ist" (*Wiss. der Logik,* Bd. II, p. 9; *Science of Logic,* p. 396).

[52] "Das Wesen ist das An-und-Für-sichsein, aber dasselbe in der Bestimmung des Ansichseins" (*Wiss. der Logik,* Bd. II, p. 5; *Science of Logic,* p. 391).

very opposition of being and thought which it both recognizes and avoids.[53] It is this avoidance that leads Hegel to dub Kantian thought as servile, for it is the essence of the servile consciousness to recognize its limit outside of itself in the master. Moreover, it may retreat within out of fear (the resignation of the Stoic).[54] For the Kantian limit is not a physical one; it does not cut off knowledge at some boundary. It is an ideal limit; that is, it cuts off knowledge from itself. It deprives knowledge, not only of any claim to infinity, but also of its autonomy and integrity. The Hegelian reply to Kant's question: What can I know? is: The nature and aim of knowledge is to grasp itself *and* being in a unity. In rejoining thought to being, then, Hegel sees himself reclaiming the essential heritage of thought. Thought and being stand or fall together.

According to Hegel, then, the Kantian limit enervates knowledge and morality. What first seems to strike him is the Kantian limitation of practical reason to a formal imperative and an ideal postulate. It is not simply that the *ought* is unreal and unrealizable qua ought, empty of actuality in itself. It is that its otherness—its distinction from *is*—has become inert and groundless. It is simply there. The *ought* claims to regulate, to order and guide, but its claim is grounded only within its own limit, that is, within the world of subjectivity, which it serves as maxim. It can claim no value in actuality.[55] So, too, if we turn to the Kantian theory of knowledge, we find the inertia of a dead other infecting the whole structure. Consider the Kantian appearance. It is, says Hegel,[56] "a *given* content of perception." As given, it contains the affections of the subject which receives it. There are present in the subject, then, determinations which are already shaped in their own independent being. They do not, of course, belong to the thing-in-itself; but they do belong to the sensuous mode of the subject, its manifold. They have in them "an element of indifference" with respect to the categories of the understanding. Indifference here, as always with Hegel, means that the dynamic operates only by imposition from without. Then either one element masters the other, as the categories organize the manifold, or a third compares the two ele-

[53] Cf. *Phänomenologie des Geistes,* hrsg. v. Joh. Hoffmeister (Hamburg: F. Meiner, 1952⁶), p. 153 (*Hegel's Phenomenology of Spirit,* trans. A. V. Miller [Oxford: Clarendon, 1977], p. 121). For the critical edition, see *Gesammelte Werke,* Bd. 6.

[54] Thus the Kantian "ought." For the Hegelian analysis of the "ought" (*das Sollen*) and its overcoming or sublation, see *Science of Logic,* pp. 131–36 (*Wiss. der Logik,* Bd. I, pp. 119–24).

[55] *Science of Logic,* p. 396 (*Wiss. der Logik,* Bd. II, p. 9).

[56] *Science of Logic,* p. 397 (*Wiss. der Logik,* Bd. II, p. 10).

ments and joins them by an external relation, as the schematism joins pure categories to sensible data. The determinate judgment of the first *Critique*, by which sensible particulars are subsumed under universal categories, does not *transform* the elements of sensibility; it merely *combines* them. That is, it imposes an alien pattern upon them, but leaves them radically indifferent to it. The reflective judgment of the third *Critique* looks for a principle of unity between reason and nature, but withdraws from prescribing what appearances really are, and falls back upon a merely subjective principle of unity. At the root of this indifference, and its consequent subjectivism, according to Hegel is the inadequacy of the Kantian mode of reflection. Indeed, it infects everything that it touches with its dead otherness, leaving an unbridged gulf between thought and being.

In discussing the character of Kantian reflection, Hegel stresses the movement of intro-reflection by which thought falls back upon its own resources. It is a simple and immediate return of consciousness into itself: immediate reflection.[57] Now, in falling back in this way, thought finds nothing but consciousness itself and its needs; there is nothing of the thing-in-itself, of being or reality. Indeed, in the end, there is no genuine otherness at all, only the pure "I think" without any manifold, a pretender to synthetic unity which reduces to analyticity. There is no mediation in and through another. Drawn out of itself, of course, Kantian thought recognizes the other and even starts out from it in order to integrate the manifold of sensibility which it finds before it. Nevertheless, such a reflective thought holds on to its own simple self-identity, and does not give itself up to the other. Such reflection recognizes (posits) the other, and presupposes it (*voraussetzt*), but it does so from a distance which it never closes.[58] The other is left as an external other, and so Kantian thought does not pass over into the other in order to return out of it to an enriched and transformed self-knowledge. This is why it remains a consciousness, and never attains to genuine self-consciousness. Instead, Kantian thought subsumes the sensible particulars under categories that are already universal and determined. It thus produces only an appearance, a phenomenal object, i.e., one subject to the conditions of intro-reflection. The alien manifold of sense has been permitted to intervene between the aim and the result of reason. Moreover, the data

[57] Such immediate reflection is transformed (sublated: *aufgehoben*) in the *Logik* as the moment of positing (*setzende*) reflection (*Wiss. der Logik*, Bd. II, p. 15; *Science of Logic*, p. 401).

[58] This mode of recognition is transformed in the *Logik* as the moment of external (*äussere*) reflection (*Wiss. der Logik*, Bd. II, pp. 17–20; *Science of Logic*, pp. 402–5).

have been found as one finds an obstacle; but they have not been mediated. The result is a world that falls short of reality and settles for appearance. Now it is just this inertia, this inoperativeness and indifference, this ineffectuality of an element in the knowledge structure, that leads Hegel to say that Kant has grasped matters wrongly. That wrong or inadequate grasping is a restrictive way of reflecting thought back into itself.

In all of this, reflective thought has kept to its initial predilection: its withdrawal back into itself. Moreover, it has lent to the elements of its phenomenal world just that same self-isolating dynamic of withdrawal into oneself. In taking its own projected otherness back into itself, while retaining a relation to the given determinations of the manifold, thought has given to its own products the same character of self-withdrawal. Each element in its isolation turns only its external surface to the others, so that nothing interior, nothing genuinely its own, is disclosed. Everything is bound to the other by external connections: one part of the manifold is bound to another by parts of space and moments of time, one category is bound to another in some unexplained way. Everywhere self-identities are combined by external connections with each other under a priori principles of combination.

Because of this withdrawal of thought into itself, Kantian thought never says: "It is"; it only says: "It seems." And it treats all claims to reality as show (*Schein, Erscheinung*). This is the domain of skepticism, but also of critical idealism.[59] For the Kantian appearance puts forth a sort of false independence. It is not indifferent to thought as something genuinely independent. It appears as something drawn into itself, yet it is wholly dependent upon the subject which is consciousness, for it is nothing if the relation to consciousness is withdrawn. This is its transcendental ideality, without which it would not be empirically real.[60] That is, it is nothing in itself but only something for consciousness. Its independence, then, is the dynamic of consciousness's own withdrawal into itself projected onto the manifold. The indifference of the given phenomenon is simply a reflection of the isolated self-identity of the understanding and its self-reflection, whose creature the phenomenon is. And so, critical idealism does not

[59] *Wiss. der Logik,* Bd. II, pp. 9–10 (*Science of Logic,* p. 396). Hegel writes (*Science of Logic,* p. 396): "The various forms of idealism, Leibnizian, Kantian, Fichtean, and others, have not advanced beyond being as determinateness [*über das Sein als Bestimmtheit*], have not advanced beyond this immediacy, any more than scepticism did" (*Wiss. der Logik,* Bd. II, p. 10).

[60] Kant, *Kritik der reinen Vernunft,* A35, B52 (*Kant's Critique of Pure Reason,* trans. N. Kemp Smith [London: Macmillan, 1950], p. 78).

permit itself to regard knowledge as a knowing of reality, of the thing-in-itself. "The thing-in-itself was not supposed to enter knowledge." For knowledge was supposed to be an inward domain that must place any genuine otherness beyond it.

It is of especial interest, therefore, to consider the career of the *other* in Hegel's philosophy. In a passage in the *Science of Logic* Hegel turns to explicitly consider the nature of the *other.*[61] He has been developing the category of determinate being with its predilection for the affirmative and positive features of things. So far, negation has played a merely subordinate role. It is time, he says, to face the *other* as bravely as Plato faced up to *to heteron,* the pure other taken up in its own right. This moment of isolation of the other is necessary so that the other can establish a nature of its *own.* Unless otherness comes into its own, it will remain latent, a possibility will pass unexploited, opposition and conflict will be glossed over. Hegel finds the "other in its own self" to be the paradigm of a natural existence that stands outside of thought. The philosopher must find as strong a stomach as Plato, therefore, if he is to enter into a domain of thoughtless contingency. Only thought in the form of spirit—that is, thought which has not endorsed the presupposition of its own limitation, yet which has reconciled itself to its own negation (even to its own death, prefigured in religion)—can find the courage to pursue the other into its own lair. No metaphysical philosophy, says Hegel, not even the critical philosophy of Kant, can free itself from the affirmative presuppositions of the category of being, viz., that being simply *is.* And as long as thought remains under the affirmative forms of being, then otherness and negation cannot come into their full native power. Hegel insists that only the dialectic of spirit can release the full force of the negative and can take up the other seriously. The source of the Kantian flaw, according to Hegel, then, is a false and indifferent respect for the domain of positive reality, for what is simply there, for what is given. Kantian thought secretly chains itself to the positive form of being, for positing is part of the armory of reflection, even as affirmative unity is part of the furniture of being as thing.

The passage about the *other* is one of a series throughout the *Logic* in which the negative and the other make their appearance. It is a first foray, and little more than a declaration of intent on Hegel's part. In the book on essence, however, thought wins its spurs, for it passes over from the merely relative negation of beings to one another to the

[61] *Wiss. der Logik,* Bd. II, pp. 105–6 (*Science of Logic,* pp. 118–19).

absolute negation of being and all of its forms and determinations.[62] That is, thought breaks free from the immediate and thingly relation to being. At first this seems to be that very withdrawal of thought into itself that Hegel criticizes in Kant. Nor, indeed, is the freedom complete. For it is just here that the crisis in Hegel's "refutation" of Kant reaches its mortal climax. Hegel is convinced that the Kantian withdrawal is a concession to defeat in the face of obdurate reality, a retreat into a self-isolating thought that is still held captive to positive being. Hegelian reflection intends to break that chain and to free thought, so that it may come into its own full and infinite nature—not only for theoretical knowledge, but for the practical tasks of building social reality as well. In breaking free, Hegelian speculation recognizes that it must also let the other go free in order to be itself. In the third part of the *Logic,* the proper Hegelian sense of objectivity is explored under the concept of the proper Hegelian sense of subjectivity.[63] It is an objectivity that respects the other, its real existence and even its contingency, and yet accommodates the full theoretical and practical needs of subjectivity. In letting being go free and yet reconciling it with thought, Hegel finds the courage to write a philosophy of the other, that is, of nature as the other of spirit. And he is driven further to trace out the career of the other in history, politics, religion, and art.[64] He is convinced that he has broken free of Kant's self-isolating reflection with its conception of consciousness as something in itself (*Ansichsein*). Has he broken free? The moment of withdrawal into self remains, even when it is sublated and placed in a more generous context. It is the original fall of thought, a fall which Kant raises to its extreme in a philosophy of finite understanding. It is, moreover, a fall that the Hegelian philosophy needs to suffer over and over in each new situation in order to rise again.

Finally, Kant's conception of consciousness as an ideal something in itself is the correlate to his conception of philosophy as the architectonic system of knowledge. Kant makes a distinction between a merely scholastic organization of knowledge and a genuine philosophical sys-

[62] *Wiss. der Logik,* Bd. I, pp. 397–98 (*Science of Logic,* pp. 383–85). Writing of the "absolute indifference" with which the logic of being (Bk. I) ends, Hegel points to the sublation of "this fundamental onesidedness of being in itself [*Ansichsein*]." And, in the beginning of the logic of essence (Bk. II), he remarks that "essence is the absolute negativity of being" (*Science of Logic,* p. 395; *Wiss. der Logik,* Bd. II, p. 9).

[63] That is, in the subjective logic of the concept (*Begriff*) (*Wiss. der Logik,* Bd. II, pp. 213ff.; *Science of Logic,* pp. 577ff.).

[64] That is, in the philosophy of nature (*Encyclopedia,* Pt. II), in the philosophy of spirit (ibid., Pt. III), and in the Berlin lectures on aesthetics, religion, history, and philosophy itself.

tem.[65] The former produces a mechanical collection ordered contingently by the particular and partial aims of this or that human inquiry, whereas a genuine philosophical system can be brought about only in accordance with the essential ends of human reason. Now these essential ends are pursued in line with Kant's famous questions: What can I know? What ought I to do? and, What may I hope?[66] In the end, all the achievements of reason as such can be traced back through these questions to the one single principle of pure reason in its theoretical and practical roles. And this gives to the unity of rational endeavors that genuine philosophical system for which Kant reserved the noble name: architectonic.

But, even though Kant extolled such a system as intrinsic and organic, it was not sufficiently unified to satisfy Hegel. The Fichtean form of absolute reflection made the contradiction among the elements of the system—implicit all along in Kant—unavoidably clear. Moreover, in Fichte's conception of positing, Hegel found an intimation of a unitary speculative principle that, if freed from the limitations of Fichtean reflection, could resolve the Kantian dualism. Indeed, we might even see in it Kant's unknown unitary root. But it brought with it also the anticipation of a tighter and more comprehensive systematic unity. The more extreme the contradictions the principle could survive and integrate, the more the convertibility of thought and being could be realized. Kant had emphasized synthesis as combination (*Verbindung*), but this had led to a relatively loose and tolerant systematic unity. Fichte had emphasized positing in the interests of a finite ego. While divesting the conception of positing of its subjective associations, Hegel appropriated it for his own absolute system. Through Fichte's eyes, Hegel read Kant as the philosopher who had brought the bitter conflicts of modern life, its dichotomies, to the point of utter contradiction, without actually resolving them, or rather, by "resolving" them in an external and ideal manner. The key to Kant's solution was to find epistemic, objective and moral "space" for the various interests of human reason within the concept of rational totality. His solution to the first two antinomies, for example, was, if not to leave the field to the two contending parties, at least to seek "higher ground" (if not safer quarters), and from that ground, to deny to the contending parties their claim to a manifold of content. In the Hegelian clash of opposites, on the contrary, the parties do contend directly with one another. They do so because each is driven on

[65] *Kritik der reinen Vernunft,* A838, B866 (*Critique,* p. 657).
[66] Ibid., A805, B833 (*Critique,* p. 635).

by the prospect of realizing their hidden unity, viz., their membership in the absolute and infinite system. From the vantage point of the Hegelian spirit with its systematic requirements, the Kantian reflection with its conception of itself and its objects as somethings in themselves (*Ansichsein*) can only be a stage along the way, the self-imprisonment and exile of thought from itself. But the exile and imprisonment is necessary from the vantage point of that same Hegelian spirit. For in the absolute system with its emphasis upon negation and opposition, there can be no freedom without imprisonment, no homecoming without exile. Kant's reflection is no dalliance along the way of thought, but rather thought's own shadow without which there could be no Hegelian light, no "grey on grey."

Trinity College
University of Toronto

Index